EASY PIANO

Arranged by DAN F(

MW01040155

THE BEATLES BEST

This publication is not for sale in
the E.C. and/or Australia
or New Zealand.

HAL•LEONARD®
CORPORATION

7777 W. BLUEMOUND RD. P.O. BOX 13819 MILWAUKEE, WI 53213

THE BEATLES BEST

CONTENTS

ACROSS THE UNIVERSE

Words and Music by JOHN LENNON
and PAUL McCARTNEY

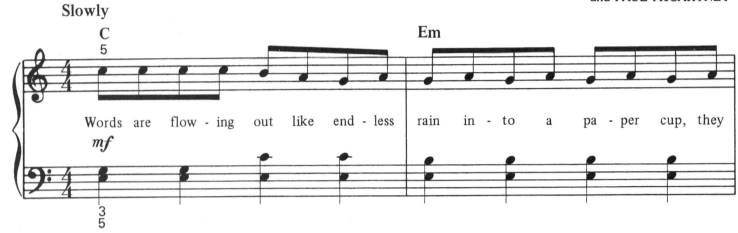

Words are flow -ing out like end -less rain in -to a pa -per cup, they

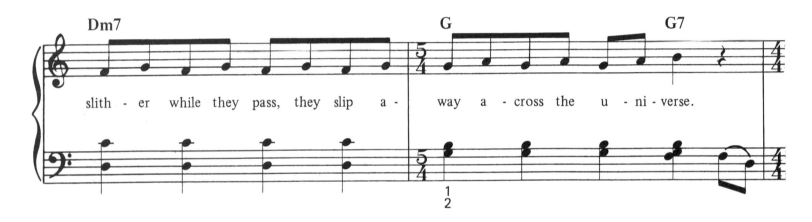

slith -er while they pass, they slip a - way a -cross the u - ni -verse.

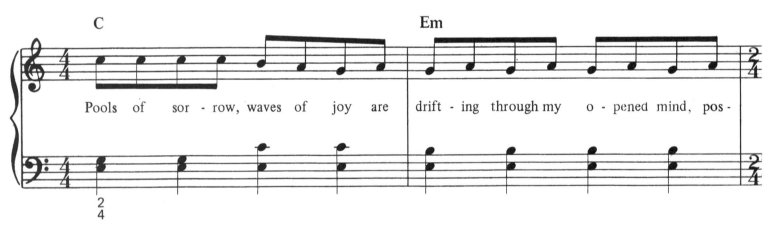

Pools of sor -row, waves of joy are drift -ing through my o -pened mind, pos-

sess -ing and ca - ress -ing me.___ Jai___ Gu -ru___

5

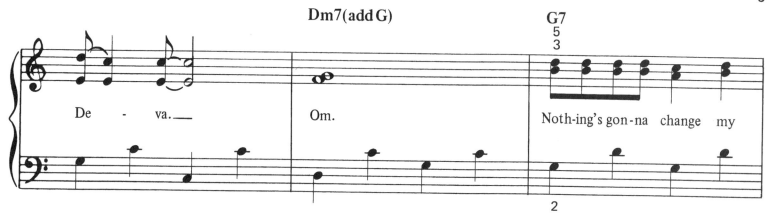

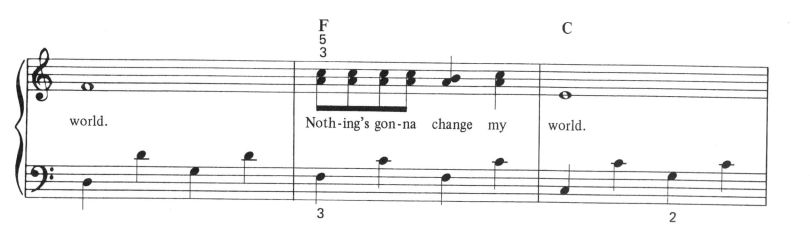

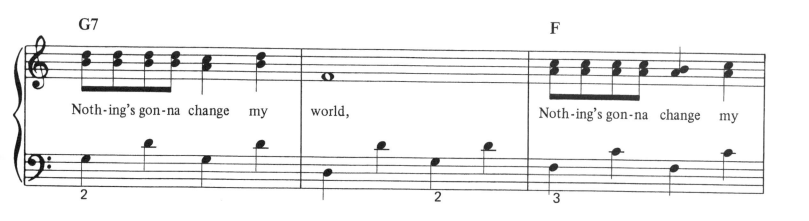

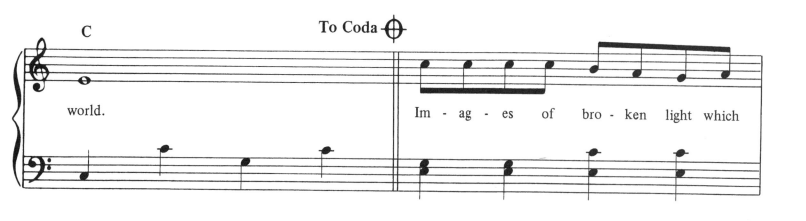

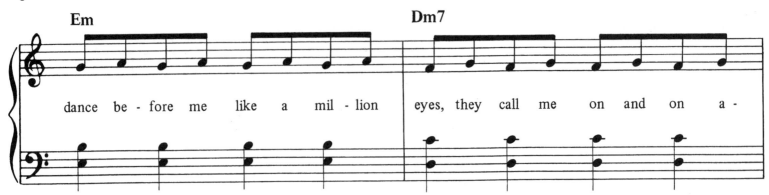

dance be-fore me like a mil-lion eyes, they call me on and on a-

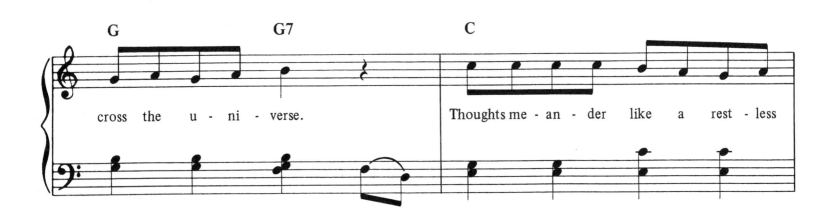

cross the u-ni-verse. Thoughts me-an-der like a rest-less

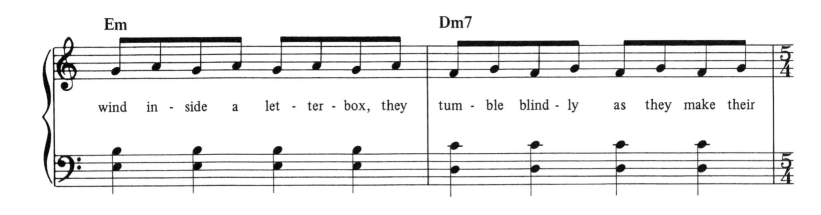

wind in-side a let-ter-box, they tum-ble blind-ly as they make their

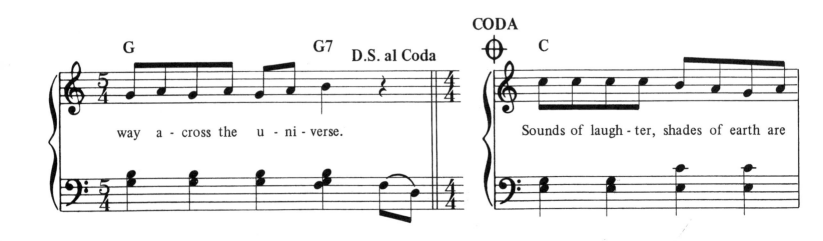

way a-cross the u-ni-verse. Sounds of laugh-ter, shades of earth are

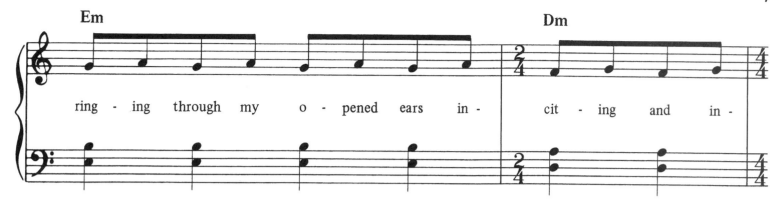

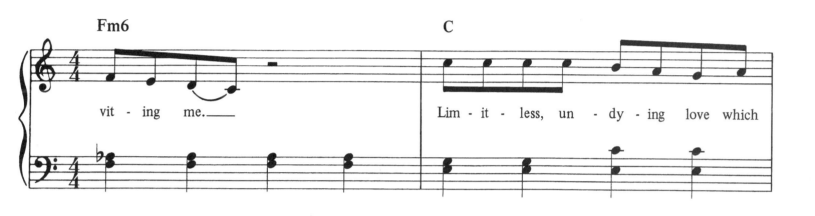

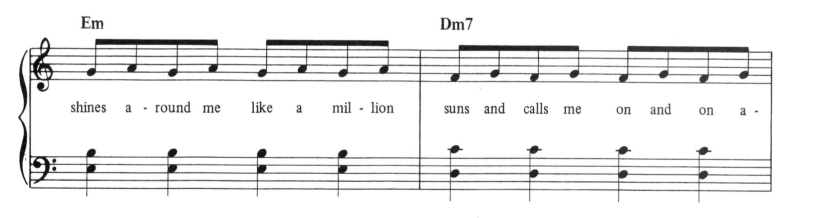

ALL MY LOVING

Words and Music by JOHN LENNON
and PAUL McCARTNEY

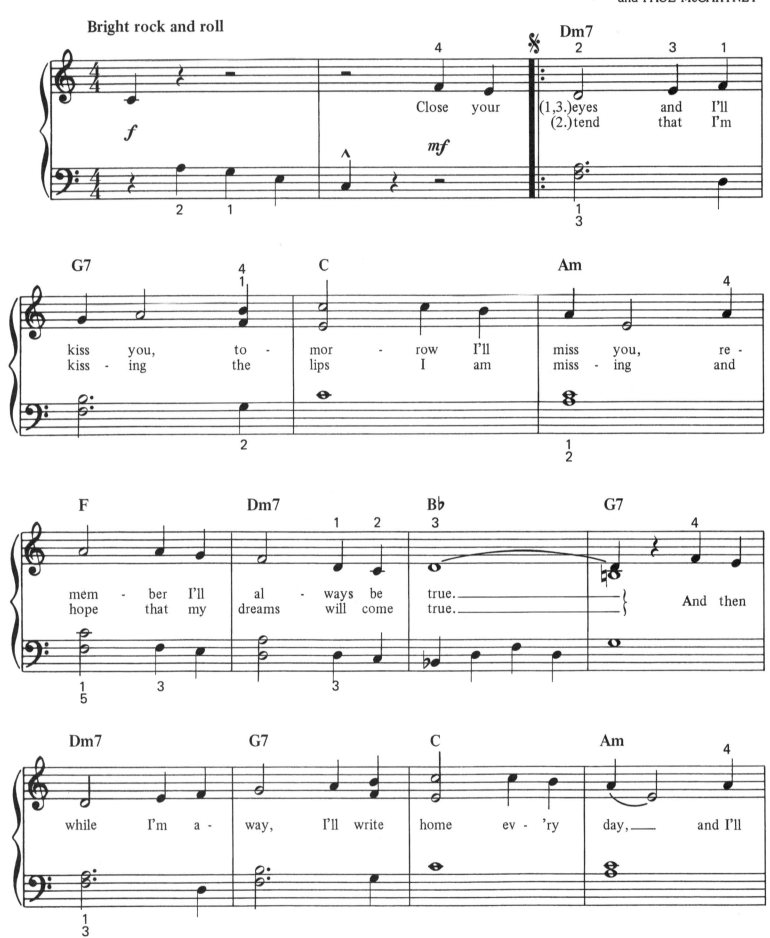

Close your (1,3.)eyes and I'll (2.)tend that I'm kiss you, to- mor- row I'll miss you, re- kiss -ing to the lips I am miss -ing and mem- ber I'll al- ways be true. hope that my dreams will come true. And then while I'm a- way, I'll write home ev- 'ry day, and I'll

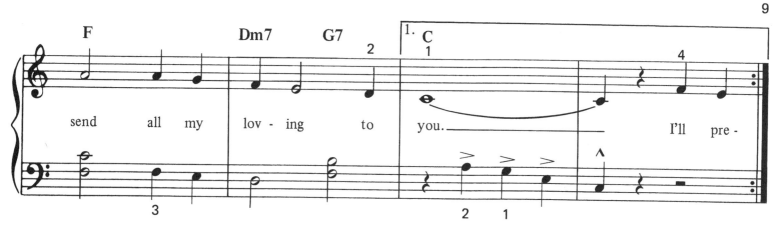

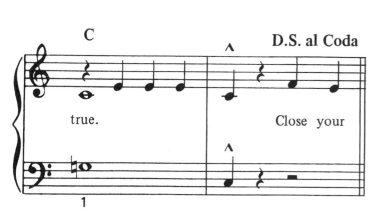

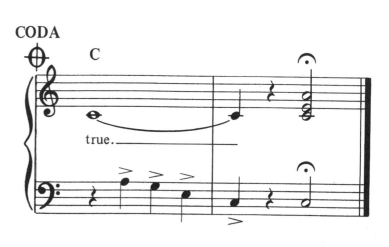

ALL TOGETHER NOW

Words and Music by JOHN LENNON
and PAUL McCARTNEY

Moderate singalong tempo

One, two, three, four, can I have a lit-tle more?_ Five, six, sev-en, eight, nine, ten,_ I love you._ A, B, C, D, can I bring my friend to tea?_ E, F, G, H, I, J,_

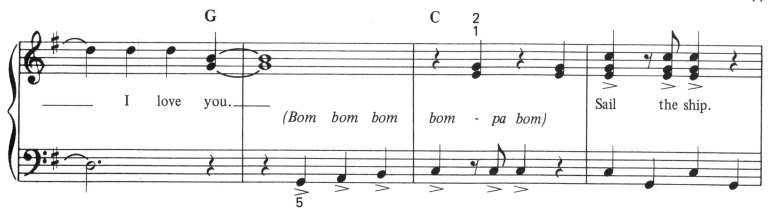

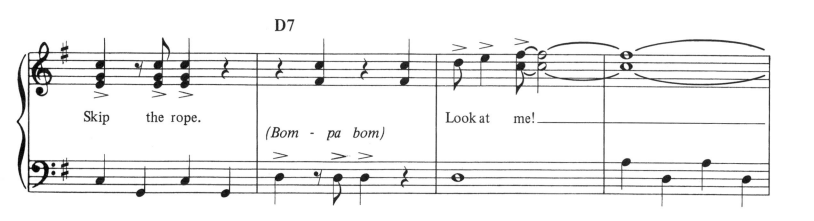

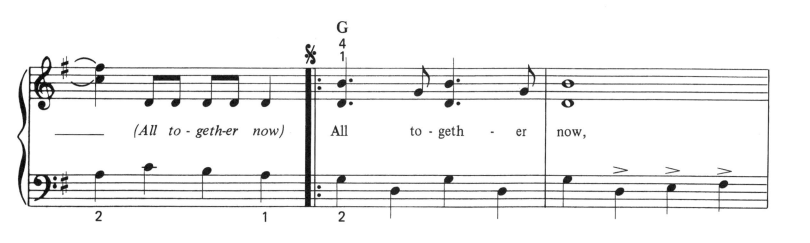

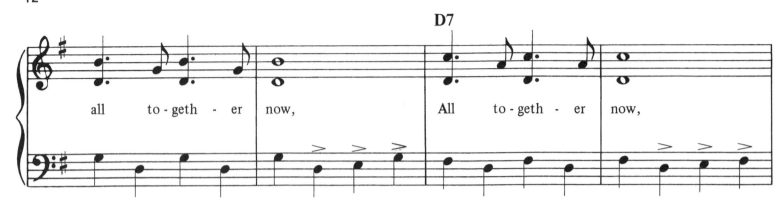

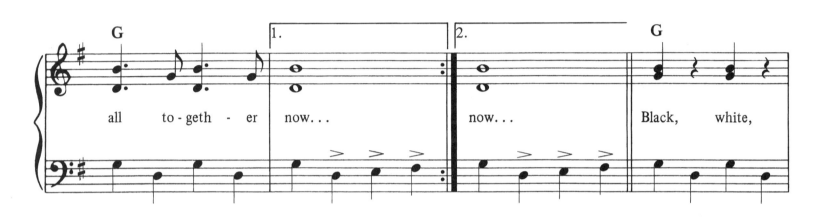

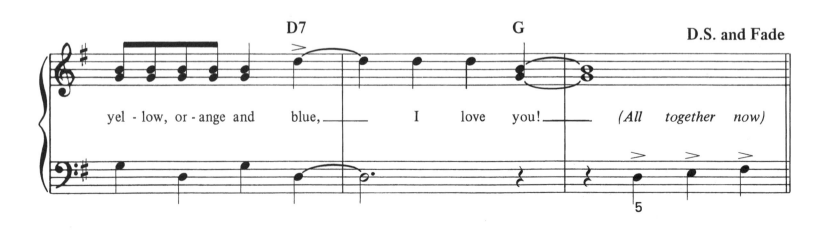

ALL YOU NEED IS LOVE

Words and Music by JOHN LENNON
and PAUL McCARTNEY

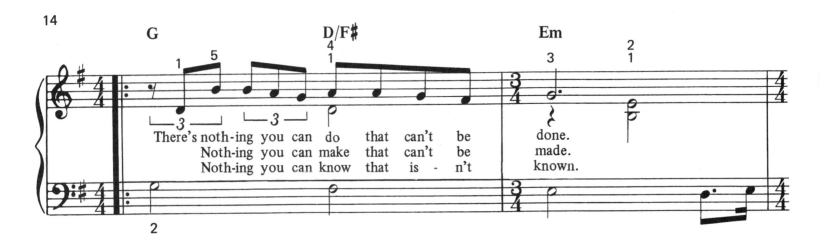

There's noth-ing you can do that can't be done.
Noth-ing you can make that can't be made.
Noth-ing you can know that is - n't known.

Noth-ing you can sing that can't be sung.
No one you can save that can't be saved.
Noth-ing you can see that is - n't shown.

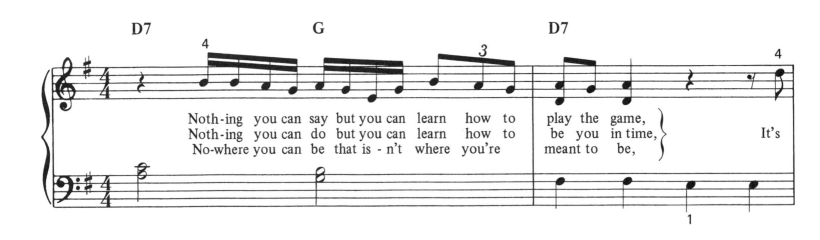

Noth-ing you can say but you can learn how to play the game,
Noth-ing you can do but you can learn how to be you in time,
No-where you can be that is - n't where you're meant to be,

It's

eas - y:

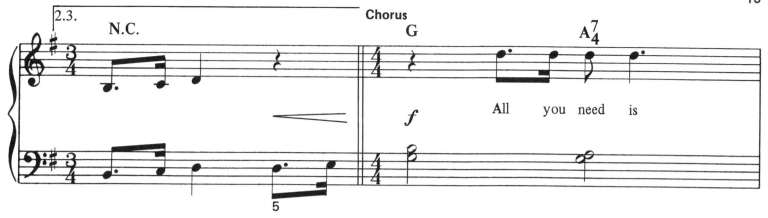

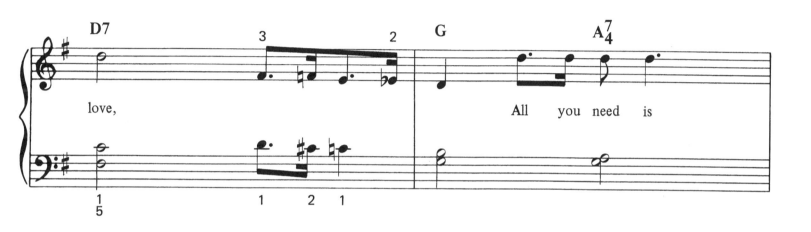

AND I LOVE HER

Words and Music by JOHN LENNON
and PAUL McCARTNEY

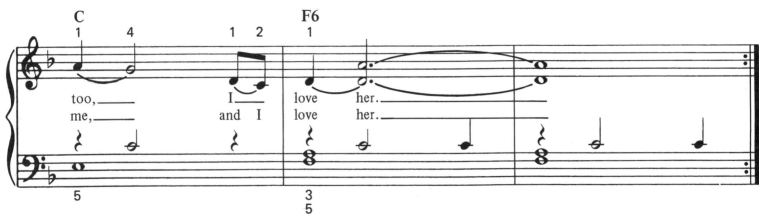

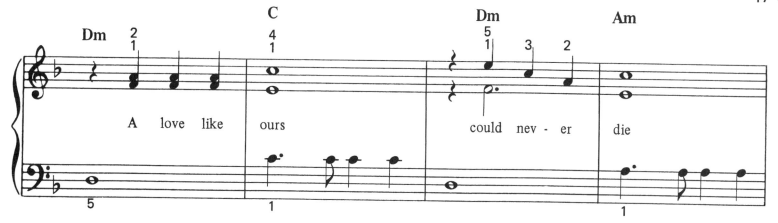

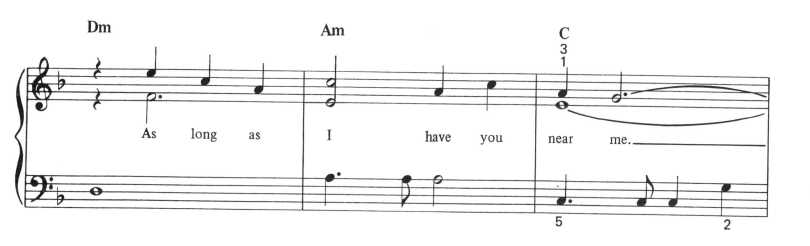

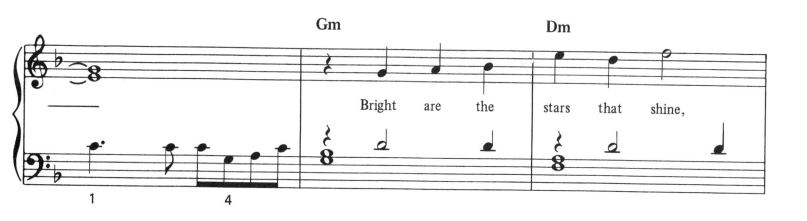

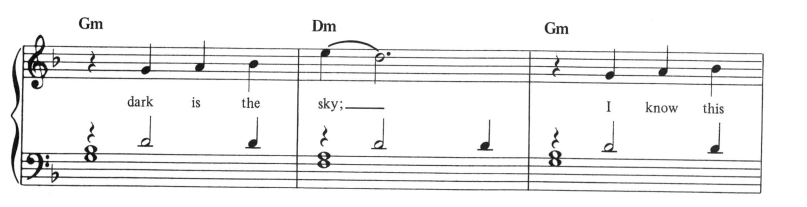

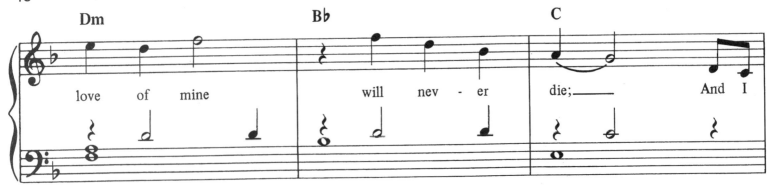

love of mine   will nev - er   die;_____   And I

love her._____

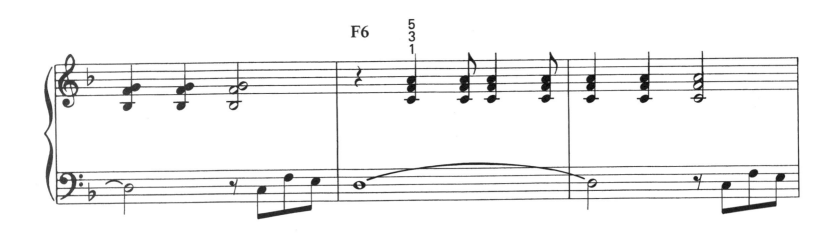

slowing

BABY, YOU'RE A RICH MAN

Moderate Rock

Words and Music by JOHN LENNON
and PAUL McCARTNEY

1. How does it feel ___ to be one of the beau - ti - ful
2. How does it feel ___ to be one of the beau - ti - ful
3. How does it feel ___ to be one of the beau - ti - ful

peo - ple?
peo - ple?
peo - ple?

Now that you know ___ who you
How of - ten have ___ you been
Tuned to a nat - u - ral

are,
there,
E,

what do you want ___ to
of - ten e - nough ___ to
hap - py to be ___ that

be?
know?
way;

And have you trav - eled ver - y
What did you see ___ when you were
Now that you've found ___ an - oth - er

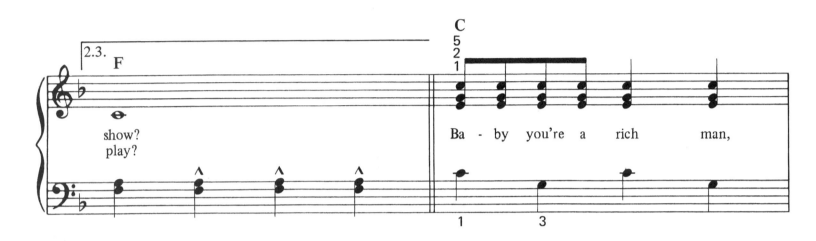

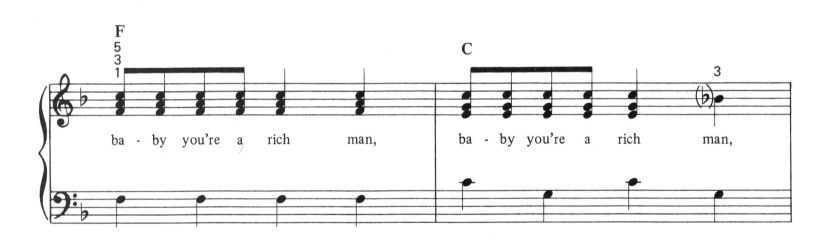

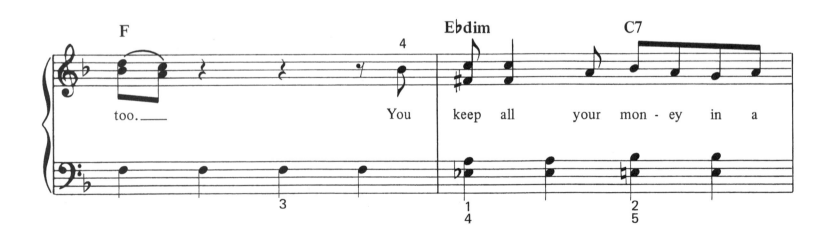

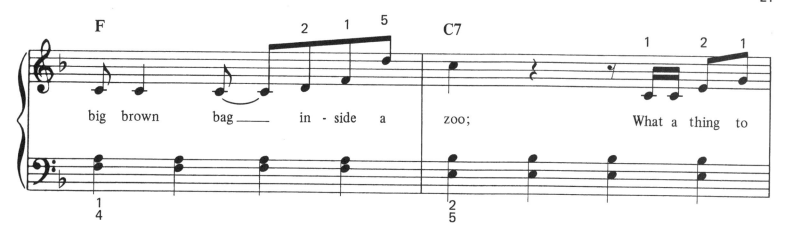

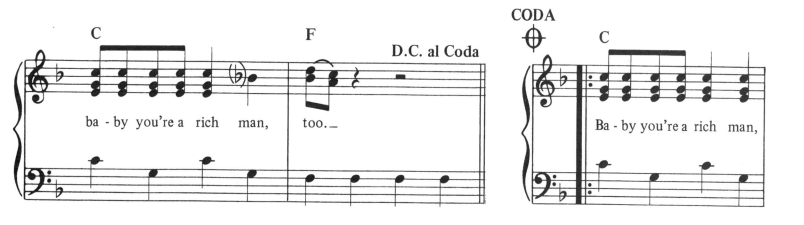

ANYTIME AT ALL

Words and Music by JOHN LENNON
and PAUL McCARTNEY

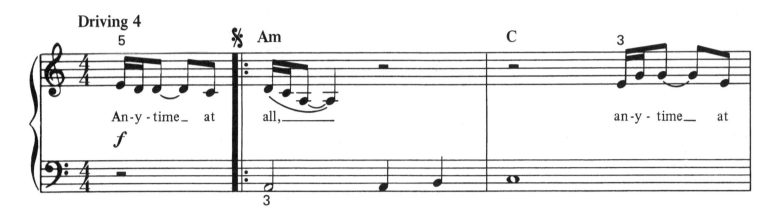

An-y-time at all, an-y-time at

all, An-y-time at all, all you got-ta do is

call and I'll be there.

1.,2. To next strain

Fine

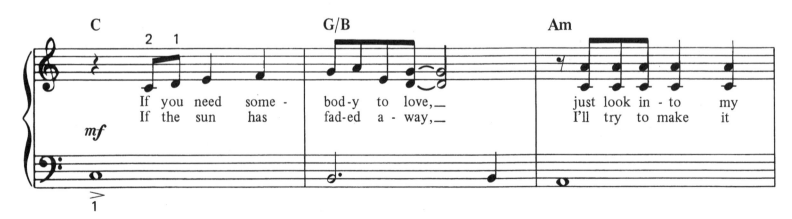

If you need some-bod-y to love, just look in-to my
If the sun has fad-ed a-way, I'll try to make it

BABY'S IN BLACK

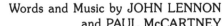

Words and Music by JOHN LENNON
and PAUL McCARTNEY

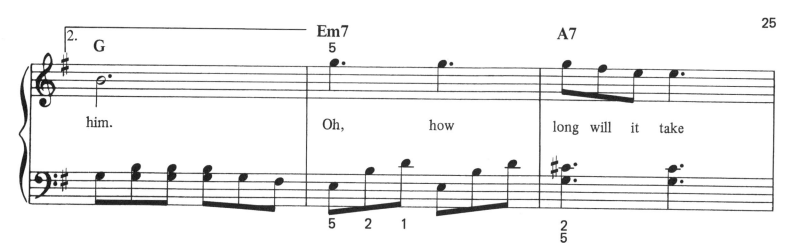

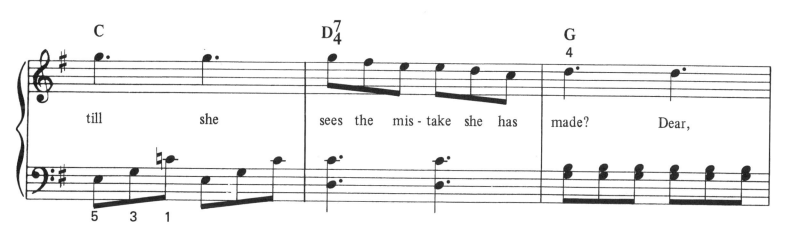

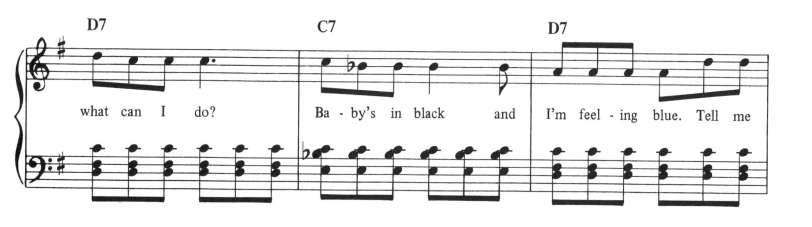

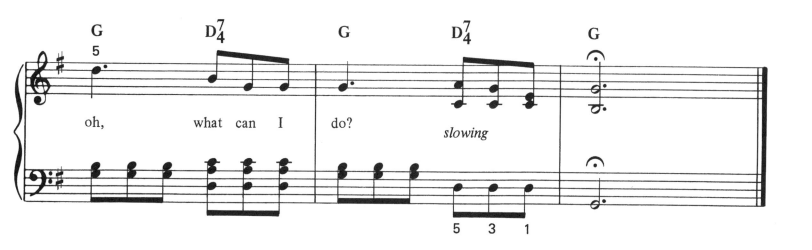

BACK IN THE U.S.S.R.

Words and Music by JOHN LENNON
and PAUL McCARTNEY

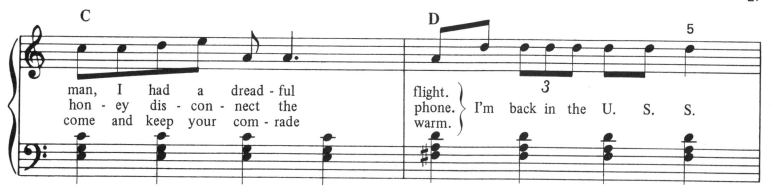

man, I had a dread - ful
hon - ey dis - con - nect the
come and keep your com - rade
flight.
phone.
warm.
I'm back in the U. S. S.

R.,
You don't know how luck-y you are, boy,—

Last time
to Coda

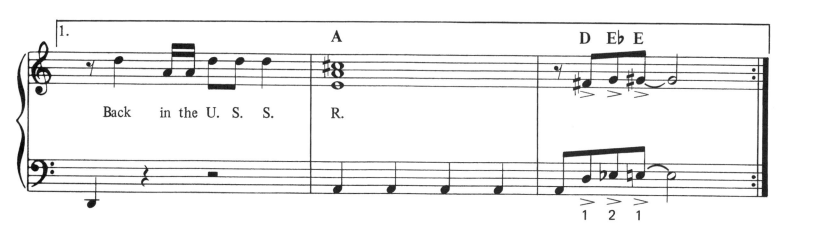

Back in the U. S. S. R.

Back in the U. S.,
Back in the U. S.,
Back in the U. S. S.

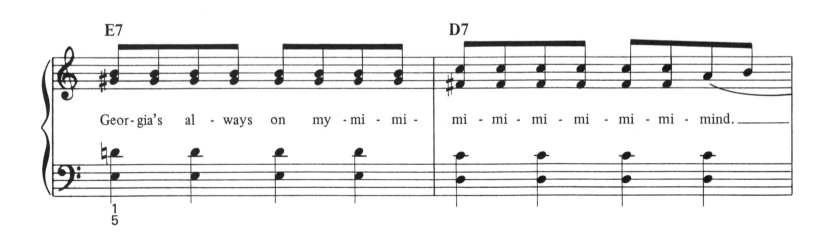

THE BALLAD OF JOHN AND YOKO

Words and Music by JOHN LENNON
and PAUL McCARTNEY

did - n't e - ven give us a chance.
mar - ried in Gib - ral - tar near Spain." Christ! you know it ain't eas-
on - ly try'n to get us some peace."

F

-y,___   you know how hard it can be;___

C

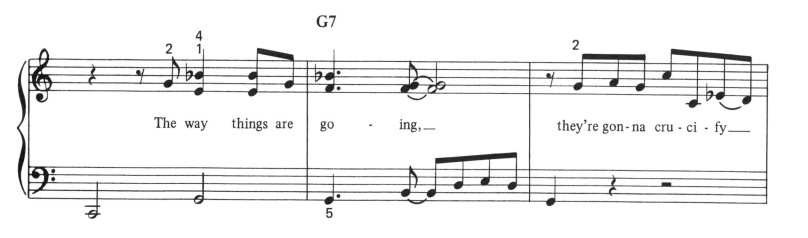

G7

The way things are go - ing,___   they're gon-na cru-ci-fy___

C

me.   3. Drove from

32

Sav - ing up your mon - ey for a

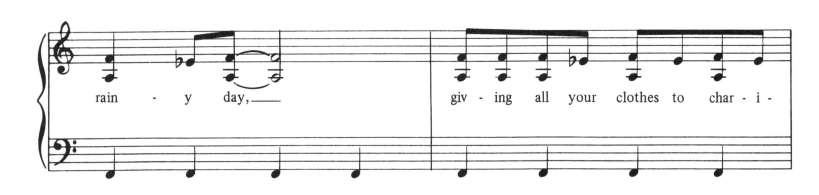

rain - y day, _____ giv - ing all your clothes to char - i -

ty, Last night the wife said, "Oh boy, when you're dead, you

don't take noth - ing with you but your soul." _____ Think!

33

4. Made a light-ning trip to Vi-en - na, — eat-ing choc-'late cake in a bag, —
5. Caught the ear - ly plane back to Lon - don, — fif - ty a - corns tied in a sack,

The news-pa-pers said, — "She's gone to his head; — They
The men from the press— said, "We wish you suc-cess; — It's

look just like two gu-rus in drag." — } Christ! You know it ain't eas-
good to have the both of you back." —

- y, — you know how hard it can be. —

BECAUSE

Words and Music by JOHN LENNON
and PAUL McCARTNEY

Moderately Slow

36

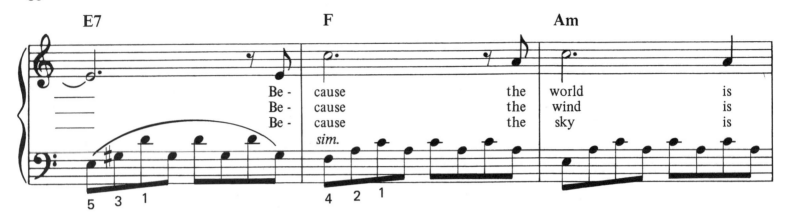

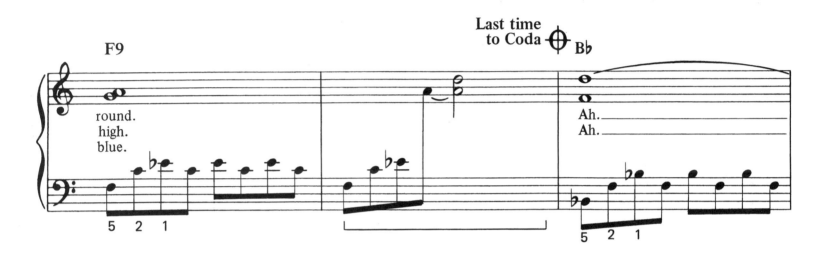

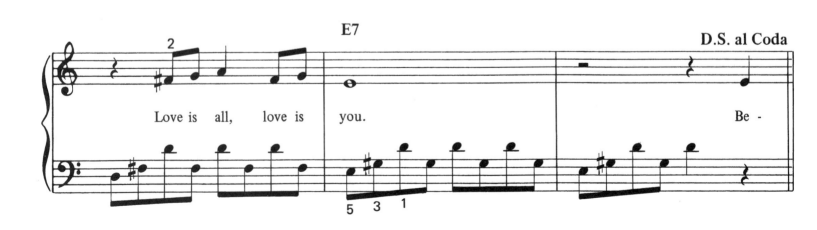

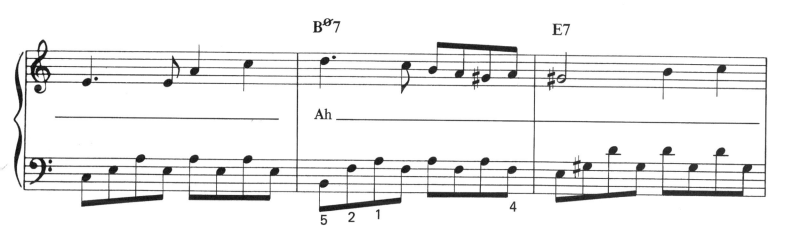

BIRTHDAY

Words and Music by JOHN LENNON
and PAUL McCARTNEY

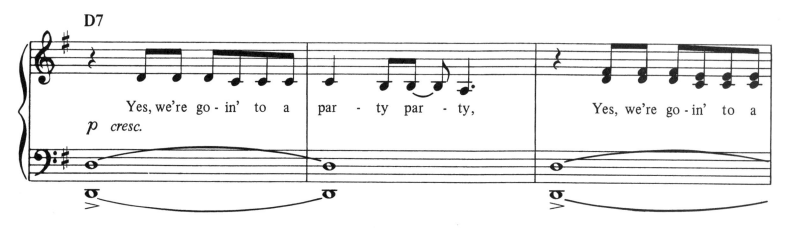

I would like you to dance,—

dance!

p cresc.

D.C. al Coda

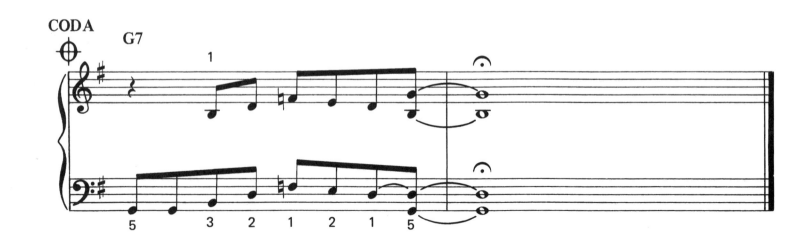

CODA

COME TOGETHER

Words and Music by JOHN LENNON
and PAUL McCARTNEY

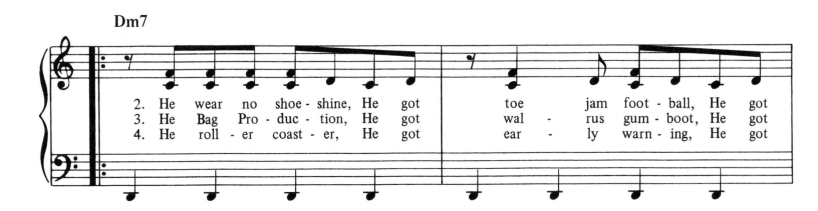

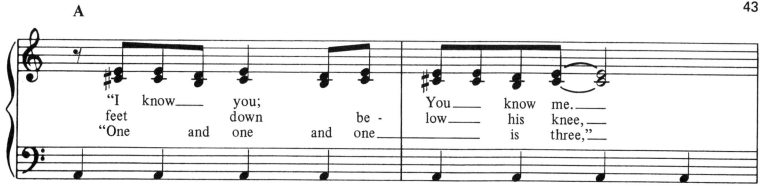

A

"I know____ you; You____ know me.____
feet down be- low____ his knee,____
"One and one and one____ is three,"

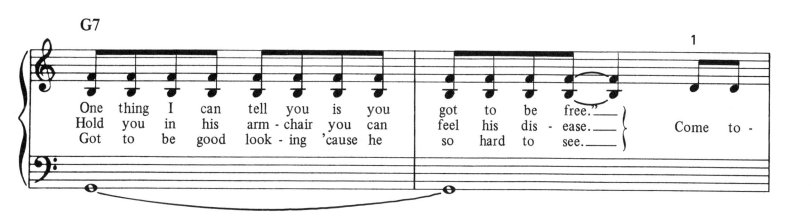

G7

One thing I can tell you is you got to be free."____
Hold you in his arm-chair you can feel his dis-ease.____
Got to be good look-ing 'cause he so hard to see.____

1 Come to-

Bm **G** **Dm7**

geth-er,____ right now,____ o-ver me!

After 4th verse, D.C. and fade

BLACKBIRD

Words and Music by JOHN LENNON
and PAUL McCARTNEY

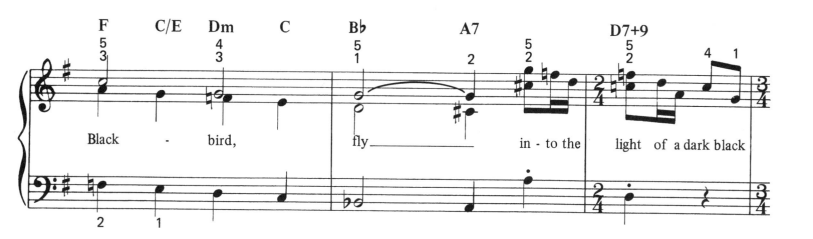

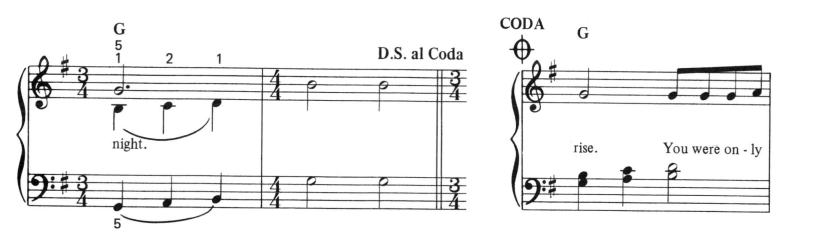

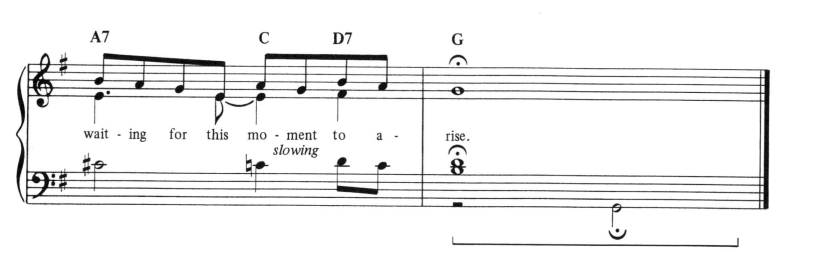

CAN'T BUY ME LOVE

Words and Music by JOHN LENNON
and PAUL McCARTNEY

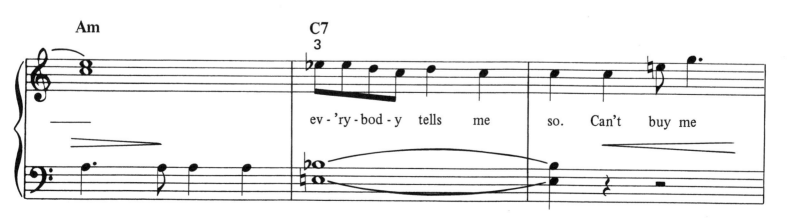

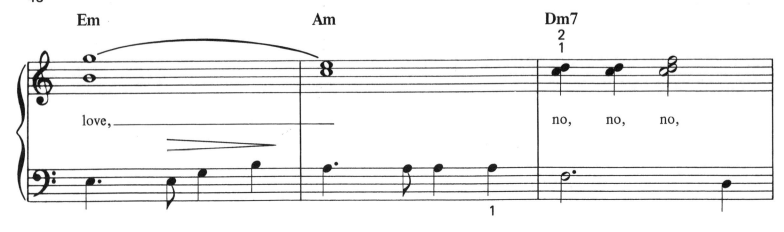

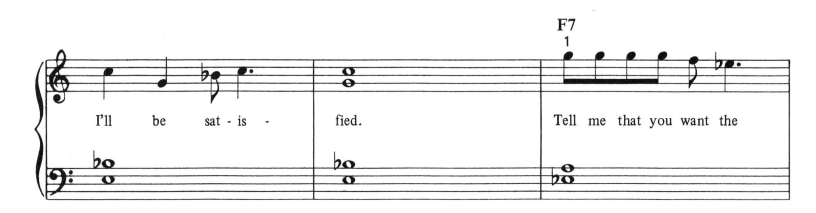

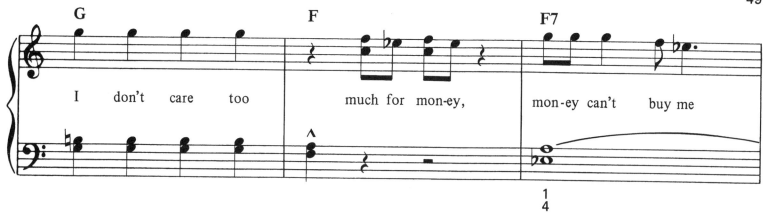

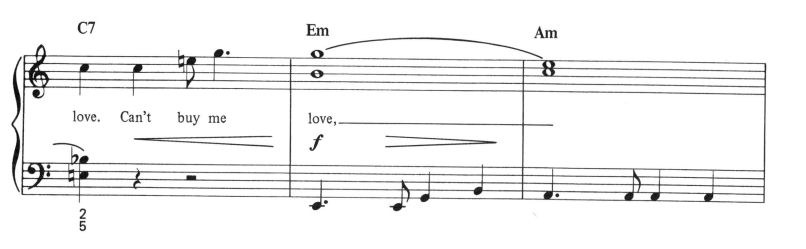

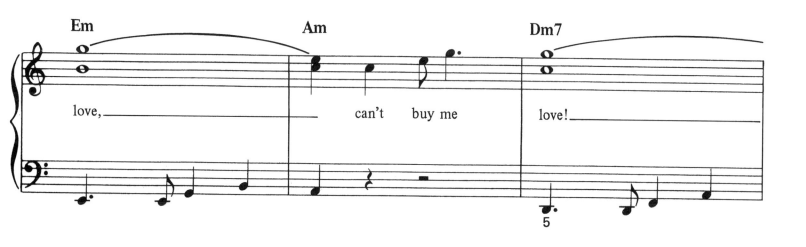

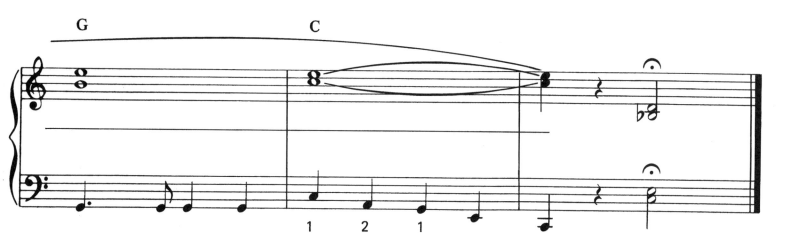

CARRY THAT WEIGHT

Words and Music by JOHN LENNON
and PAUL McCARTNEY

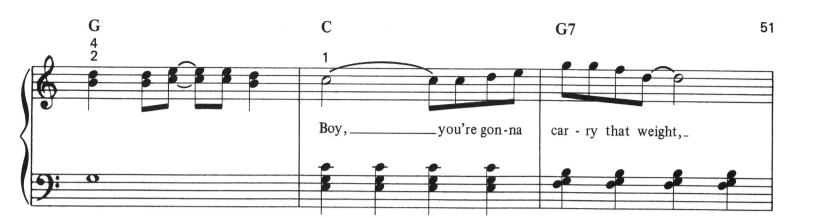

G   C   G7

Boy, _____ you're gon-na   car - ry that weight,_

C

car - ry that weight_ a   long time._   Boy, _____ you're gon-na

G7   C   G

car - ry that weight,_   car - ry that weight_ a   long time._

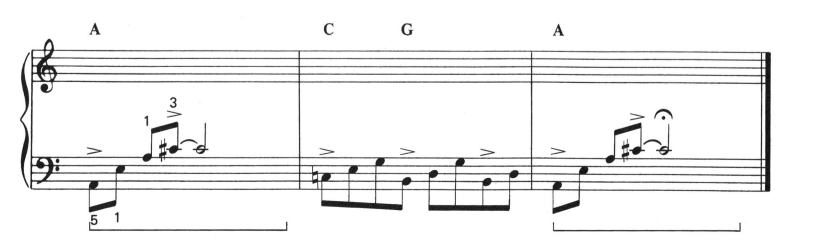

A   C   G   A

A DAY IN THE LIFE

Words and Music by JOHN LENNON
and PAUL McCARTNEY

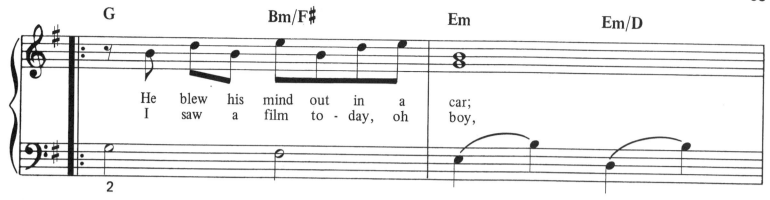

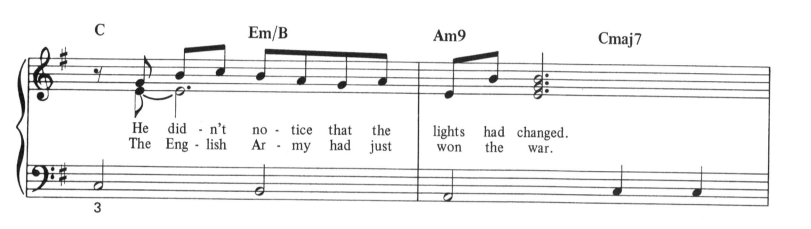

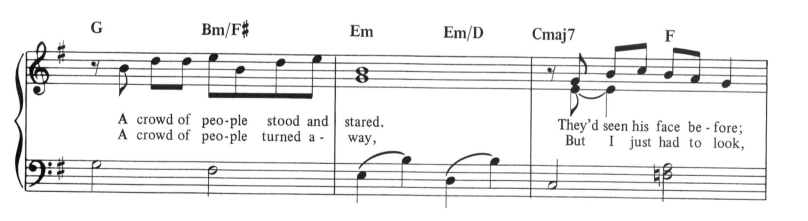

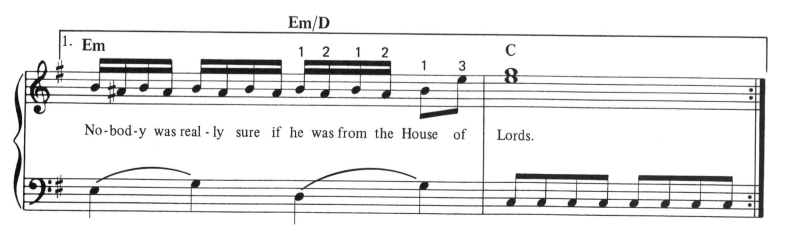

2.

Em | Em/D | C | Bm/D

Hav-ing read the book, I'd love to turn _____

Em | Am7 | Em

you _____ on. _____

Twice as fast (♪=♩)

E (maj)

Woke up, got out of bed; Dragged a comb a-cross my

D | E

head. Found my way down stairs and

55

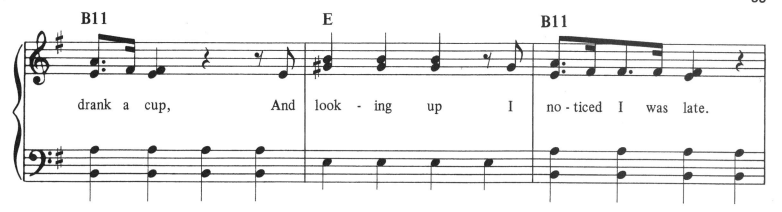

drank a cup, And look - ing up I no - ticed I was late.

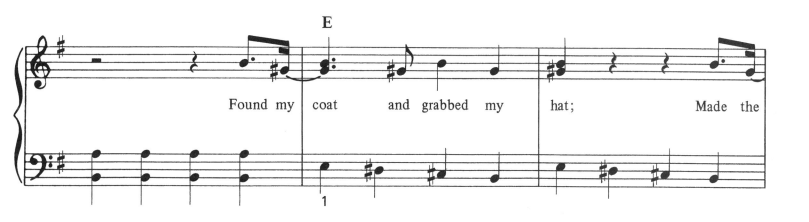

Found my coat and grabbed my hat; Made the

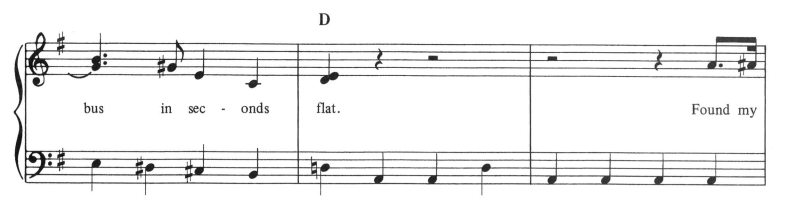

bus in sec - onds flat. Found my

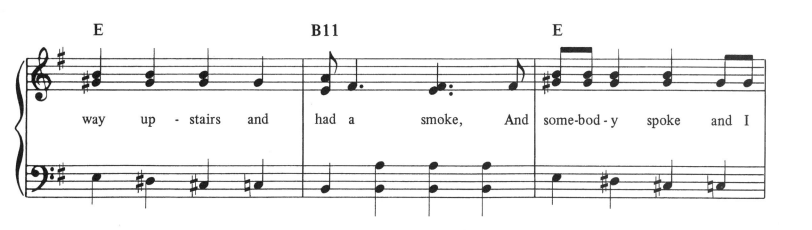

way up - stairs and had a smoke, And some-bod - y spoke and I

Original tempo

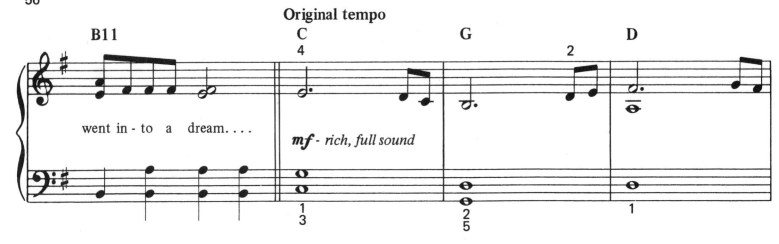

went in-to a dream....

mf - rich, full sound

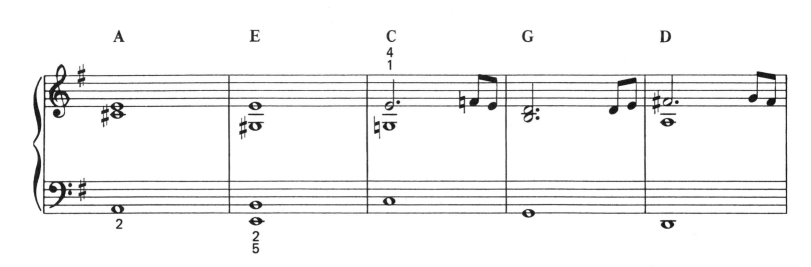

I read the news to-day, oh

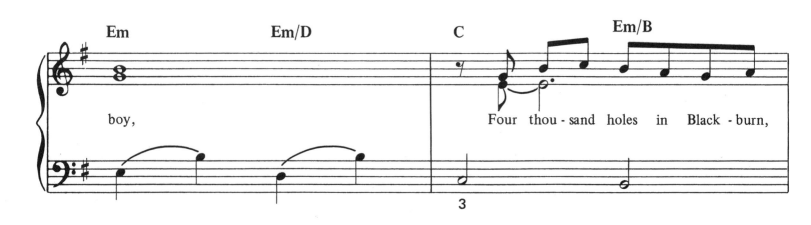

boy,

Four thou-sand holes in Black-burn,

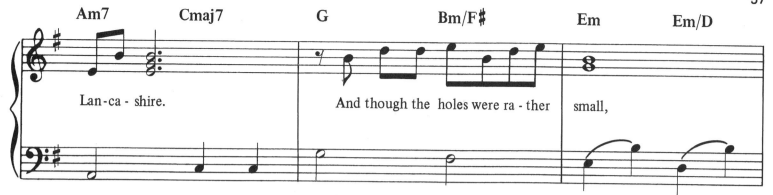

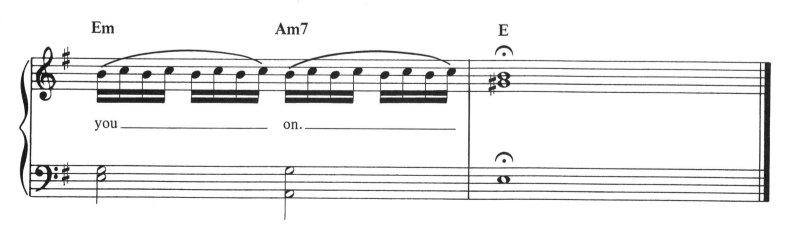

DAY TRIPPER

Words and Music by JOHN LENNON
and PAUL McCARTNEY

for / she / she

tak - ing the eas - y way / took me half___ the way / on - ly played_ one night

out, / there, / stands

now; / now; / now;

She was a / She was a / She was a

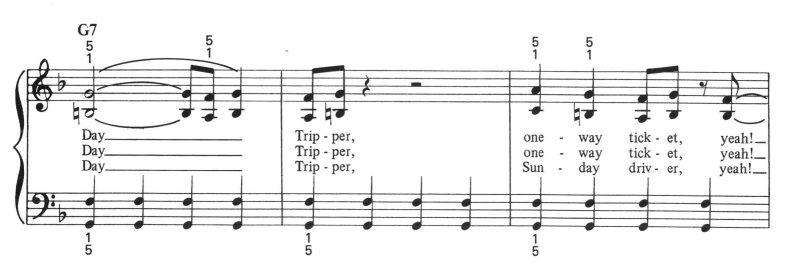

Day_____ / Day_____ / Day_____

Trip - per, / Trip - per, / Trip - per,

one - way / one - way / Sun - day

tick - et, / tick - et, / driv - er,

yeah!_ / yeah!_ / yeah!_

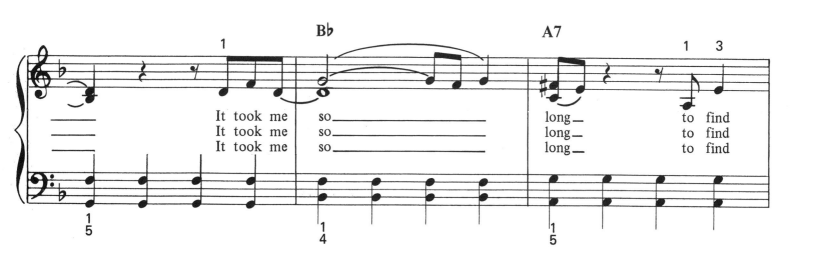

It took me / It took me / It took me

so_____ / so_____ / so_____

long_ / long_ / long_

to find / to find / to find

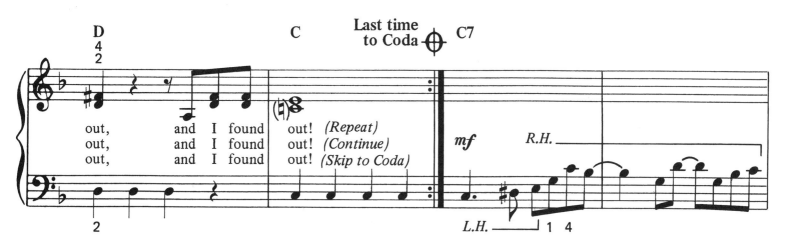

out, / out, / out,

and I found / and I found / and I found

out! *(Repeat)* / out! *(Continue)* / out! *(Skip to Coda)*

Last time
to Coda

mf

R.H.

L.H.

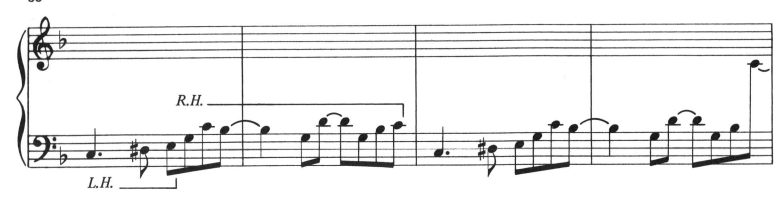

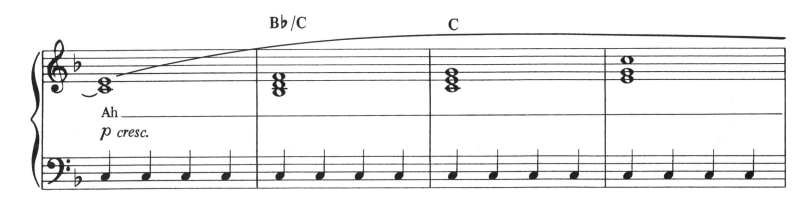

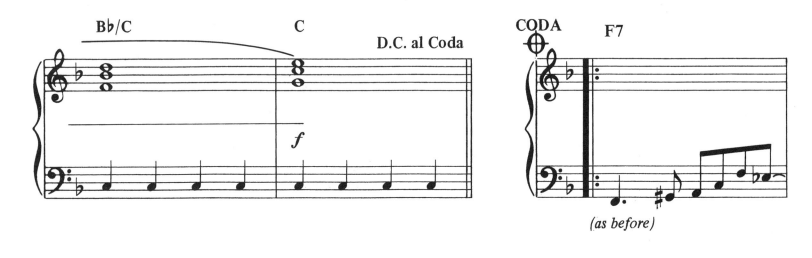

DON'T LET ME DOWN

Words and Music by JOHN LENNON
and PAUL McCARTNEY

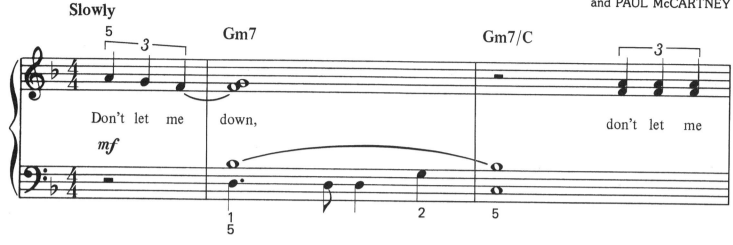

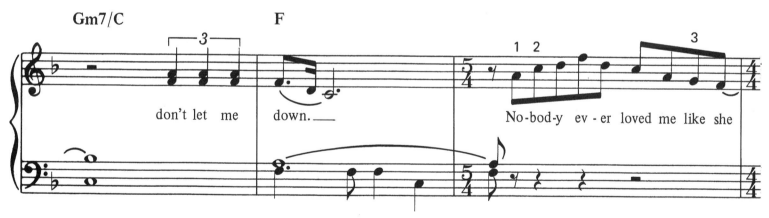

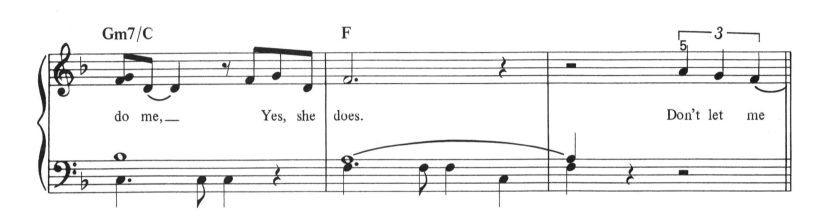

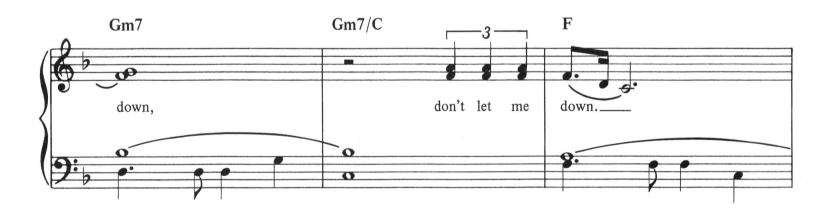

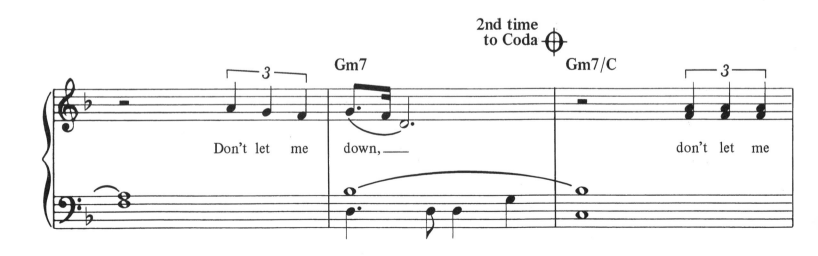

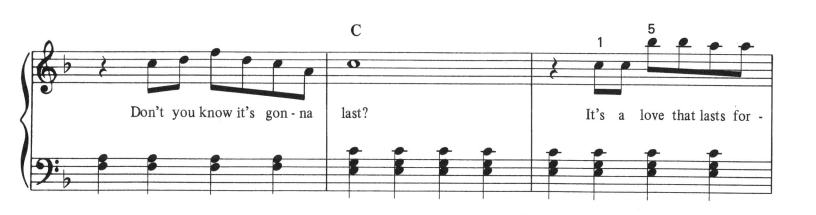

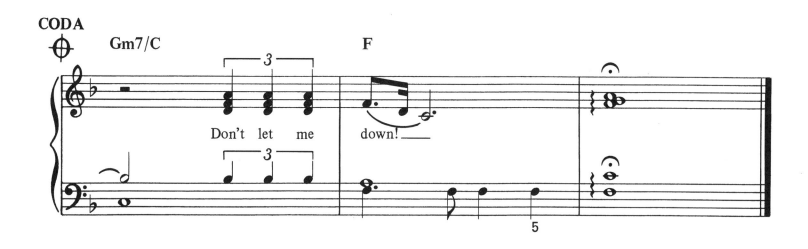

DEAR PRUDENCE

Slowly, in 2 (♩ = 1 beat)

Words and Music by JOHN LENNON
and PAUL McCARTNEY

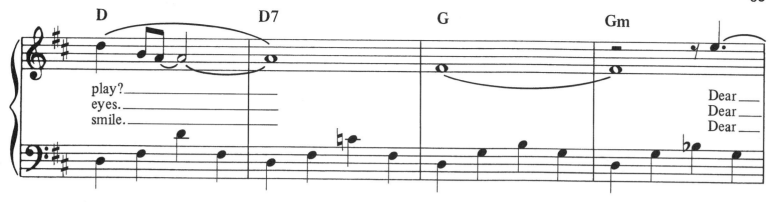

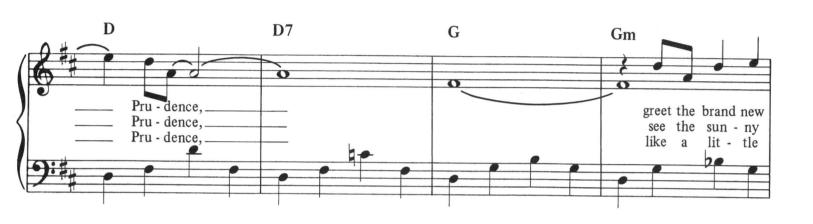

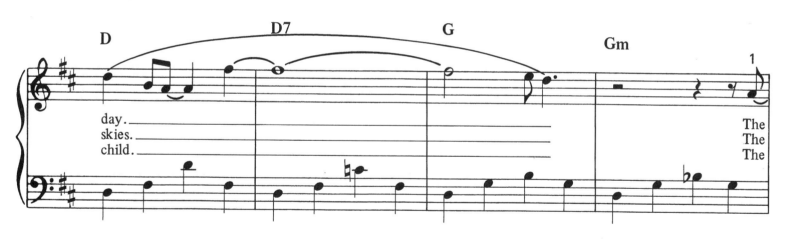

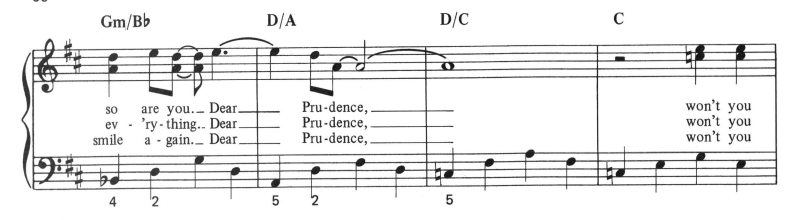

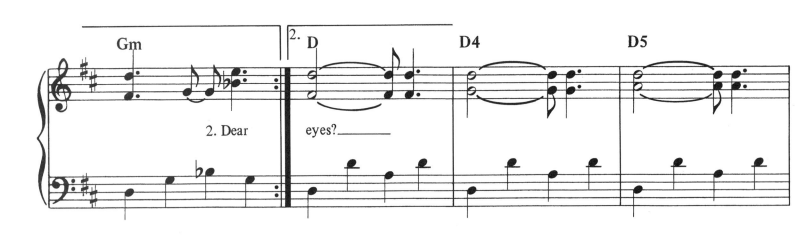

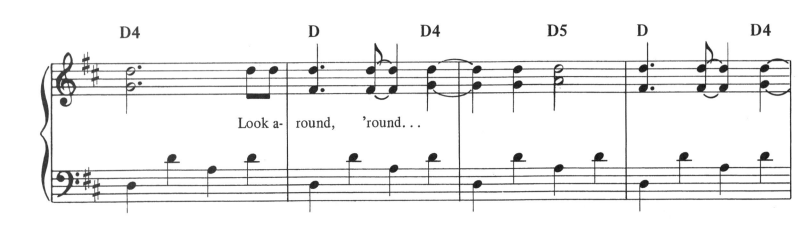

Look a - round, round...

Look a - round.

D.S. al Coda

1

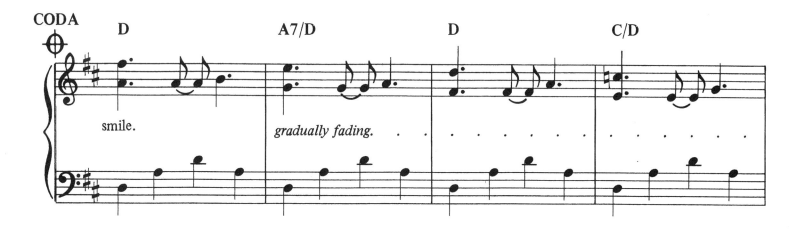

CODA

smile.

gradually fading. . . . .

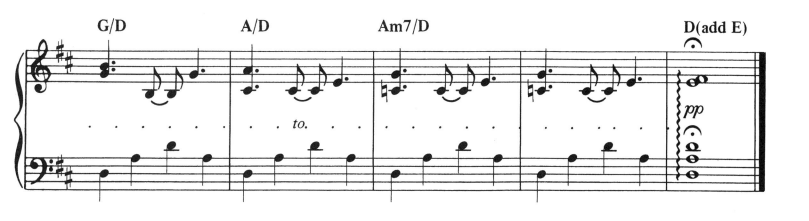

. . . . *to.* . . . .

DO YOU WANT TO KNOW A SECRET

Words and Music by JOHN LENNON
and PAUL McCARTNEY

You'll nev-er know how much I real-ly love you; You'll nev-er know how much I real-ly care.

Lis-ten,__ (doo dah doo) do you want to know a se-cret?__ (doo dah doo) Do you prom-ise not to tell? Wo__ wo__ clos-er,__ (doo dah doo) let me whis-per in your

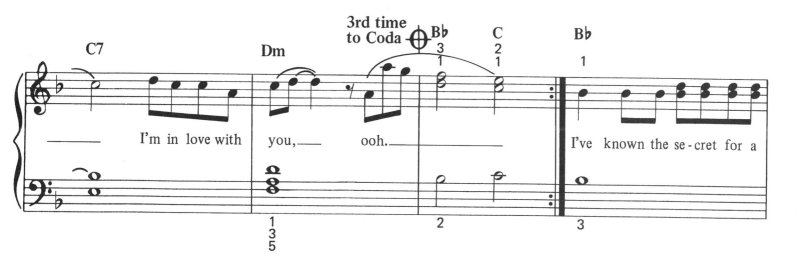

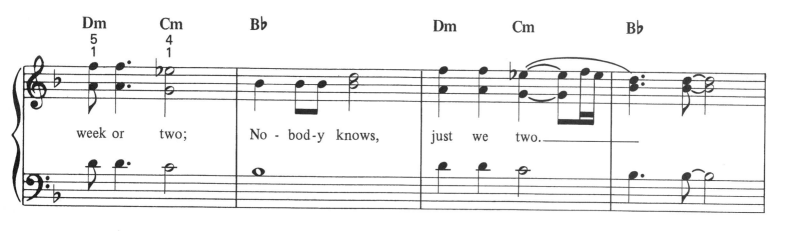

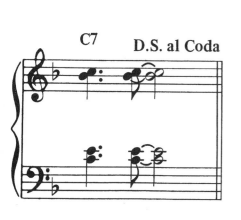

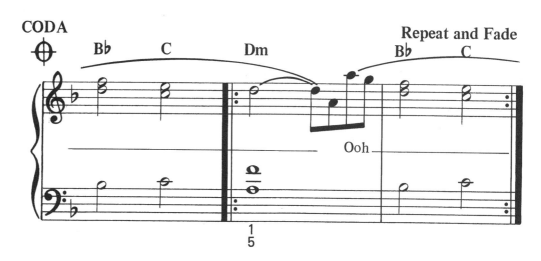

DRIVE MY CAR

Words and Music by JOHN LENNON
and PAUL McCARTNEY

With a beat

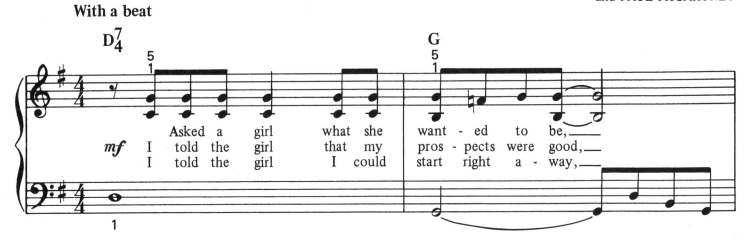

Asked a girl what she want-ed to be,___
I told the girl what that my pros-pects were good,___
I told the girl I could start right a-way,___

She said, "Ba-by, can't you see?___
And she said, "Ba-by, it's un-der-stood.___
And she said, "Listen, babe, I got some-thing to say.___

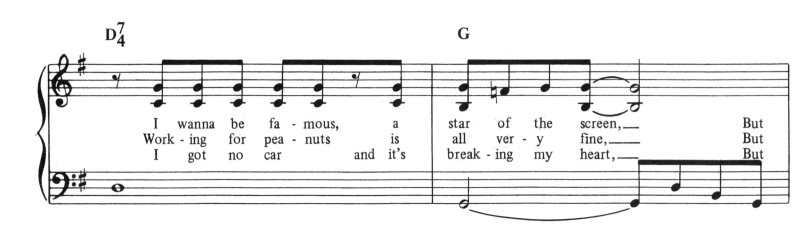

I wan-na be fa-mous, a star of the screen,___ But
Work-ing for pea-nuts is all ver-y fine,___ But
I got no car and it's break-ing my heart,___ But

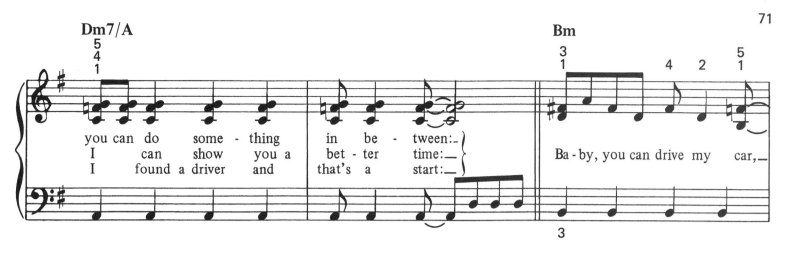

you can do some-thing in be-tween:
I can show you a bet-ter time:
I found a driver and that's a start:

Ba-by, you can drive my car,

Yes, I'm gon-na be a star,

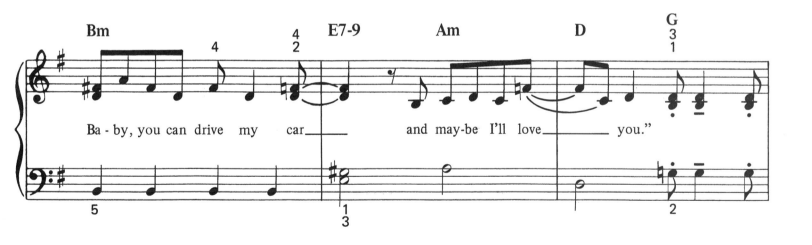

Ba-by, you can drive my car and may-be I'll love you."

Beep beep mm beep beep, yeah!

EIGHT DAYS A WEEK

Words and Music by JOHN LENNON
and PAUL McCARTNEY

Ooh I need your love, babe, guess you know it's true;
Love you ev - 'ry day, girl, al - ways on my mind;

Hope you need my love, babe, just like I need you.
One thing I can say, girl, love you all the time.

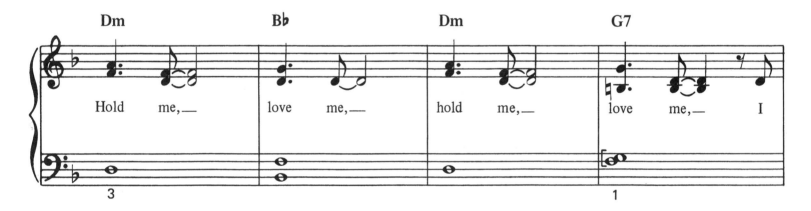

Hold me, love me, hold me, love me, I

ain't got noth-in' but love, babe, eight days a week.

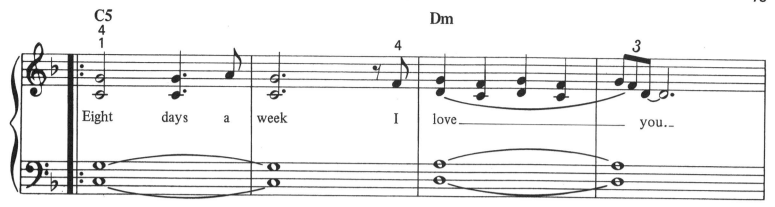

Eight days a week I love_____ you.__

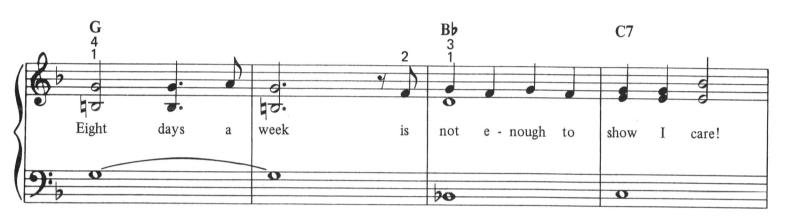

Eight days a week is not e-nough to show I care!

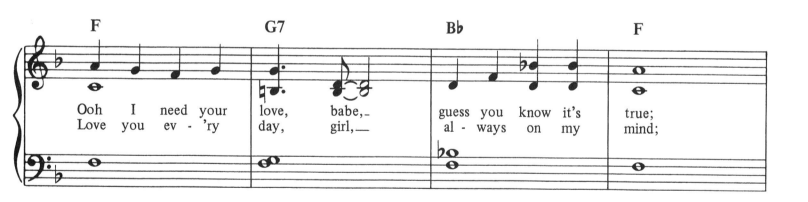

Ooh I need your love, babe,__ guess you know it's true;
Love you ev-'ry day, girl,__ al-ways on my mind;

Hope you need my love, babe,__ just like I need you.}
One thing I can say, girl,__ love you all the time.}

74

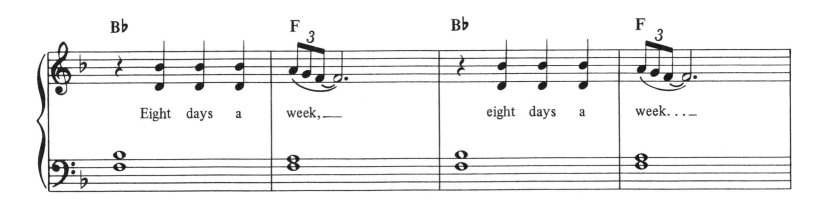

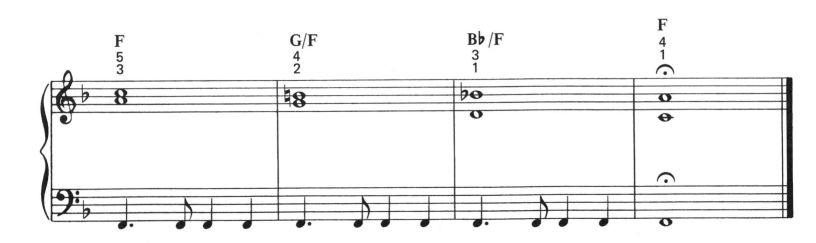

ELEANOR RIGBY

Words and Music by JOHN LENNON
and PAUL McCARTNEY

Moderately, with a steady beat

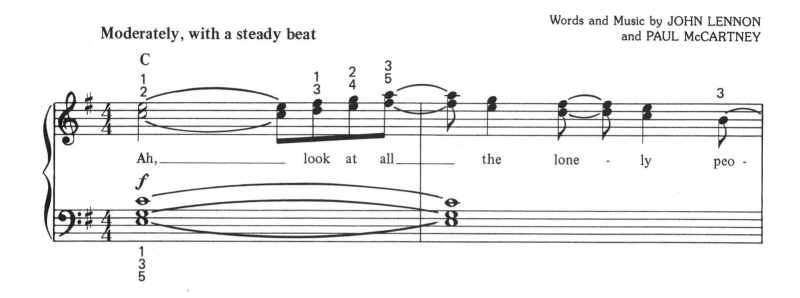

Ah, _____ look at all _____ the lone - ly peo-

- ple! _____

1. El - ea - nor Rig - by   picks up the rice _____ in the church
2. Fa - ther Mc Ken - zie,   writ - ing the words _____ of a ser-
3. El - ea - nor Rig - by,   died in the church _____ and was bur-

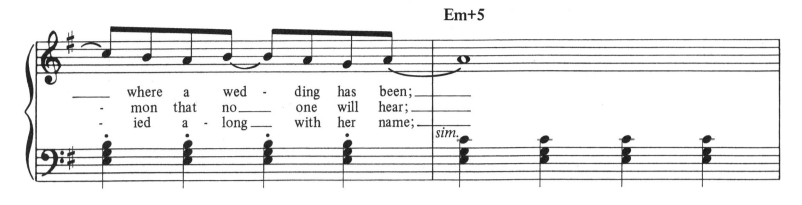

Em+5

sim.

where a wed - ding has been;
- mon that no____ one will hear;
- ied a - long____ with her name;

Em

Lives in a dream.____
No one comes near.____
No - bod - y came.____

Waits at the win - dow,
Look at him work - ing,
Fa - ther Mc Ken - zie,

1

wear - ing the face____ that she keeps____ in a jar____ by the door;
darn - ing his socks____ in the night____ when there's no - bod - y there;
wip - ing the dirt____ from his hands____ as he walks____ from the grave;

Em+5

Em

Who is it for?____
What does he care?____
No one was saved.____

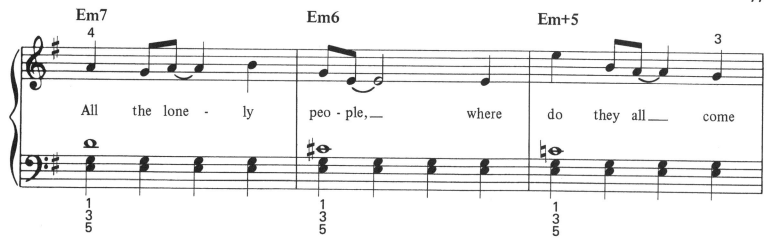

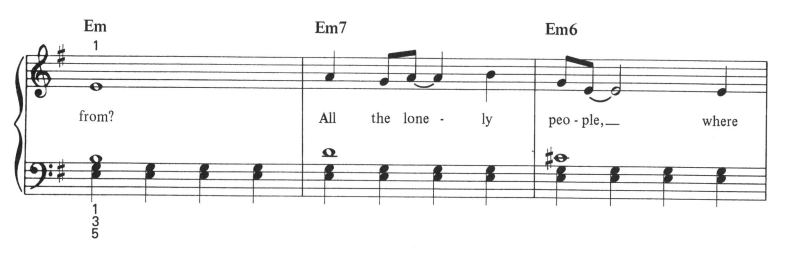

EVERY LITTLE THING

Words and Music by JOHN LENNON
and PAUL McCARTNEY

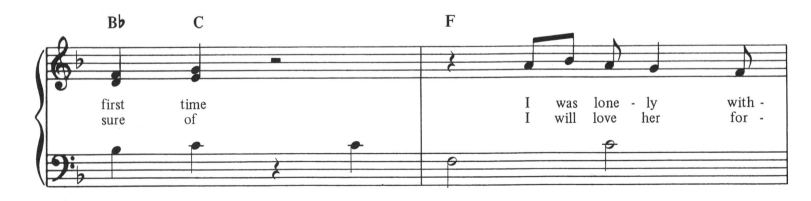

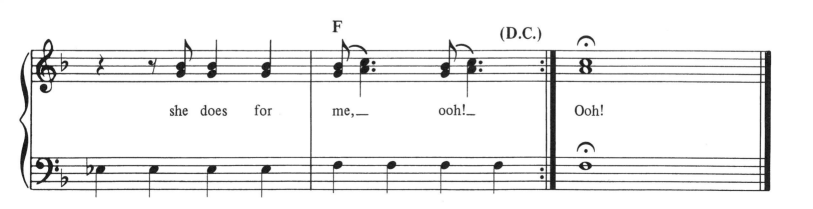

FIXING A HOLE

Words and Music by JOHN LENNON
and PAUL McCARTNEY

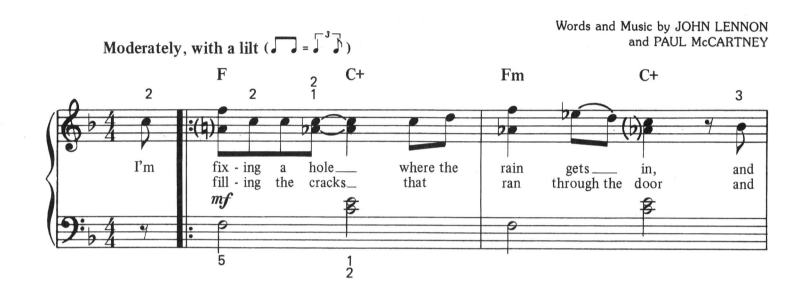

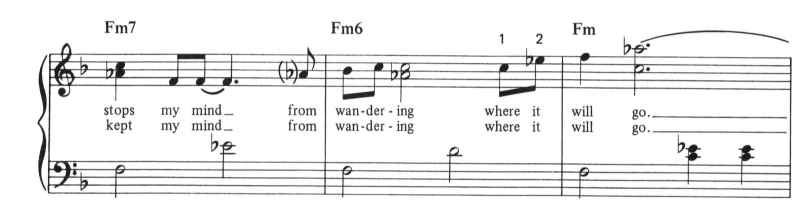

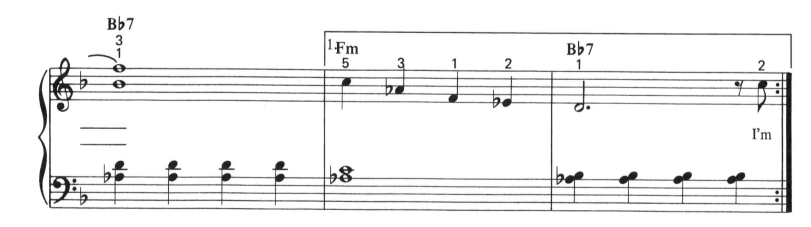

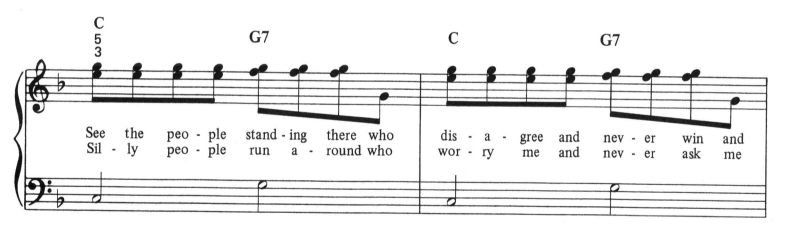

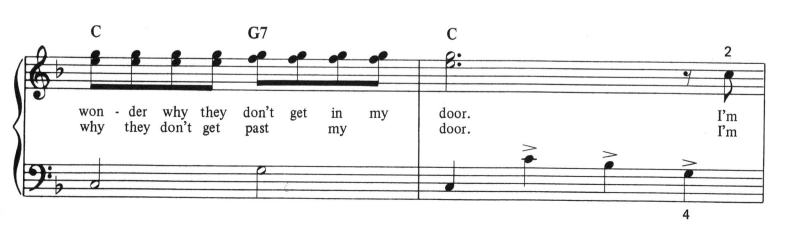

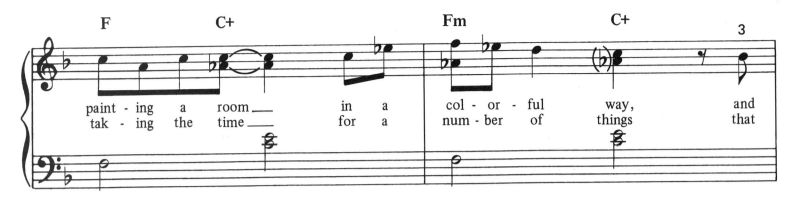

3

F   C+   Fm   C+

paint - ing   a   room ____   in a   col - or - ful   way,   and
tak - ing   the   time ____   for a   num - ber of   things   that

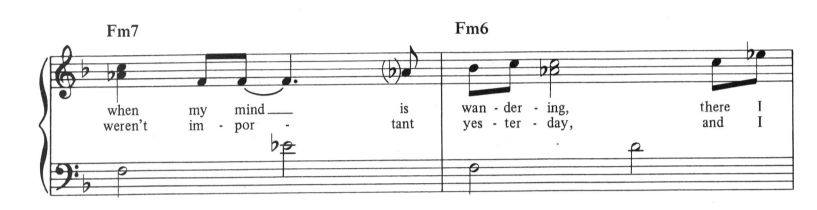

Fm7   Fm6

when   my   mind ____   is   wan - der - ing,   there   I
weren't   im - por -   tant   yes - ter - day,   and   I

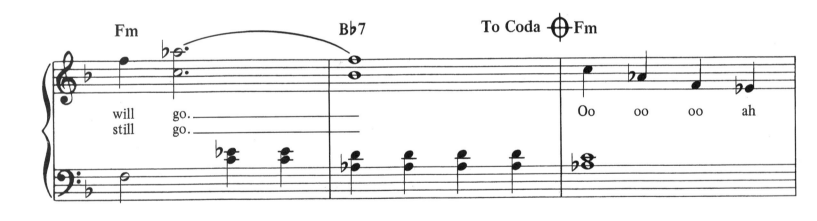

Fm   Bb7   To Coda ✛ Fm

will   go. ____   Oo   oo   oo   ah
still   go. ____

Bb7   D.S. al Coda

ah. . .   And   it

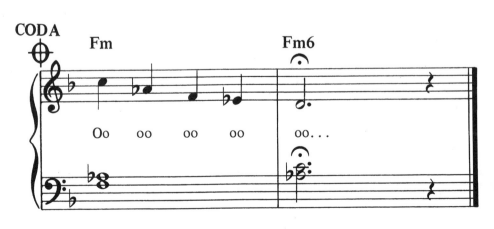

CODA ✛ Fm   Fm6

Oo   oo   oo   oo   oo. . .

THE FOOL ON THE HILL

Words and Music by JOHN LENNON
and PAUL McCARTNEY

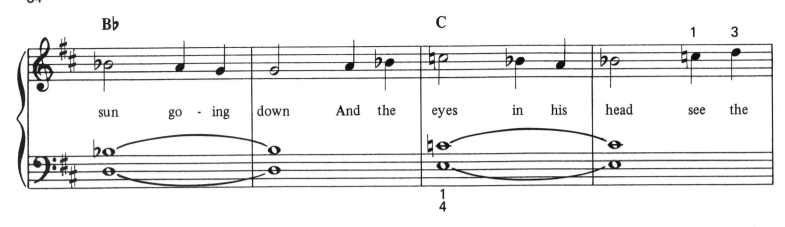

sun go - ing down And the eyes in his head see the

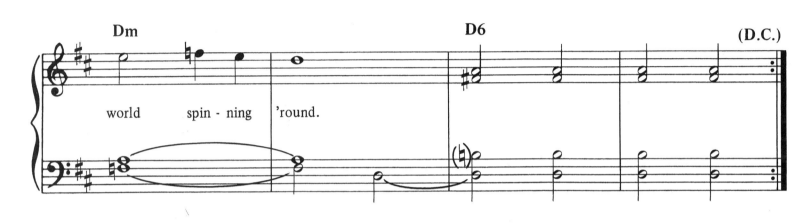

world spin - ning 'round.

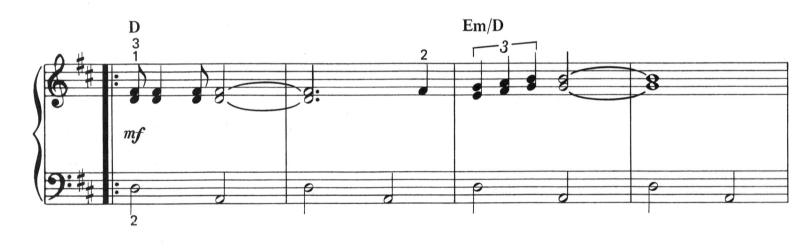

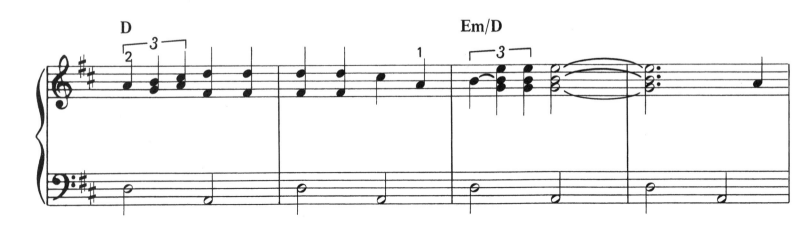

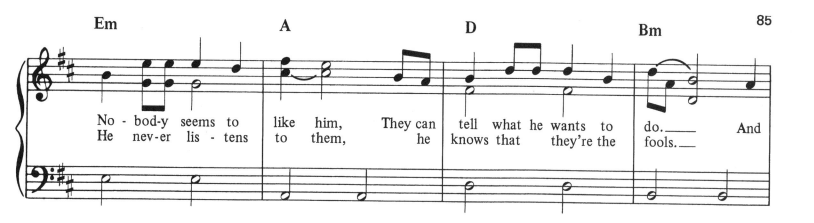

No - bod-y seems to like him, They can tell what he wants to do.____ And
He nev-er lis - tens to them, he knows that they're the fools.____

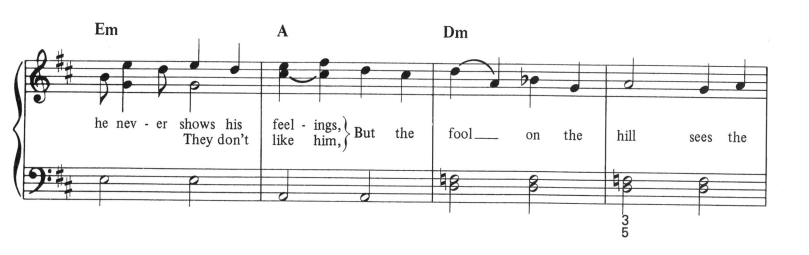

he nev - er shows his feel - ings,
They don't like him, But the fool____ on the hill sees the

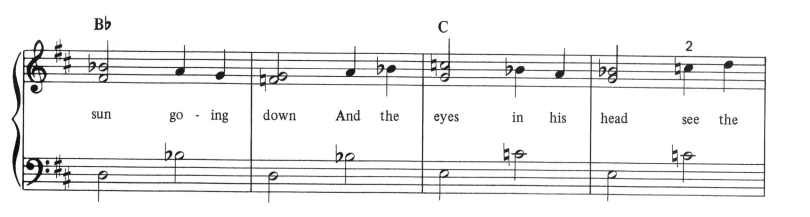

sun go - ing down And the eyes in his head see the

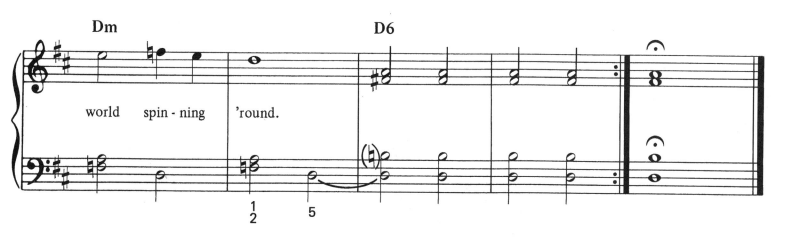

world spin - ning 'round.

FOR NO ONE

Words and Music by JOHN LENNON
and PAUL McCARTNEY

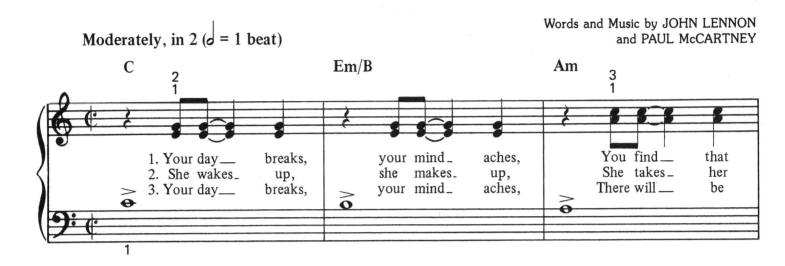

Moderately, in 2 (♩ = 1 beat)

1. Your day breaks, your mind aches, You find that
2. She wakes up, she makes up, She takes her
3. Your day breaks, your mind aches, There will be

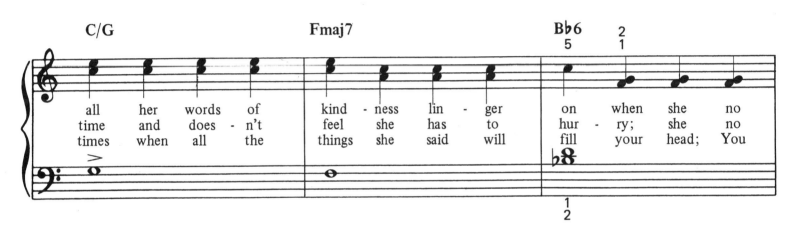

all her words of kind - ness lin - ger on when she no
time and does - n't feel she has to hur - ry; she no
times when all the things she said will fill your head; You

long - er needs you. *(Repeat to the top)*
long - er needs you. *(to 2nd ending)*
won't for - get her. *(to 3rd ending)*

And in her eyes you are

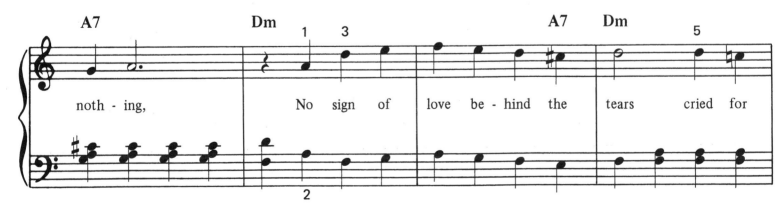

noth - ing, No sign of love be - hind the tears cried for

FROM ME TO YOU

Words and Music by JOHN LENNON
and PAUL McCARTNEY

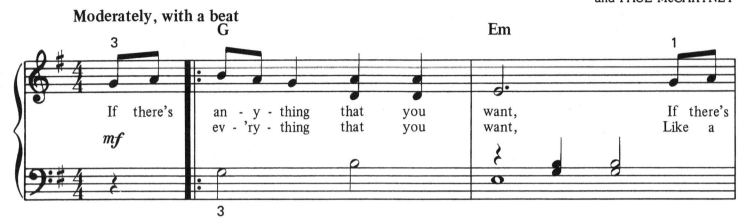

Moderately, with a beat

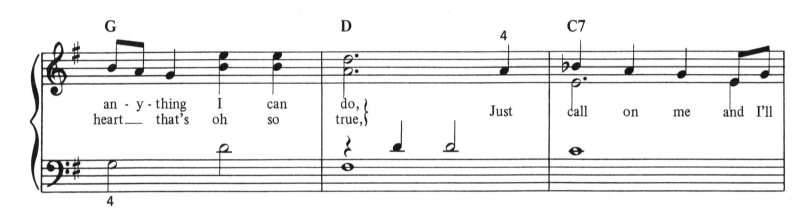

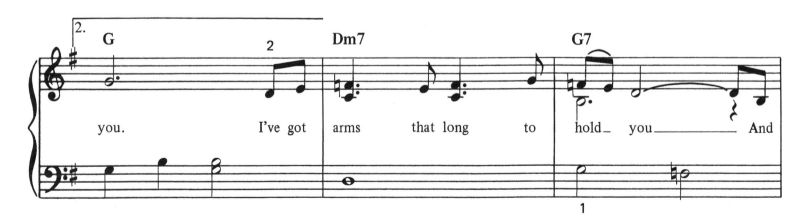

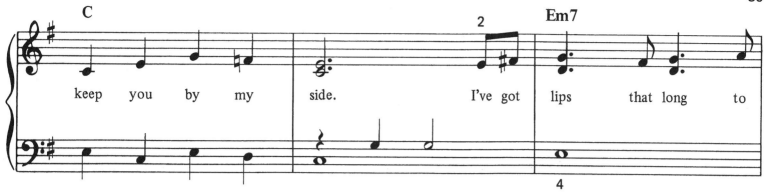

GET BACK

Words and Music by JOHN LENNON
and PAUL McCARTNEY

to where you once be - longed.___ Get back! Get back!

Get back to where you once be - longed.___ 1.(Get back, Jo Jo) 2.___

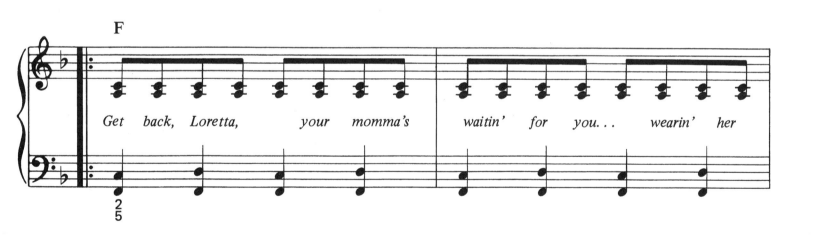

Get back, Loretta, your momma's waitin' for you... wearin' her

Repeat and Fade

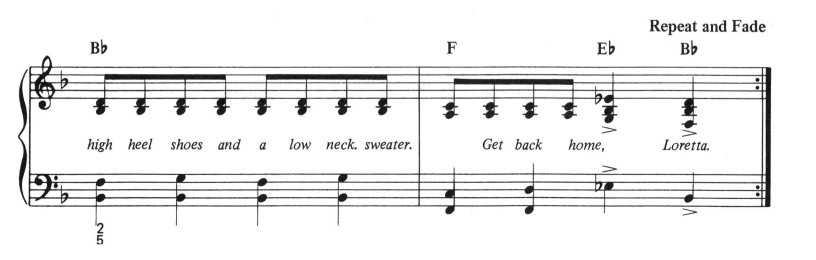

high heel shoes and a low neck sweater. Get back home, Loretta.

GETTING BETTER

Words and Music by JOHN LENNON
and PAUL McCARTNEY

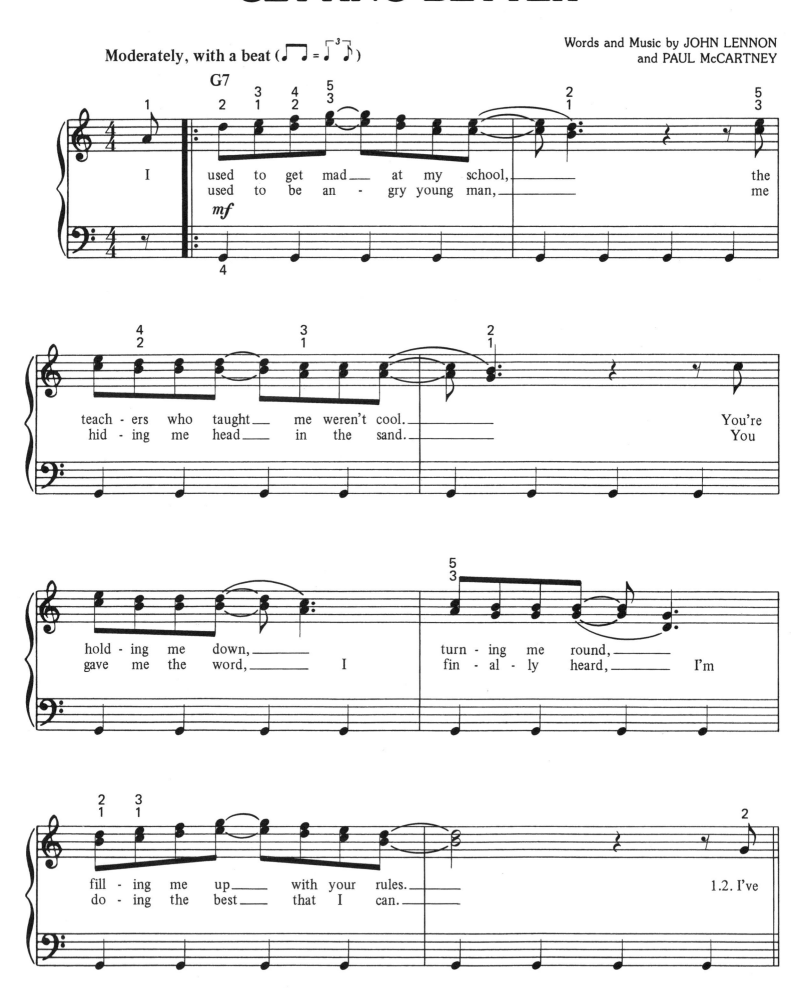

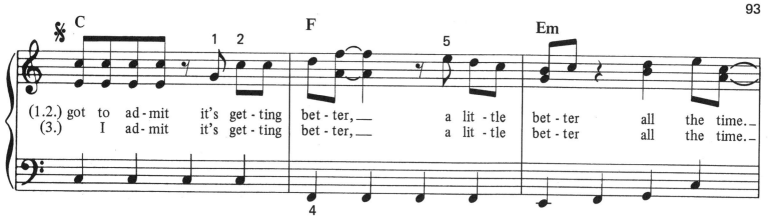

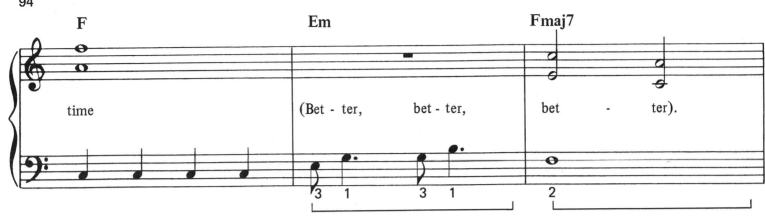

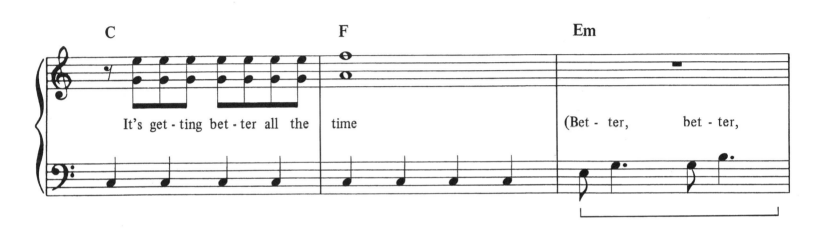

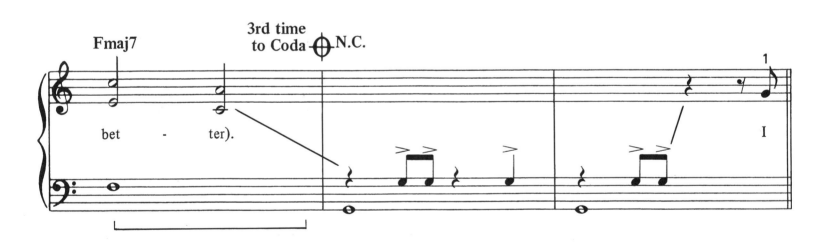

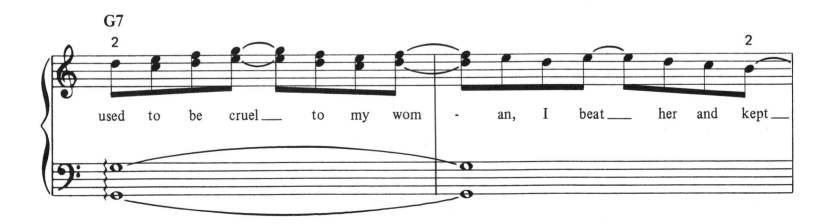

her a - part from the things that she loved.

Man, I was mean, but I'm chang - ing my scene, and I'm do -

D.S. al Coda
(take 3rd lyric
and 3rd ending)

- ing the best that I can.

CODA

F	C	F	C	F	C	F	C

Get - ting so much bet - ter all the time.

GIRL

Words and Music by JOHN LENNON
and PAUL McCARTNEY

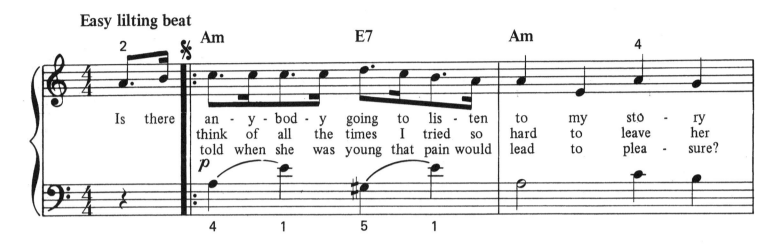

Is there an-y-bod-y going to lis-ten to my sto - ry
think of all the times I tried so hard to leave her
told when she was young that pain would lead to plea - sure?

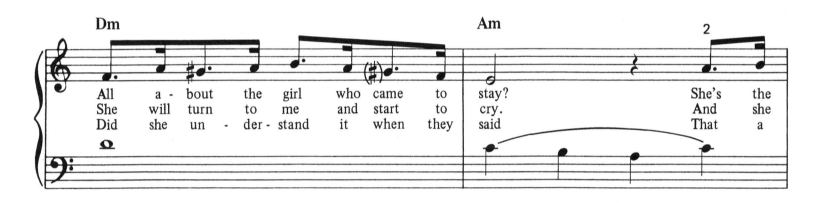

All a-bout the girl who came to stay? She's the
She will turn to me and start to cry. And she
Did she un-der-stand it when they said That a

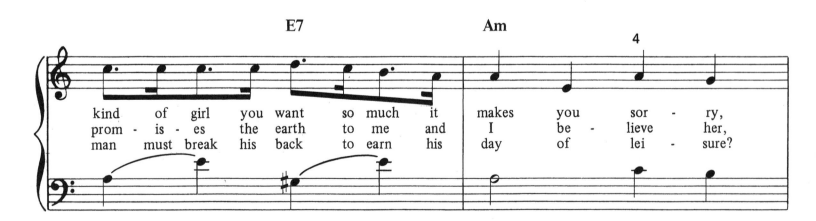

kind of girl you want so much it makes you sor - ry,
prom-is-es the earth to me and I be - lieve her,
man must break his back to earn his day of lei - sure?

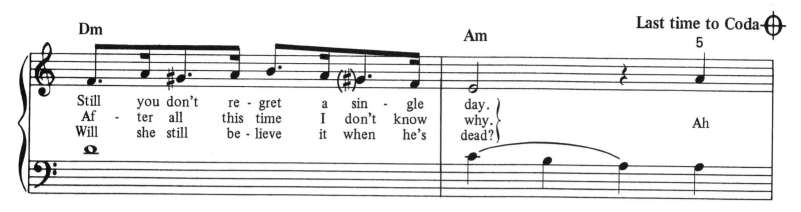

Last time to Coda

Dm   Am

Still   you don't   re - gret   a   sin - gle   day.
Af - ter all   this time   I   don't   know   why.
Will   she still   be - lieve   it   when   he's   dead?

Ah

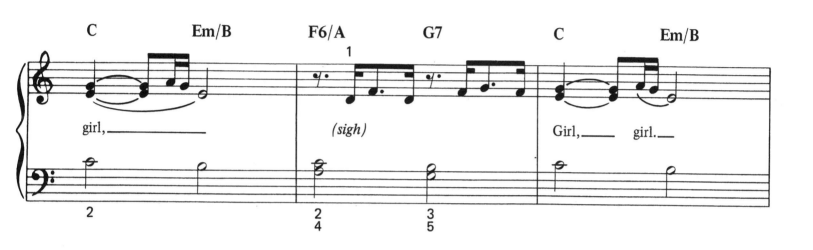

C   Em/B   F6/A   G7   C   Em/B

girl, _____   *(sigh)*   Girl, _____ girl.____

1. F6/A   G   2. F6/A   G7

2. When   I

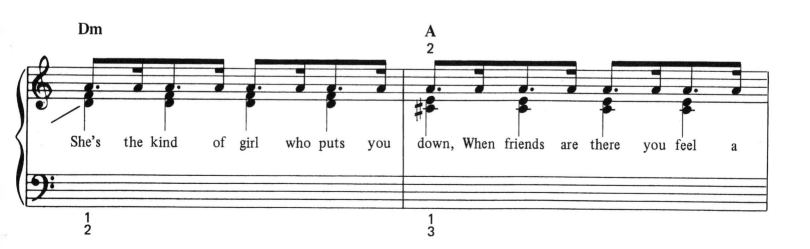

Dm   A

She's   the kind   of girl   who puts   you   down, When friends   are there   you   feel   a

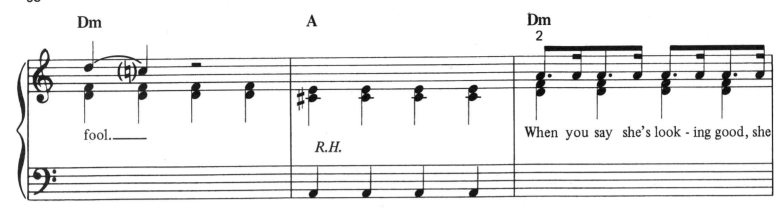

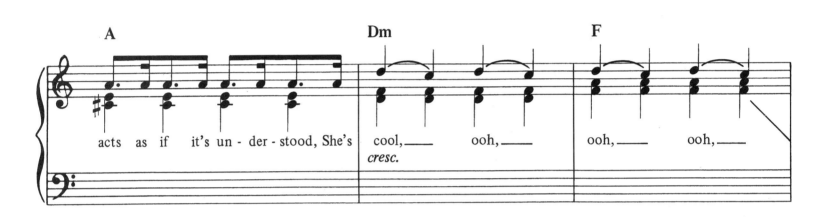

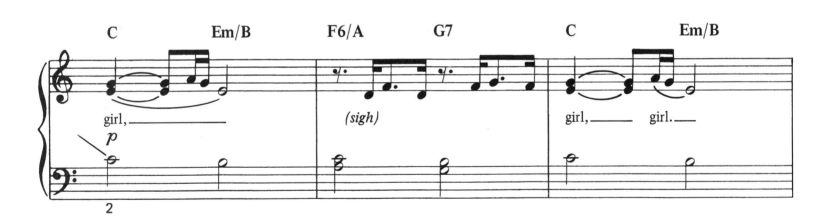

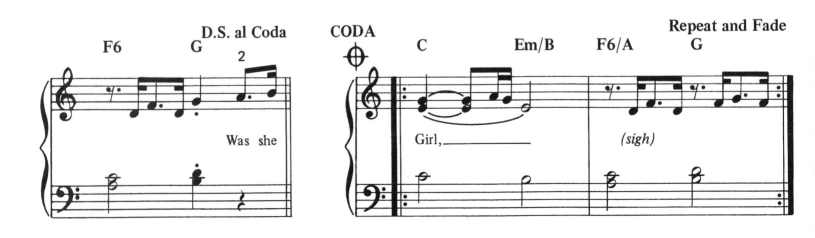

GOT TO GET YOU INTO MY LIFE

Words and Music by JOHN LENNON
and PAUL McCARTNEY

Very steady, with a lilt

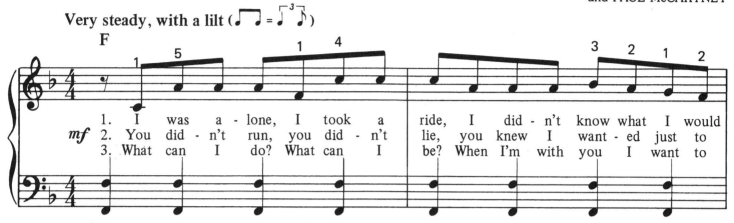

(smaller hands play lower notes only)

1. I was a - lone, I took a ride, I did - n't know what I would
2. You did - n't run, you did - n't lie, you knew I want - ed just to
3. What can I do? What can I be? When I'm with you I want to

find there._
hold you._
stay there._

An - oth - er road where may - be
And had you gone, you knew in
If I'm true I'll nev - er

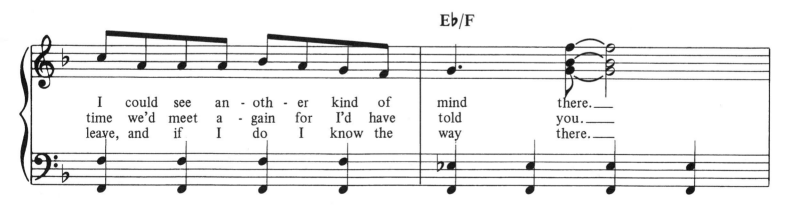

I could see an - oth - er kind of mind there._
time we'd meet a - gain for I'd have told you._
leave, and if I do I know the way there._

100

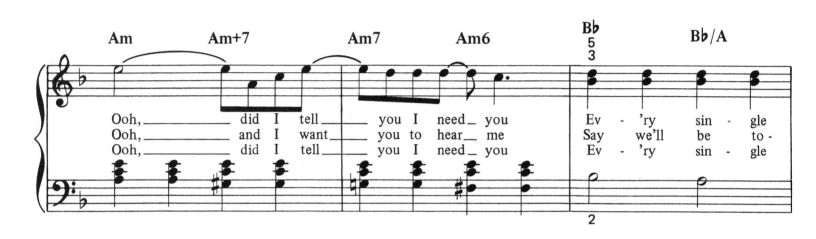

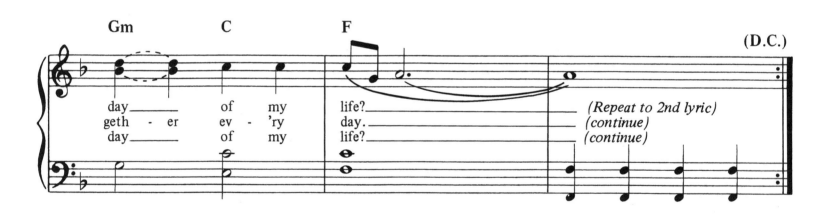

(D.C.)

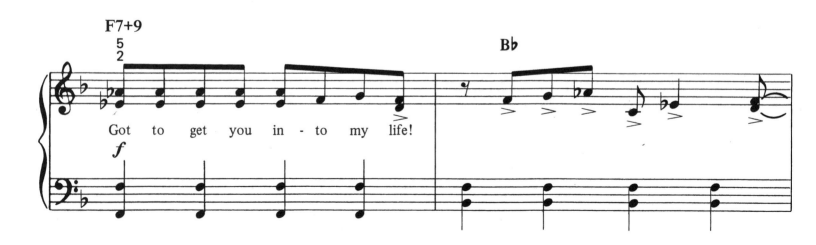

Got to get you in-to my life!

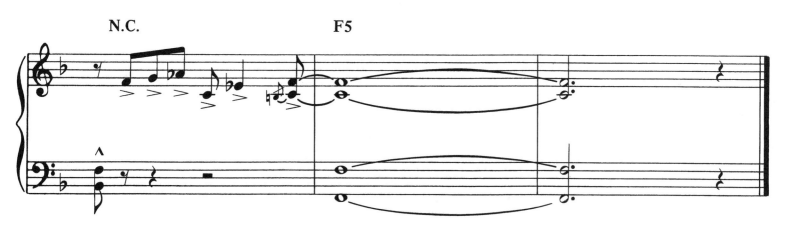

GOLDEN SLUMBERS

Words and Music by JOHN LENNON
and PAUL McCARTNEY

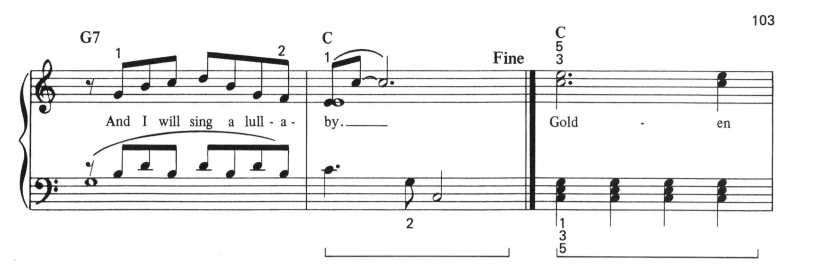

And I will sing a lull-a- by.___ Gold - en

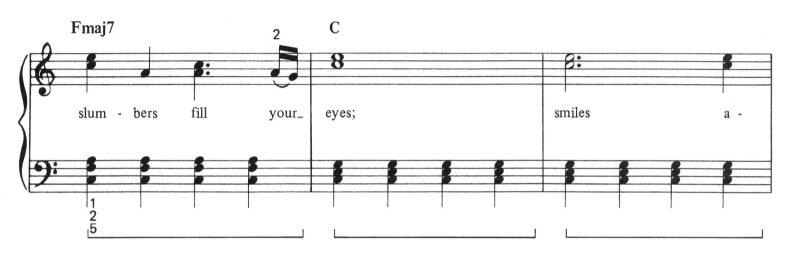

slum - bers fill your_ eyes; smiles a -

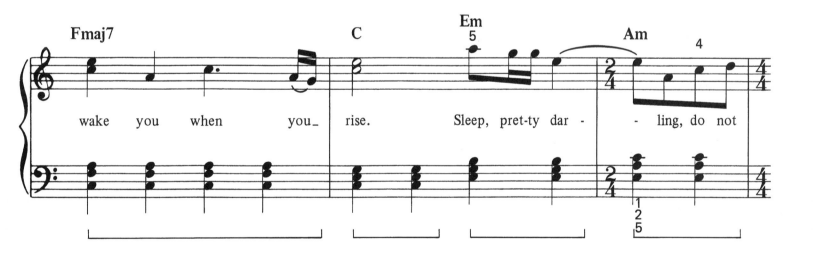

wake you when you_ rise. Sleep, pret-ty dar - - ling, do not

cry, And I will sing a lull-a- by.___

GOOD DAY SUNSHINE

Moderate barrelhouse tempo

Words and Music by JOHN LENNON
and PAUL McCARTNEY

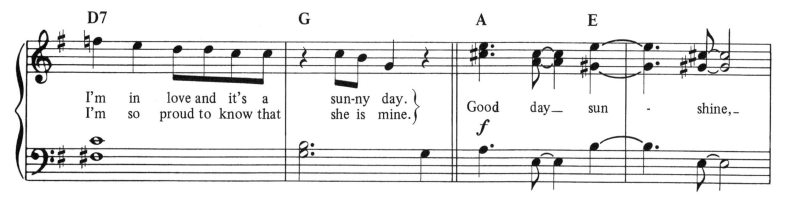

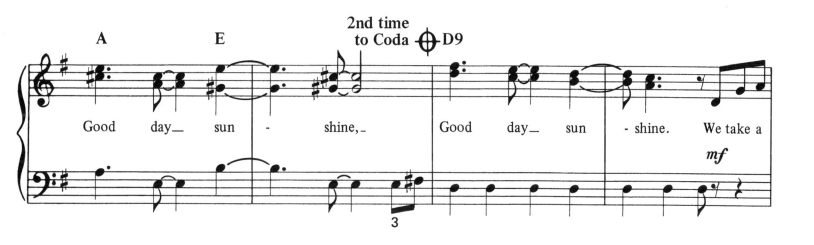

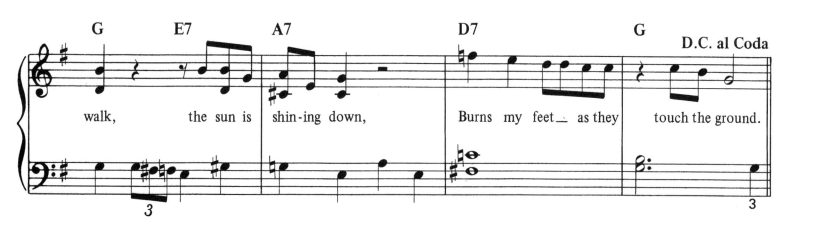

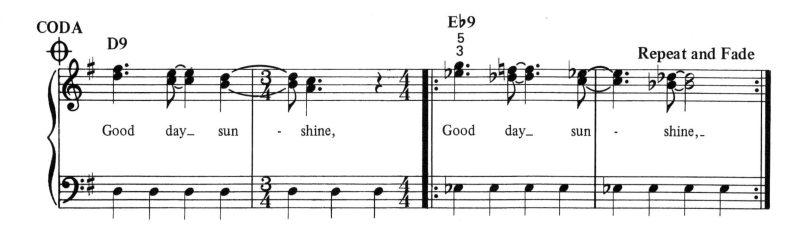

A HARD DAY'S NIGHT

Words and Music by JOHN LENNON
and PAUL McCARTNEY

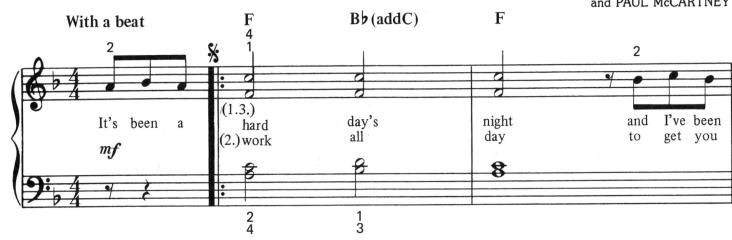

It's been a (1.3.) hard day's all night and I've been
(2.) work day to get you

work-ing like a dog. It's been a hard day's
mon-ey to buy you things. And it's worth it just to hear you

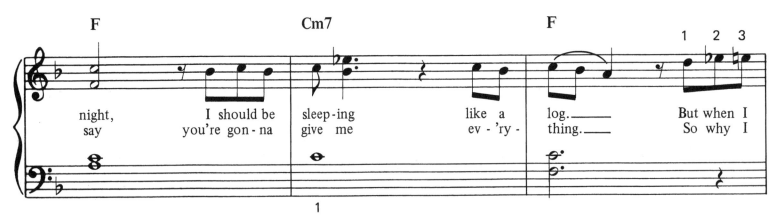

night, I should be sleep-ing like a log. But when I
say you're gon-na give me ev-'ry- thing. So why I

get home to you I find the thing that you do will make me
love to come home 'cause when I get you a-lone you know I'll

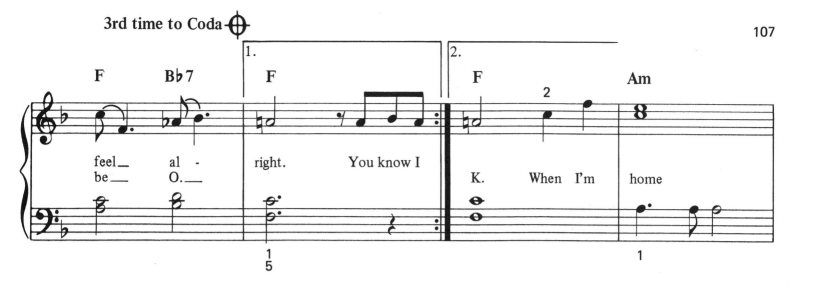
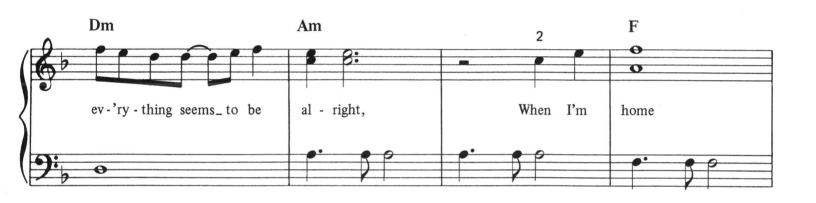
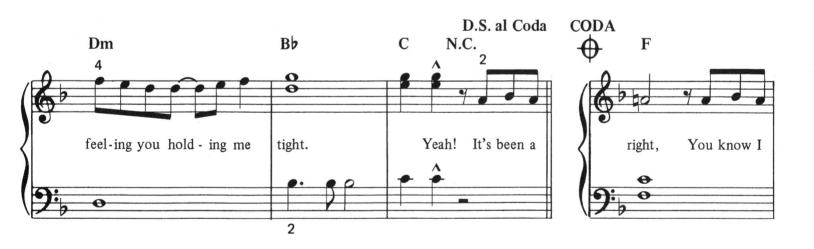

HELLO, GOODBYE

Words and Music by JOHN LENNON
and PAUL McCARTNEY

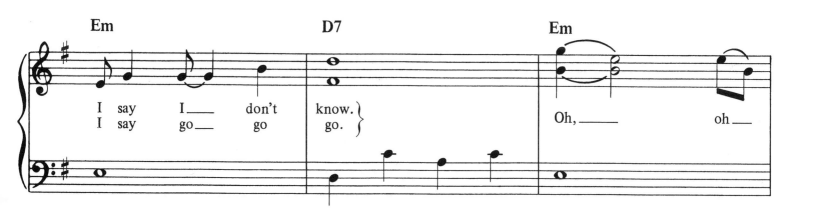

110

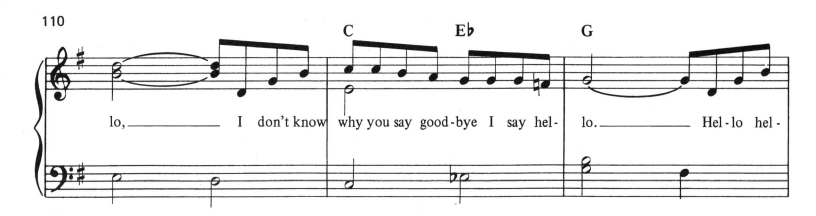

lo, _____ I don't know why you say good-bye I say hel- lo. _____ Hel-lo hel-

lo, _____ I don't know why you say good-bye I say hel- lo.

lo.   Hel - lo. _____

Hel - lo, _____ he - ba _ hel - lo - a...

Repeat and Fade

HELP!

Words and Music by JOHN LENNON
and PAUL McCARTNEY

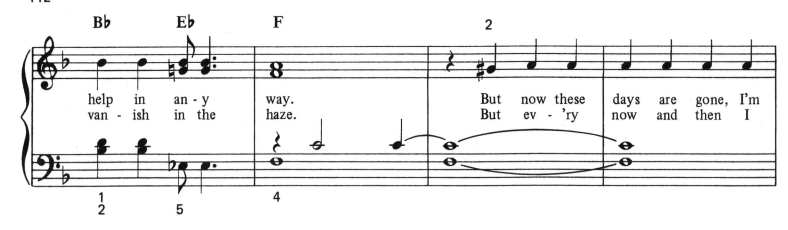

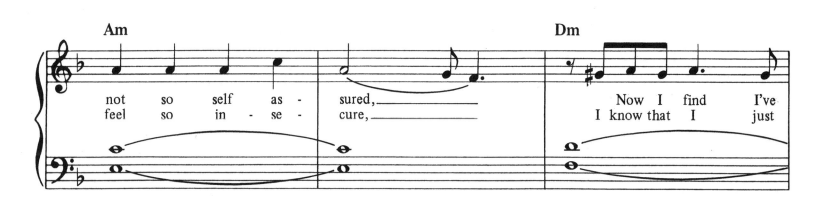

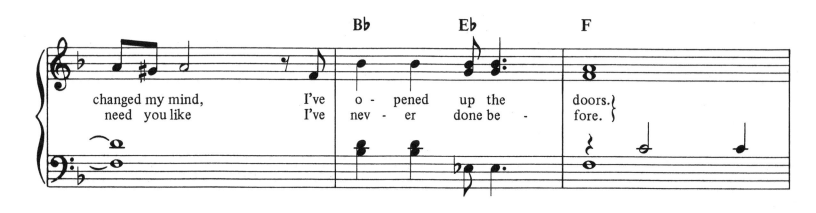

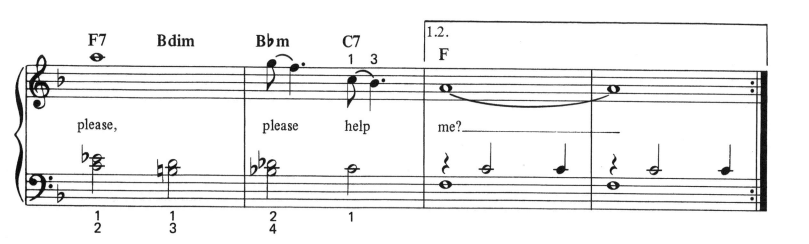

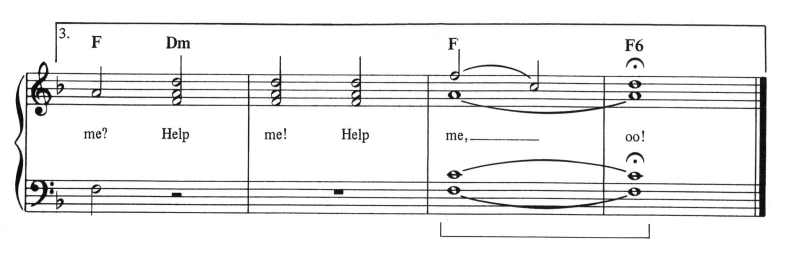

HERE COMES THE SUN

Words and Music by
GEORGE HARRISON

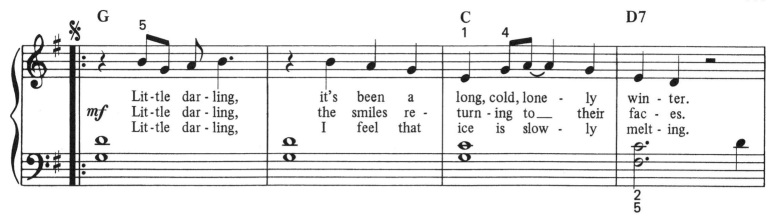

Lit-tle dar-ling, it's been a long, cold, lone-ly win-ter.
Lit-tle dar-ling, the smiles re-turn-ing to_ their fac-es.
Lit-tle dar-ling, I feel that ice is slow-ly melt-ing.

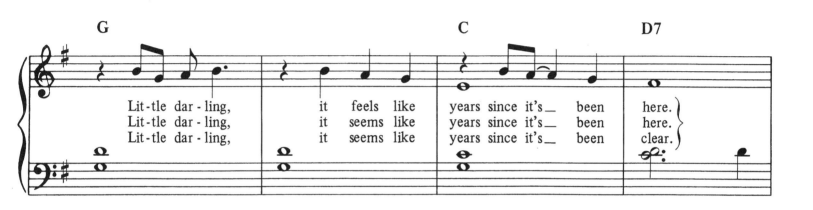

Lit-tle dar-ling, it feels like years since it's_ been here.
Lit-tle dar-ling, it seems like years since it's_ been here.
Lit-tle dar-ling, it seems like years since it's_ been clear.

Here comes_ the sun, Here comes_ the sun, and I say,

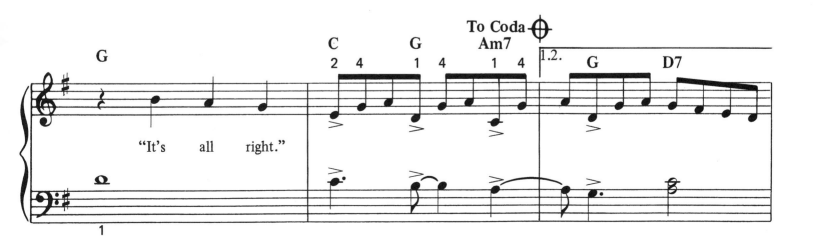

"It's all right."

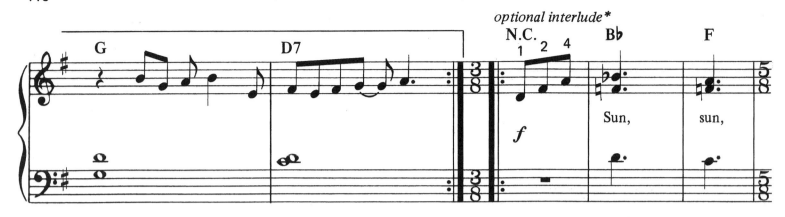

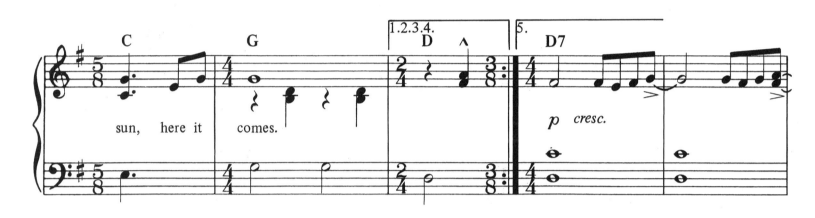

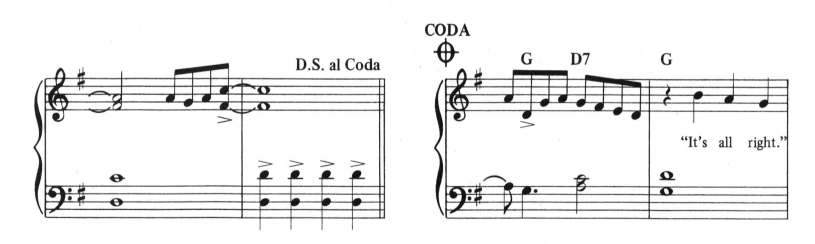

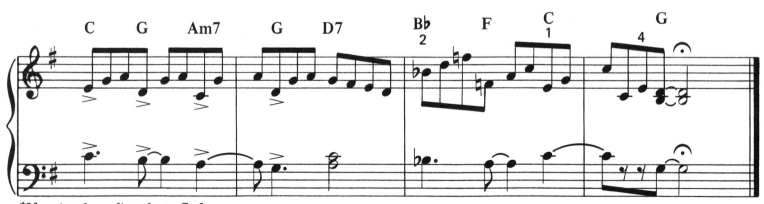

*If omitted, go directly to Coda

HERE THERE AND EVERYWHERE

Words and Music by JOHN LENNON
and PAUL McCARTNEY

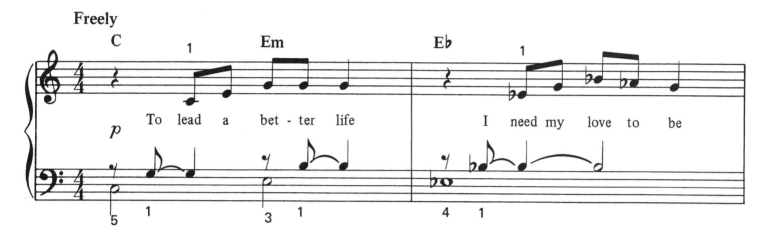

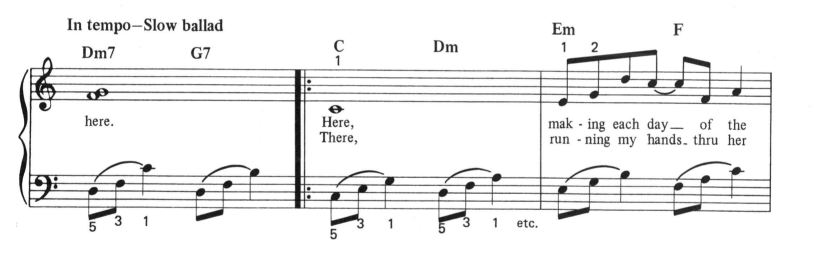

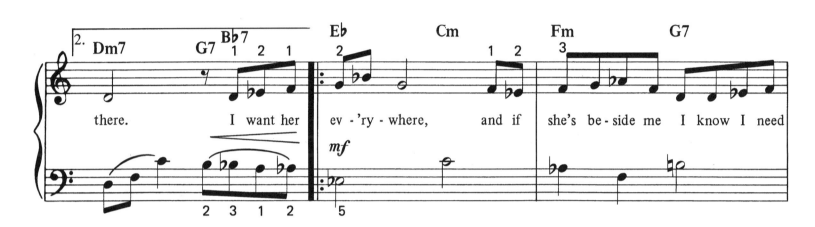

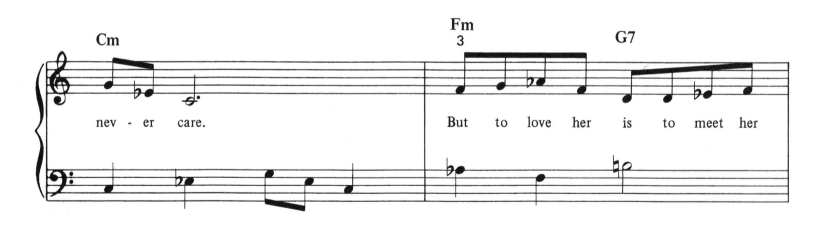

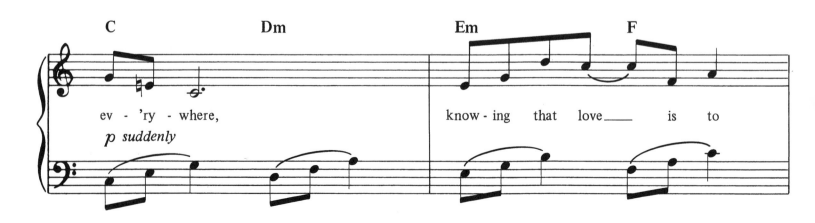

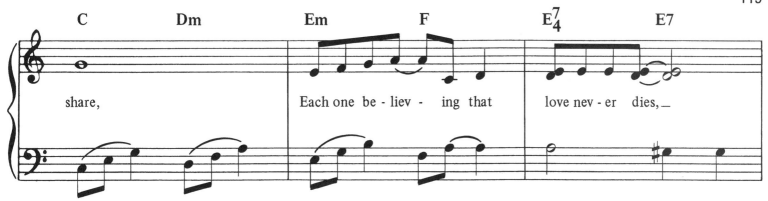

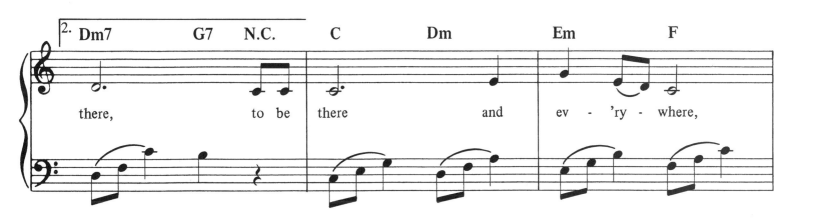

HEY JUDE

Words and Music by JOHN LENNON
and PAUL McCARTNEY
Arranged by DAN FOX

Slow and steady

Hey Jude,_____ don't make it bad, take a

sad song_____ and make it bet - ter._____ Re - mem-ber to let her in - to your

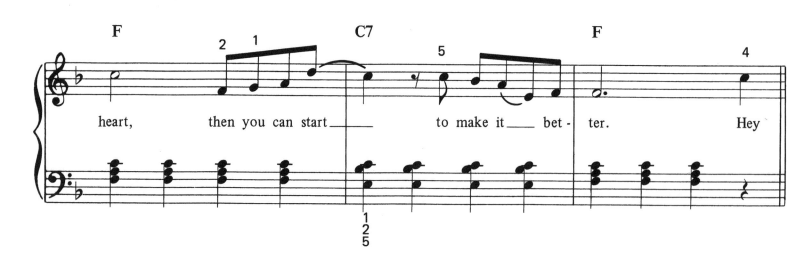

heart, then you can start_____ to make it_____ bet - ter. Hey

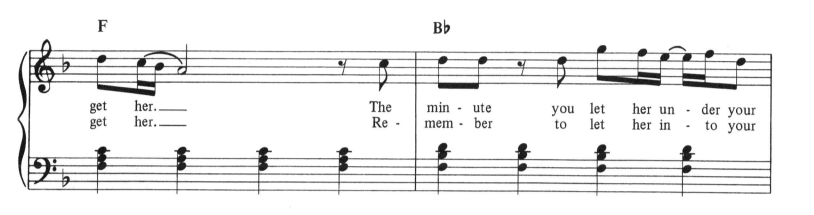

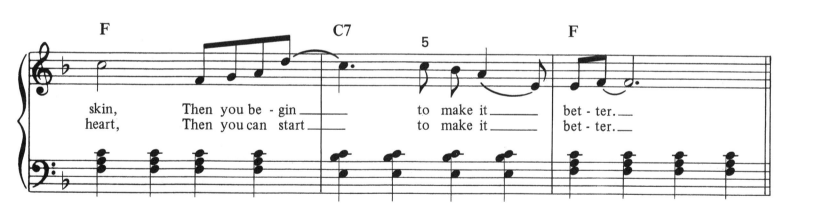

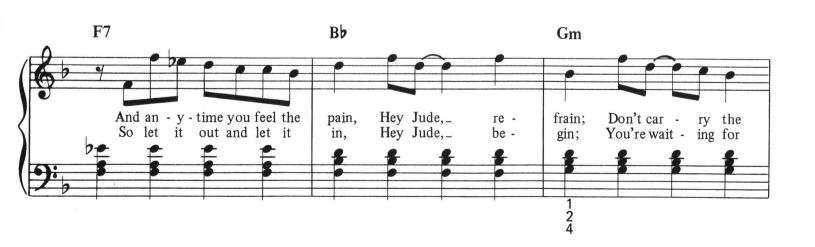

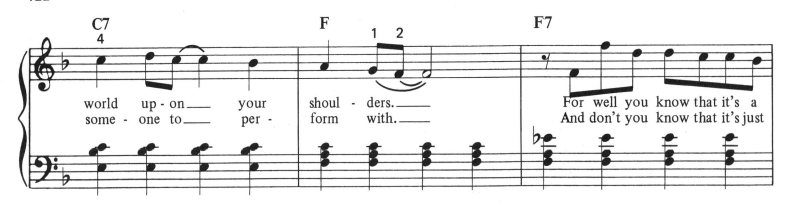

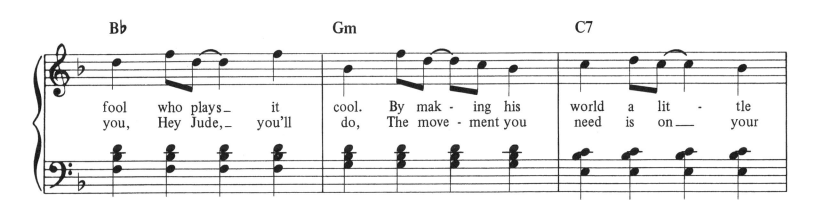

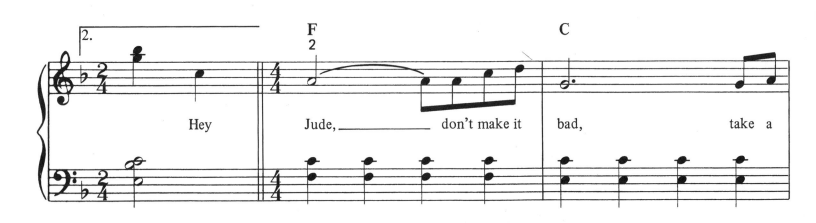

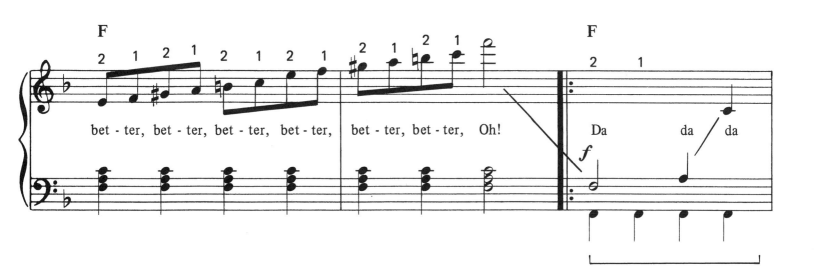

HONEY PIE

Words and Music by JOHN LENNON
and PAUL McCARTNEY

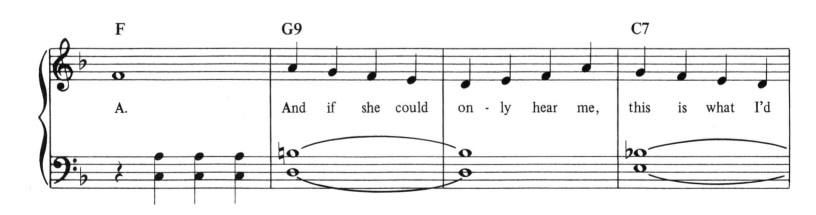

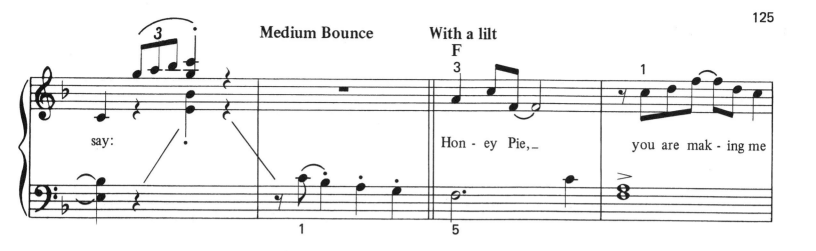

Medium Bounce With a lilt

say: Hon - ey Pie,— you are mak - ing me

cra - zy,— I'm in love— but I'm la - zy,—

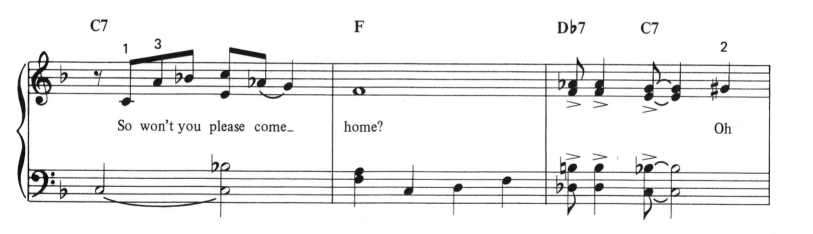

So won't you please come— home? Oh

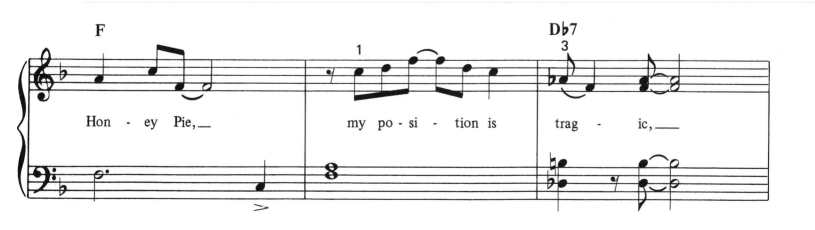

Hon - ey Pie,— my po - si - tion is trag - ic,—

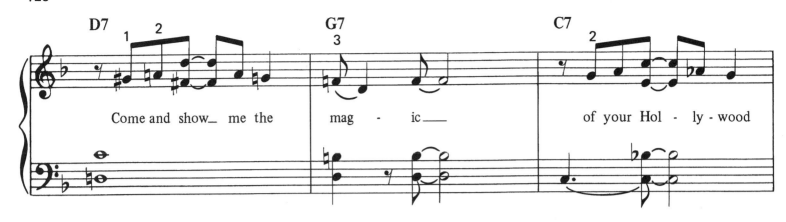

Come and show— me the mag - ic —— of your Hol - ly - wood

song.

You be - came— a
Will the wind— that

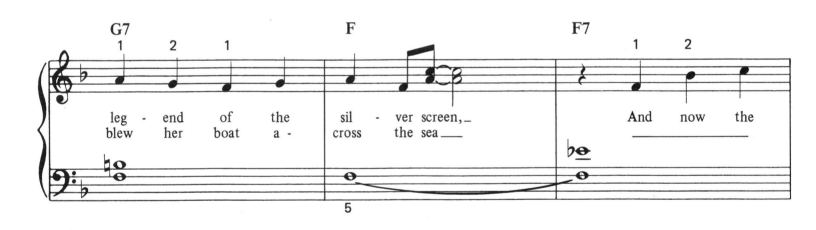

leg - end of the sil - ver screen,—
blew her boat a - cross the sea—

And now the

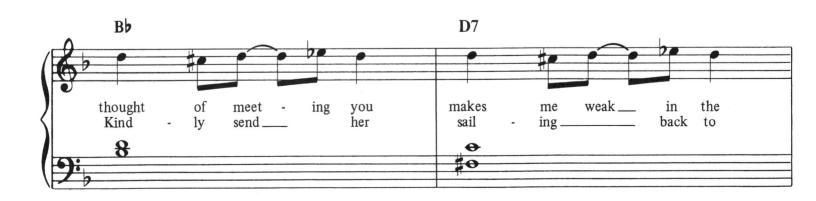

thought of meet - ing you
Kind - ly send— her

makes me weak— in the
sail - ing —— back to

I FEEL FINE

Words and Music by JOHN LENNON
and PAUL McCARTNEY

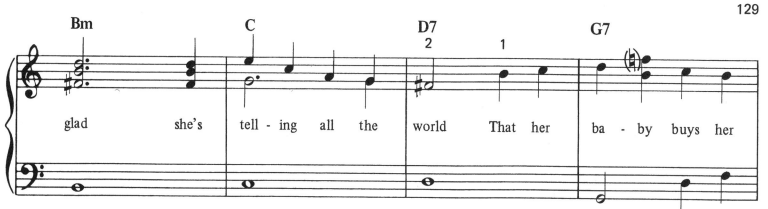

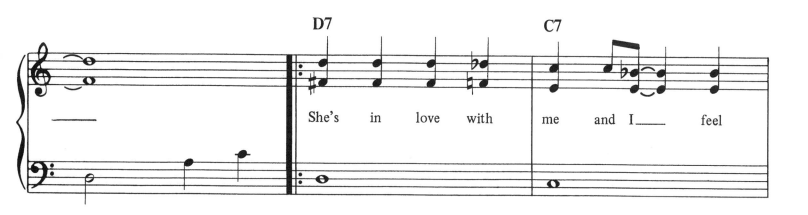

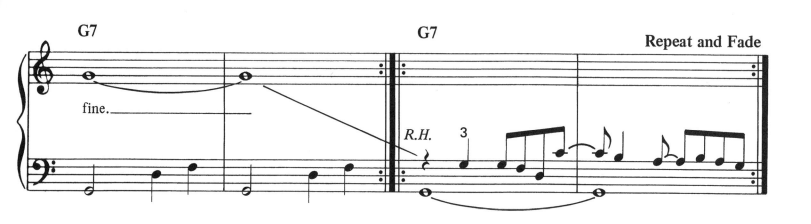

I DON'T WANT TO SPOIL THE PARTY

Words and Music by JOHN LENNON
and PAUL McCARTNEY

Brightly

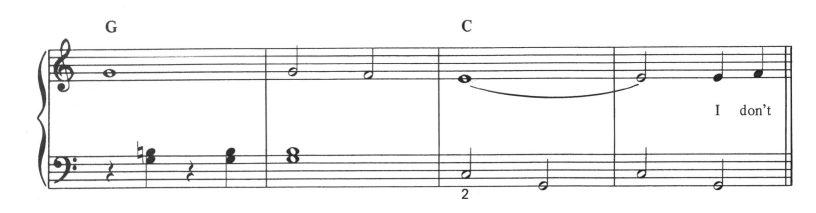

1,3. want to spoil the par - ty so I'll go, ___
2. had a drink or two and I don't care, ___

I would hate my dis - ap - point - ment to
There's no fun in what I do if she's not

show._____
there._____

There's noth-ing for me
I won-der what me went

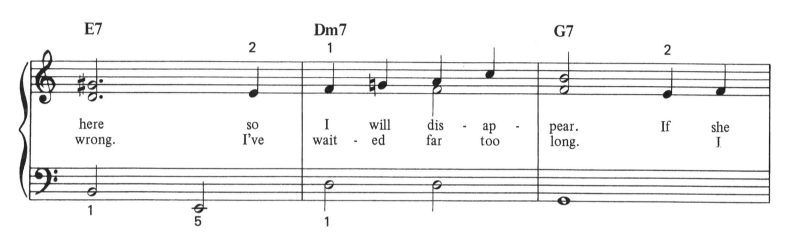

here wrong. so
wait-ed far too

I will dis-ap-pear. If she
long. I

Last time
to Coda ⊕

turns up while I'm gone please let me know._____
think I'll take a walk and look for her._____

1.

I've

2.

Though to-night she's made me sad, I

132

still | love | her. If I | find her I'll be

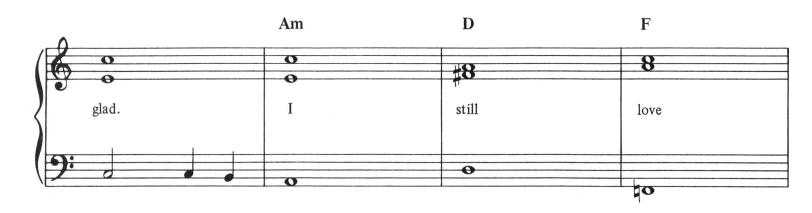

glad. | I | still | love

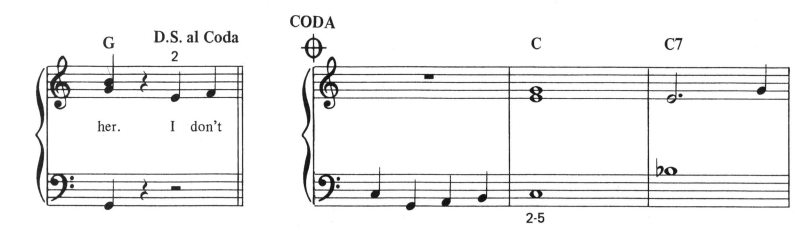

her. I don't

CODA

2-5

I SAW HER STANDING THERE

Words and Music by JOHN LENNON
and PAUL McCARTNEY

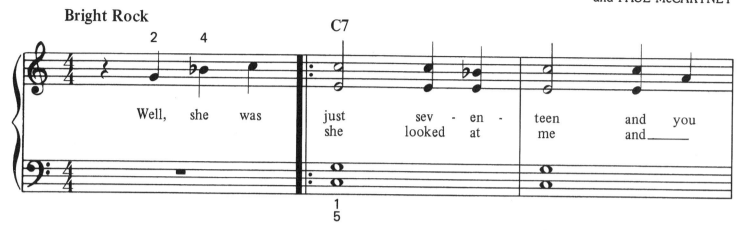

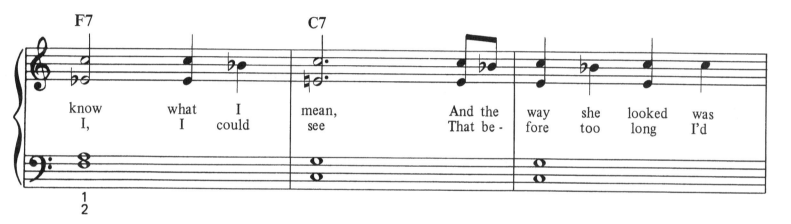

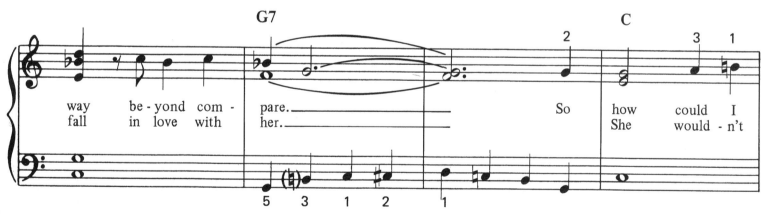

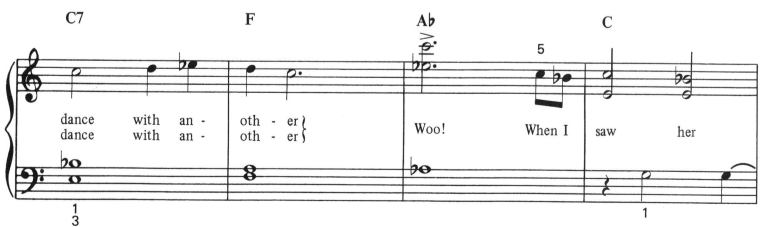

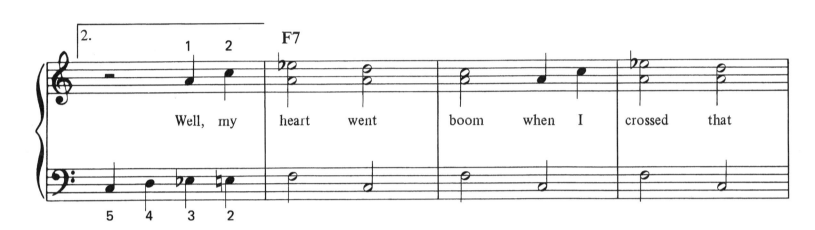

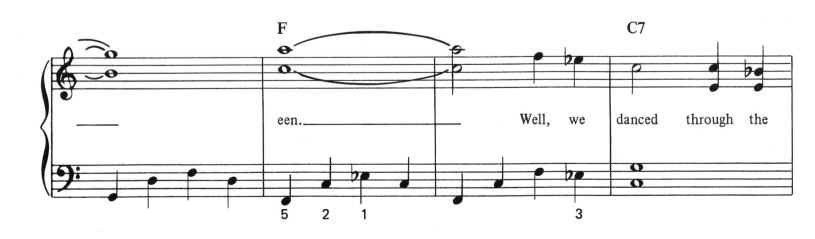

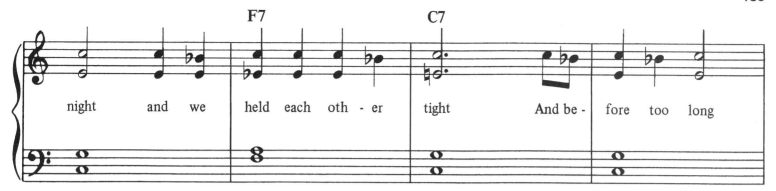

night and we held each oth - er tight And be - fore too long

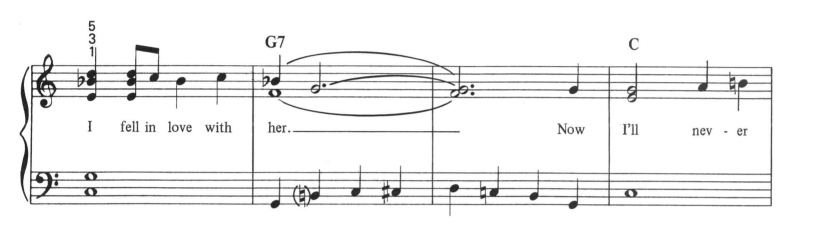

I fell in love with her._____ Now I'll nev - er

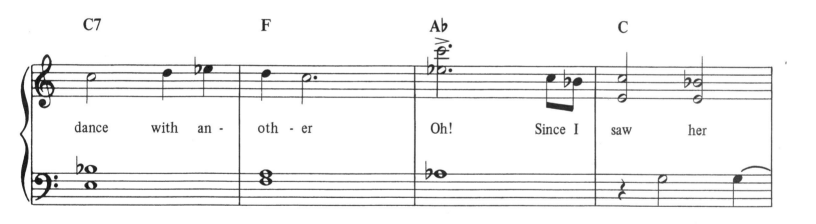

dance with an - oth - er Oh! Since I saw her

stand - ing there._____

I SHOULD HAVE KNOWN BETTER

Words and Music by JOHN LENNON
and PAUL McCARTNEY

Moderate Rock

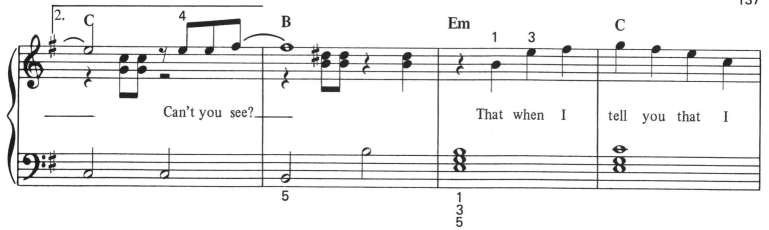

Can't you see? That when I tell you that I

love you, Oh! You're gon - na say you love me

too, hoo hoo hoo___ hoo, oh.___ And when I

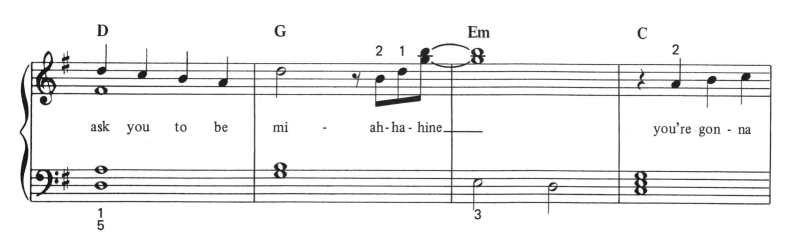

ask you to be mi - ah-ha-hine___ you're gon - na

say you love me, too. So— wo— I—

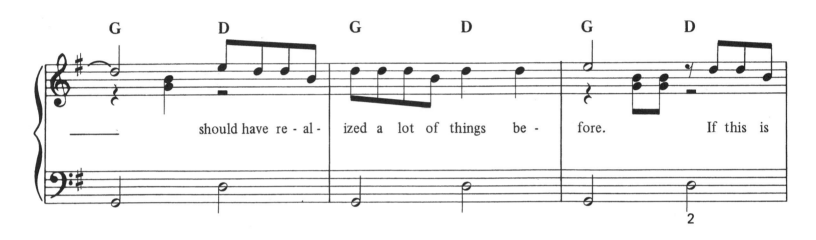

should have re - al - ized a lot of things be - fore. If this is

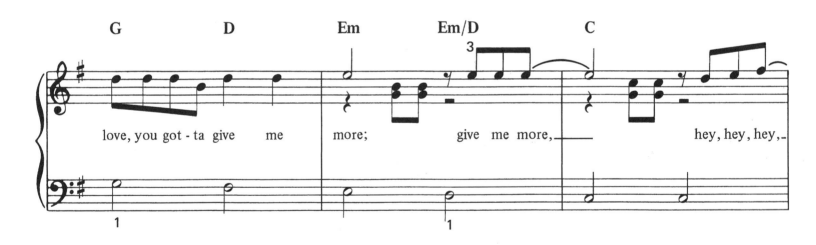

love, you got - ta give me more; give me more,— hey, hey, hey,—

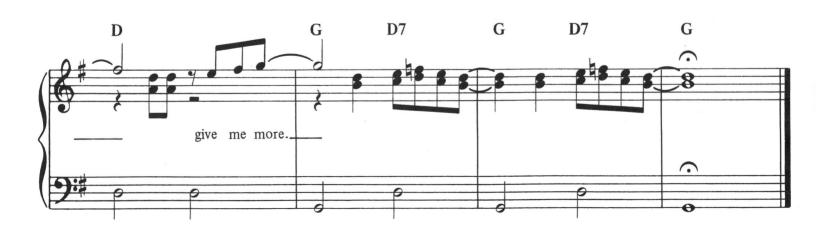

give me more.—

I WANT TO HOLD YOUR HAND

Words and Music by JOHN LENNON and PAUL McCARTNEY

MCA MUSIC PUBLISHING

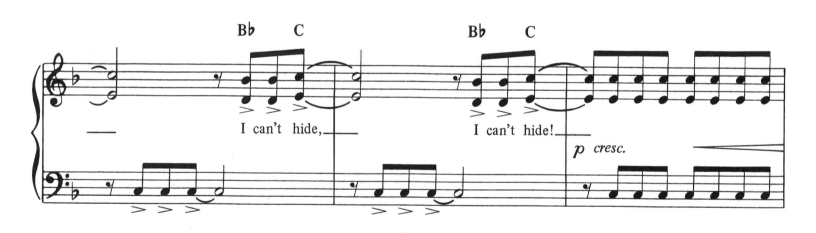

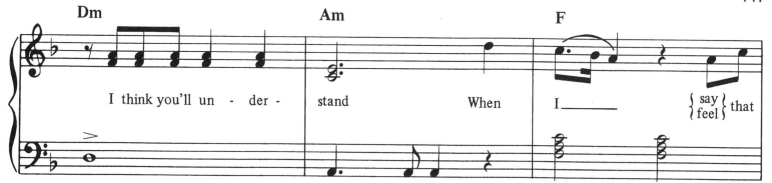

I think you'll un - der - stand   When   I _____ { say / feel } that

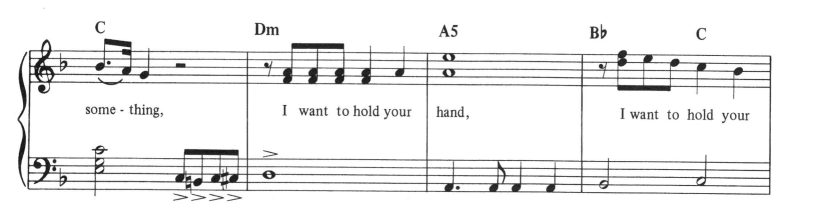

some - thing,   I want to hold your   hand,   I want to hold your

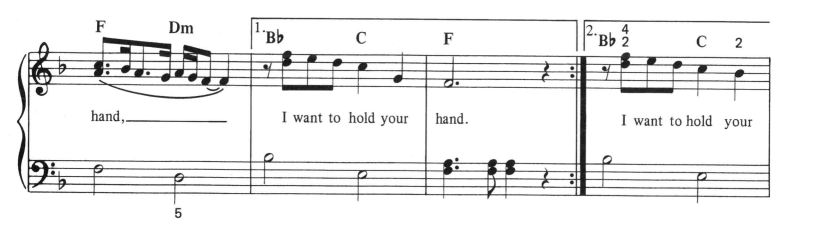

hand,_____   I want to hold your   hand.   I want to hold your

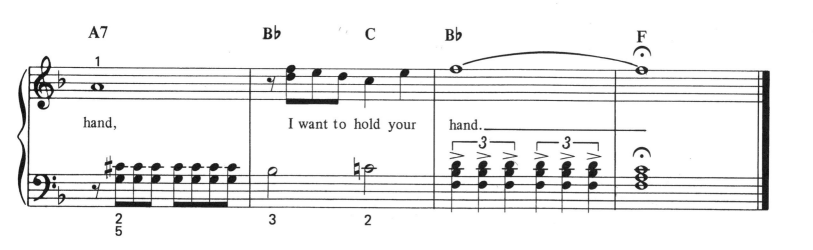

hand,   I want to hold your   hand._____

I WANNA BE YOUR MAN

Words and Music by JOHN LENNON
and PAUL McCARTNEY

Medium Rock

1.3. I wan-na be your lov-er, ba-by, I wan-na be your man;
2. Tell me that you love me, ba-by, let me un-der- stand;

I wan-na be your lov-er, ba-by, I wan-na be your man.
Tell me that you love me, ba-by, I wan-na be your man.

Love you like no oth-er, ba-by, like no oth-er can;
I wan-na be your lov-er, ba-by, I wan-na be your man;

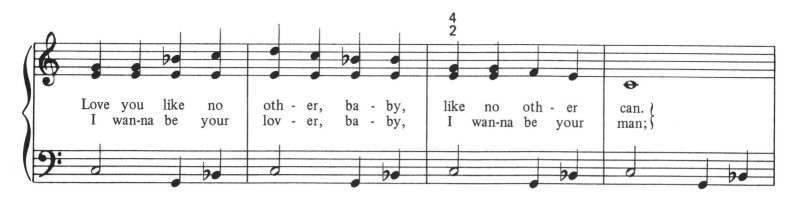

Love you like no oth - er, ba - by, like no oth - er can.
I wan-na be your lov - er, ba - by, I wan-na be your man;

N.C.   D7   G7   C

I wan-na be your man,   I wan-na be your man.

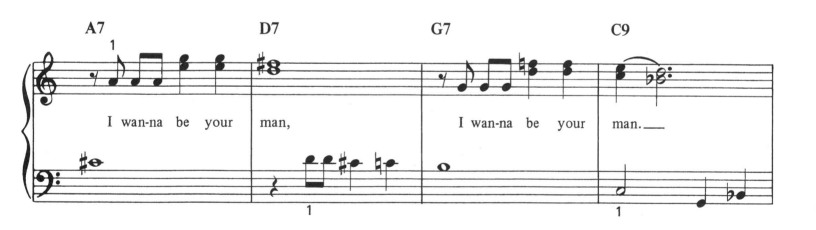

A7   D7   G7   C9

I wan-na be your man,   I wan-na be your man.___

play 3 times   C7   C   Gm7   C   Repeat and Fade

I wan-na be your man,___

I WANT YOU
(She's So Heavy)

Slowly (♩. = 1 very slow beat)

Words and Music by JOHN LENNON
and PAUL McCARTNEY

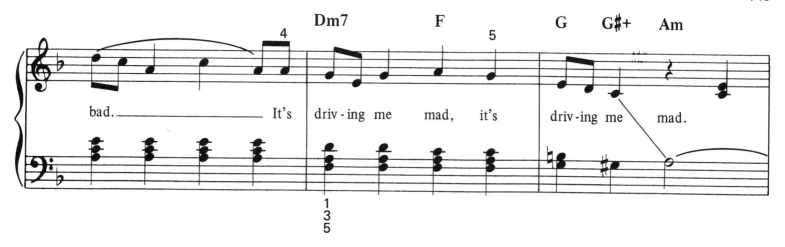

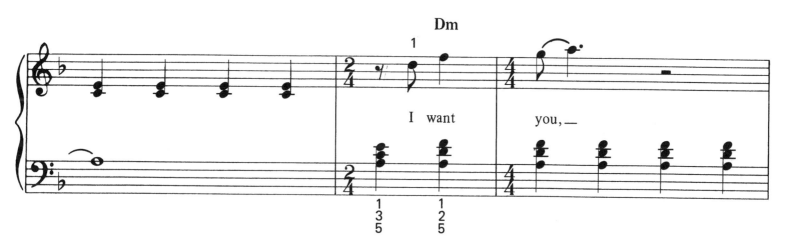

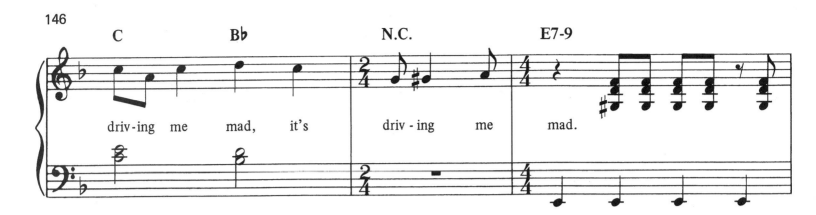

driv-ing me mad, it's driv-ing me mad.

I want   She's so   (Spoken:) HEAVY!

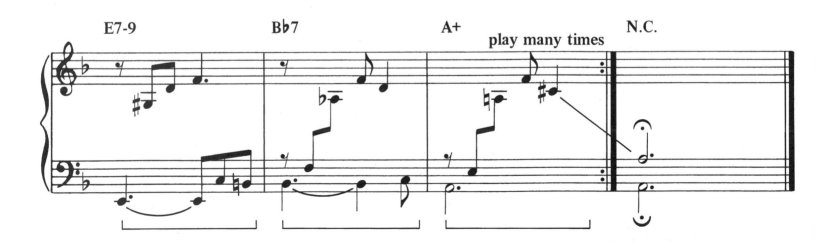

play many times

I WILL

Words and Music by JOHN LENNON
and PAUL McCARTNEY

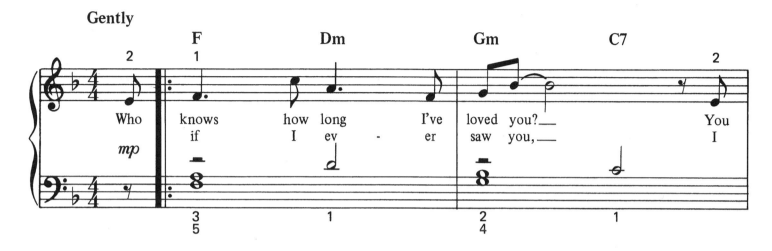

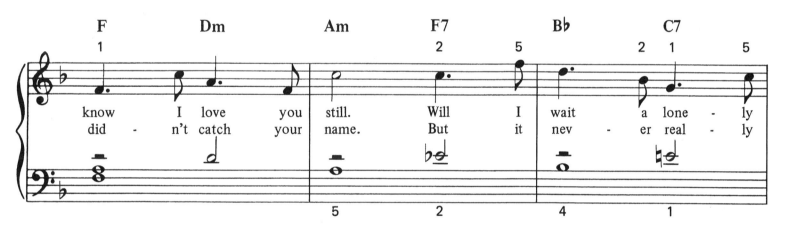

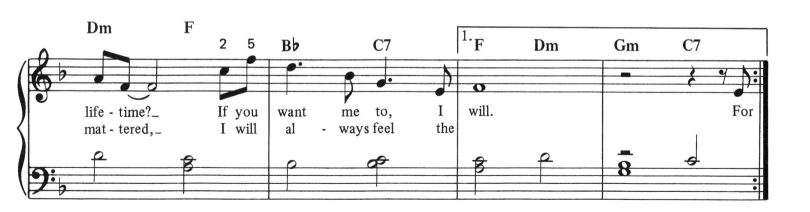

same. Love you for-ev-er and for-ev-er,

love you with all my heart, Love you when-ev-er

we're to-geth-er, love you when we're a - part. And

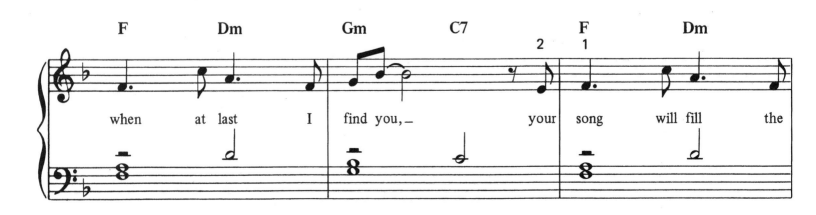

when at last I find you,— your song will fill the

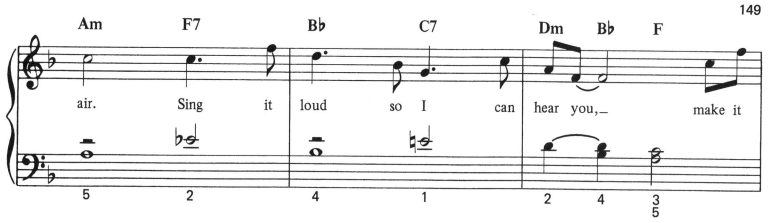

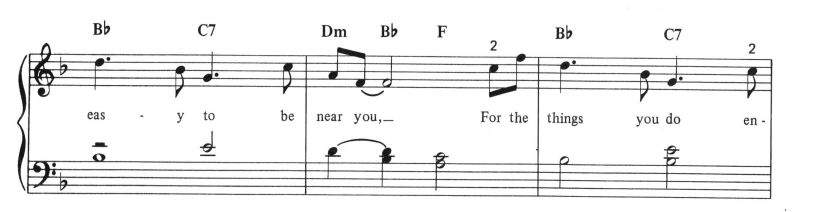

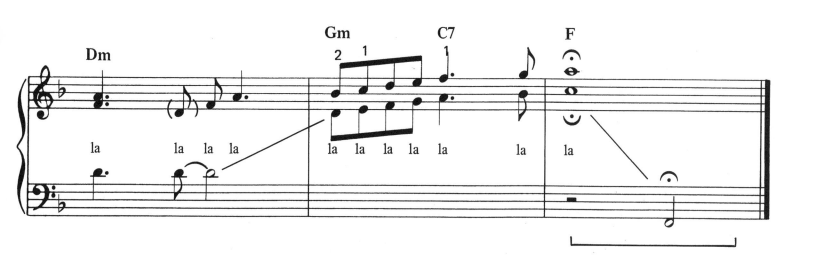

I'LL BE BACK

Words and Music by JOHN LENNON
and PAUL McCARTNEY

Yes, I'm the one who wants you, Oh ___ ho, ___ oh ___ ho.
You know I hate to leave you, Oh ___ ho, ___ oh ___ ho.

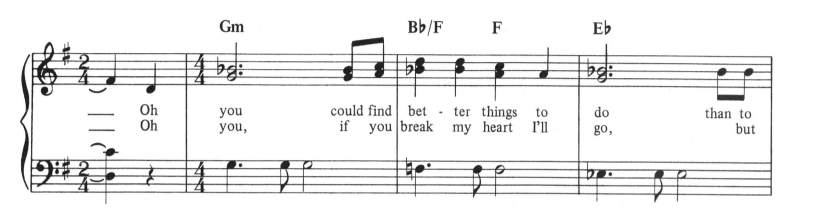

___ Oh you could find bet - ter things to do, than to
___ Oh you, if you break my heart I'll go, but

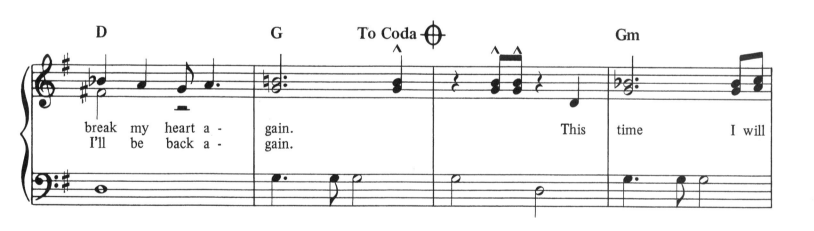

break my heart a - gain.
I'll be back a - gain. This time I will

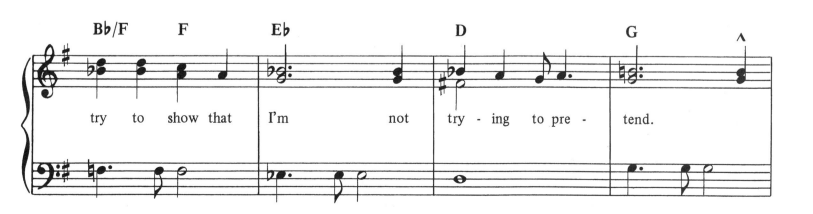

try to show that I'm not try - ing to pre - tend.

I _____ thought that you would re - al - ize ___

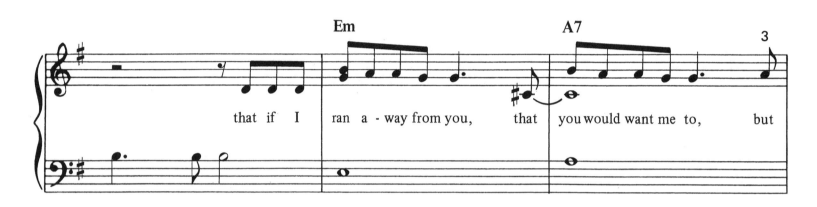

that if I ran a - way from you, that you would want me to, but

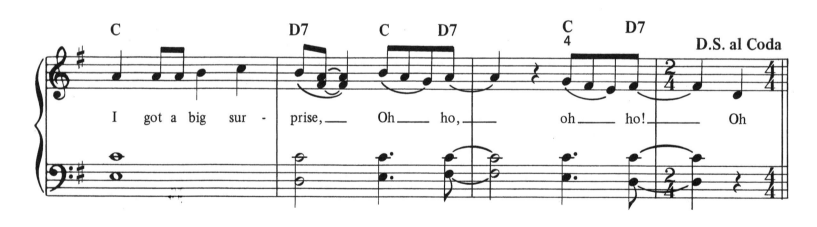

I got a big sur - prise, ___ Oh ___ ho, ___ oh ___ ho! ___ Oh

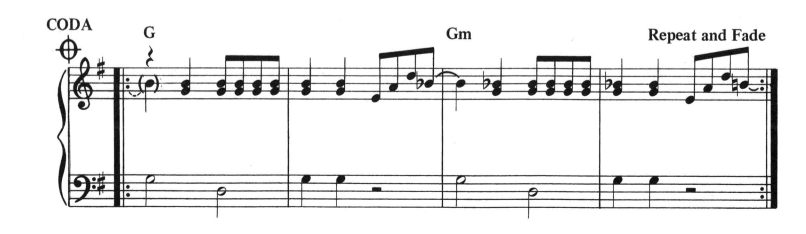

I'LL CRY INSTEAD

Words and Music by JOHN LENNON
and PAUL McCARTNEY

I've got ev-'ry rea-son on earth__ to be mad,
chip on my shoul-der that's big-ger than my feet,

'cause I've just lost the on-ly girl I had.
I can't talk to peo-ple that I meet.

If I could get my way, I'd get my-self locked
If I could see you now, I'd try to make you

up to-day;__ But I can't, so I'll cry__ in-
sad some-how;__ But I can't, so I'll cry__ in-

154

girls

'Cause I'm gon-na break their

hearts all 'round the world.

Yes, I'm gon-na break 'em in

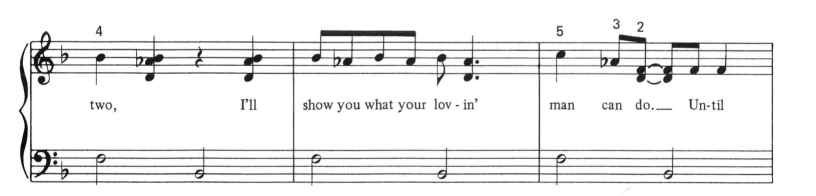

two, I'll show you what your lov-in' man can do.___ Un-til

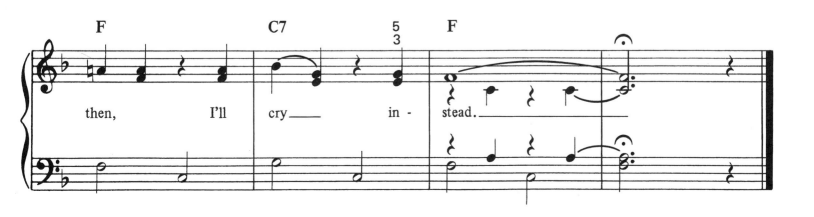

then, I'll cry___ in - stead.___

I'LL FOLLOW THE SUN

Words and Music by JOHN LENNON
and PAUL McCARTNEY

Moderate Easy Rock

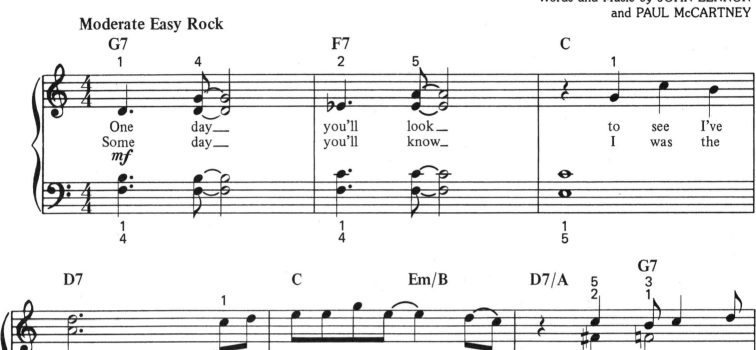

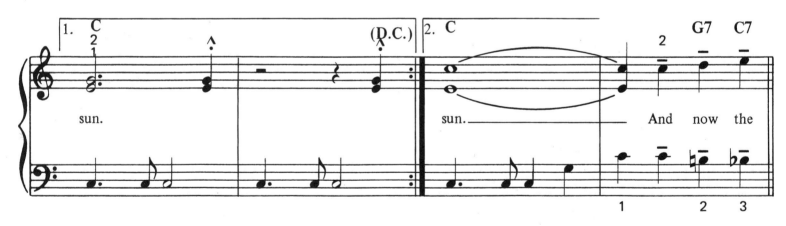

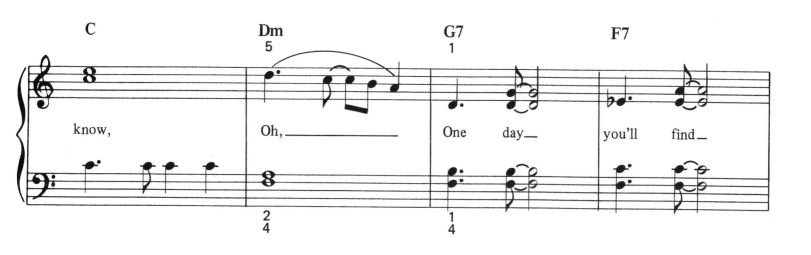

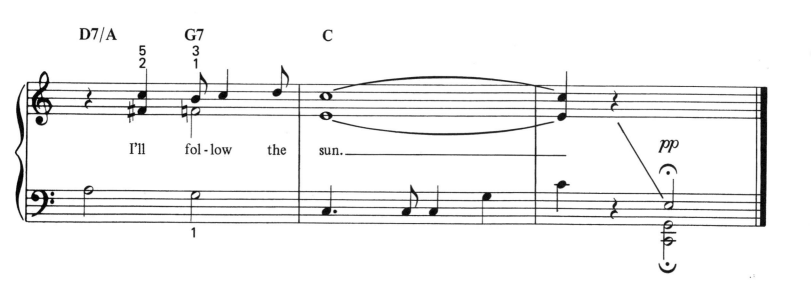

I'M A LOSER

Words and Music by JOHN LENNON
and PAUL McCARTNEY

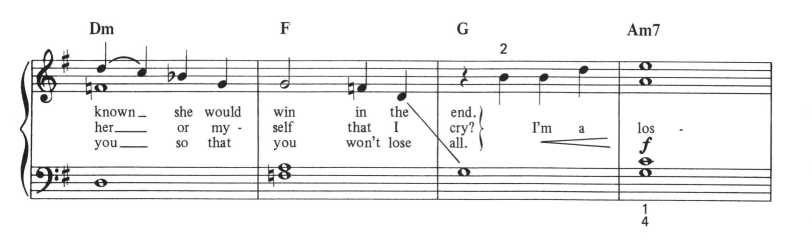

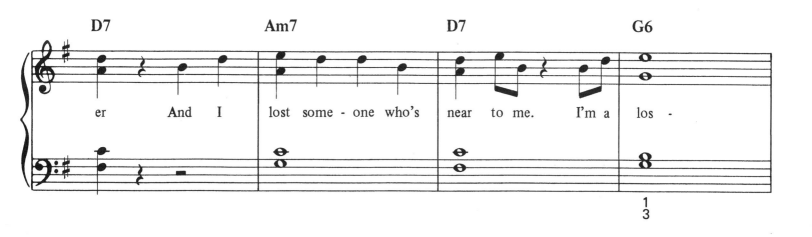

I'M HAPPY JUST TO DANCE WITH YOU

Words and Music by JOHN LENNON
and PAUL McCARTNEY

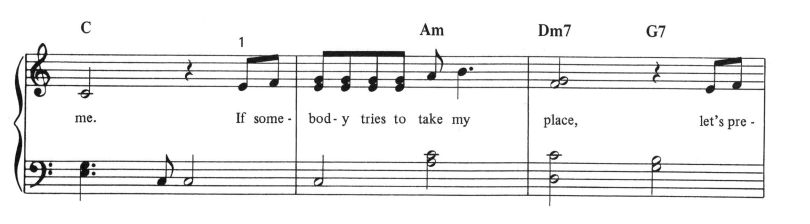

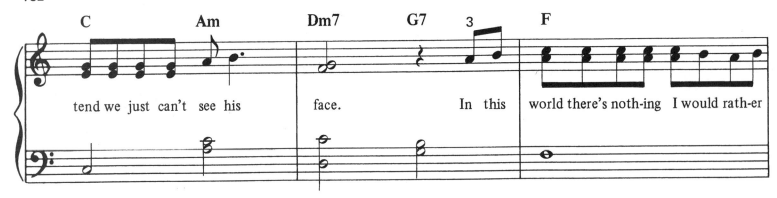

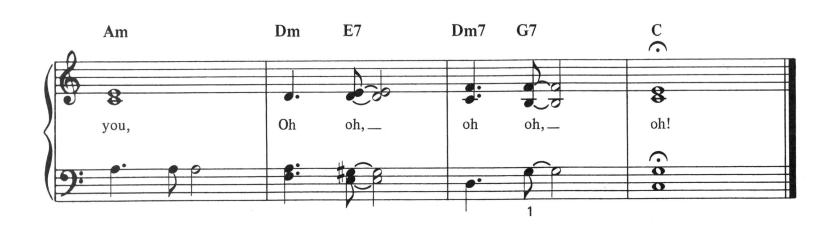

I'M LOOKING THROUGH YOU

Words and Music by JOHN LENNON
and PAUL McCARTNEY

Moderately, with a beat

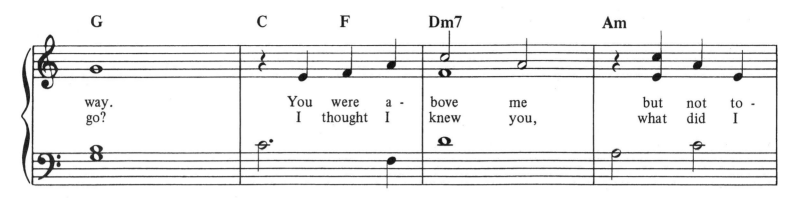

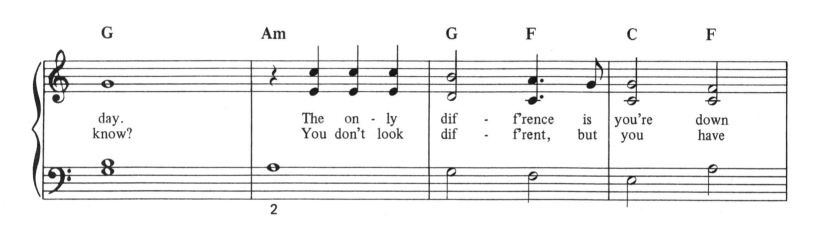

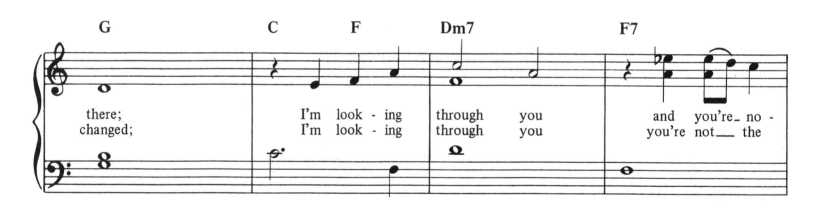

**After repeat,
fade on last 4 measures**

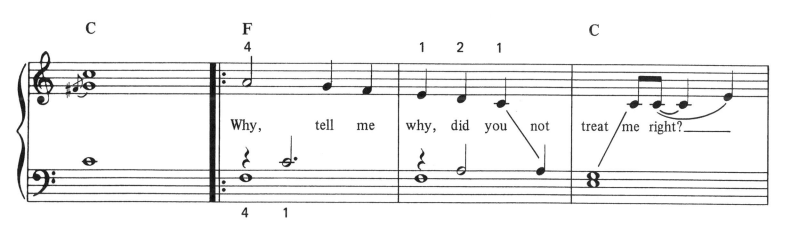

same.

Why, tell me why, did you not treat me right? _____

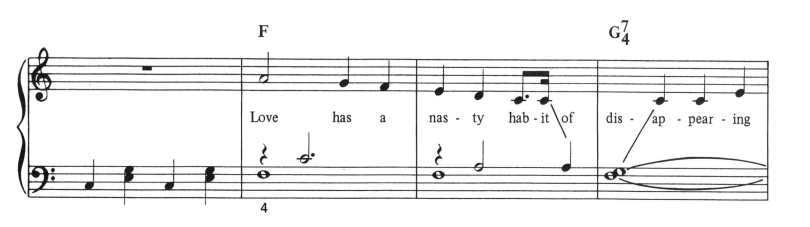

Love has a nas - ty hab - it of dis - ap - pear - ing

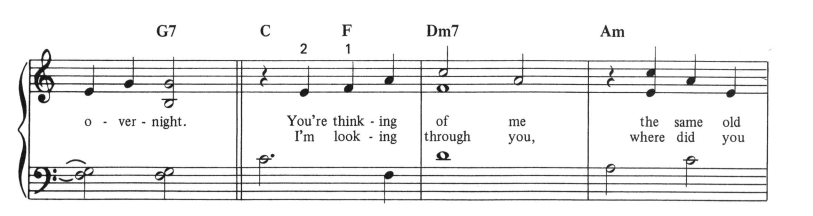

o - ver - night.

You're think - ing of me the same old
I'm look - ing through you, where did you

I'VE JUST SEEN A FACE

Words and Music by JOHN LENNON
and PAUL McCARTNEY

I've just seen a face; I can't for-get the time_ or place where we just

met. She's just the girl for me, and I want all_ the world to see we've

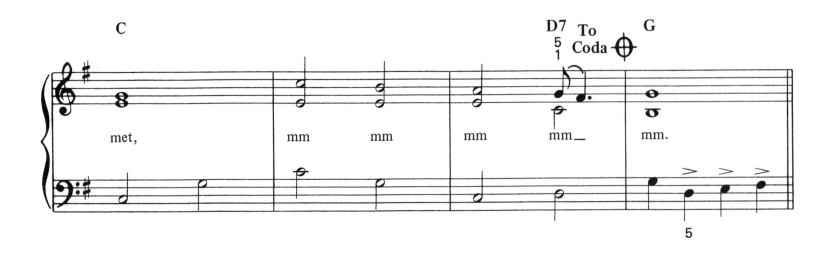

met, mm mm mm mm_ mm.

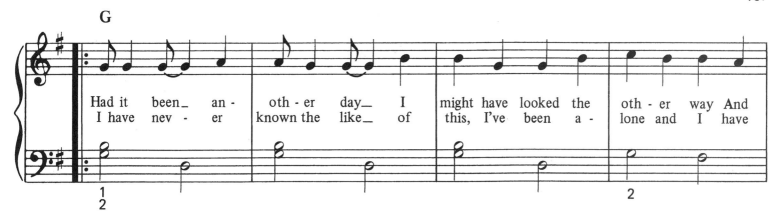

Had it been__ an-oth-er day__ I might have looked the oth-er way And
I have nev- er known the like__ of this, I've been a- lone and I have

I'd have nev- er been a-ware__ But as it is I'll dream of her to-
missed things and__ kept out of sight,__ For oth-er girls were nev-er quite like

night,
this, } da da da da da da.

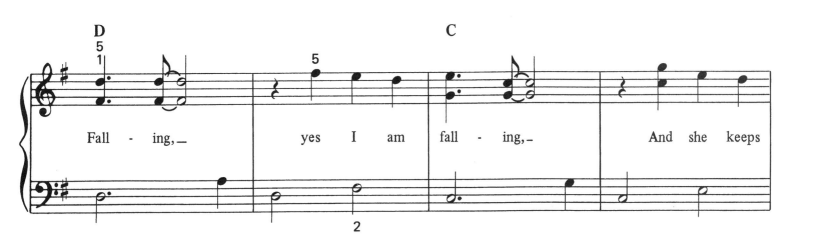

Fall- ing,__ yes I am fall- ing,__ And she keeps

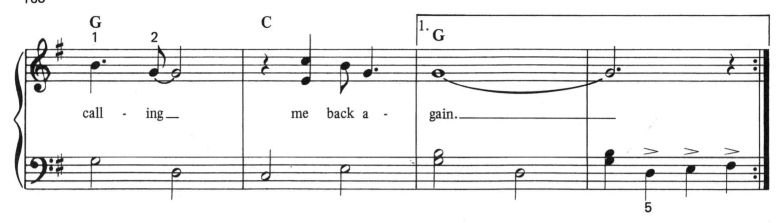

calling me back a - gain.

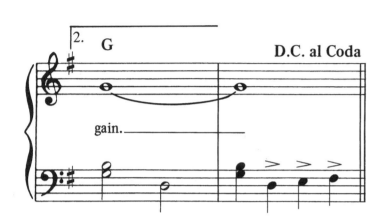

gain. D.C. al Coda

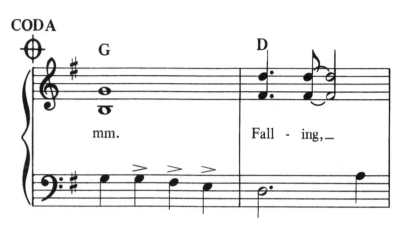

CODA

mm. Fall - ing,—

yes I am fall - ing,— and she keeps call - ing—

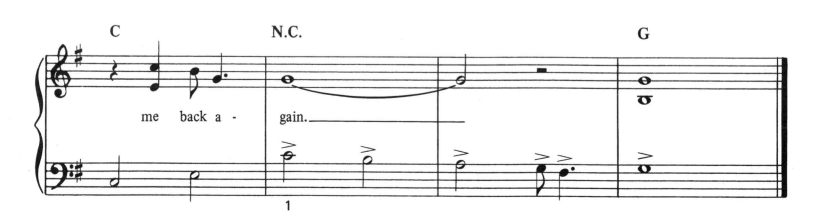

me back a - gain.

IF I FELL

Words and Music by JOHN LENNON
and PAUL McCARTNEY

Moderately Slow, but not dragging

If I fell in love with you, would you prom-ise to be true and

help me un - der - stand? 'Cause I've been in love be - fore, and I

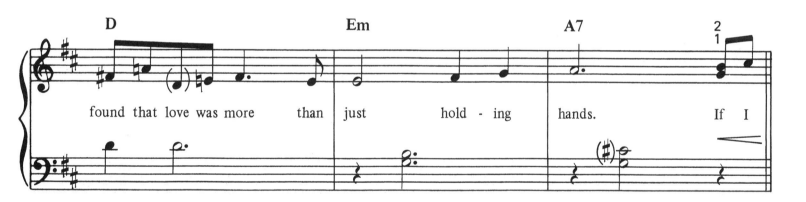

found that love was more than just hold - ing hands. If I

give my heart to you, I must be sure from the
trust in you, oh please, don't run and hide. If I

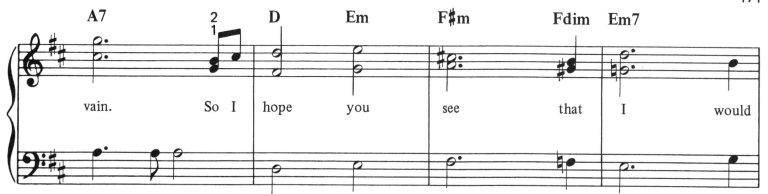

vain.   So I   hope   you   see   that   I   would

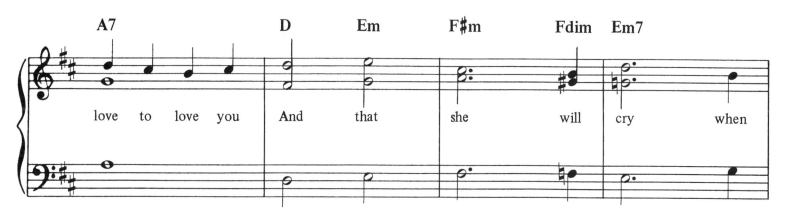

love   to   love   you   And   that   she   will   cry   when

she   learns   we   are   two.   'Cause I   she   learns   we   are   two,   If I

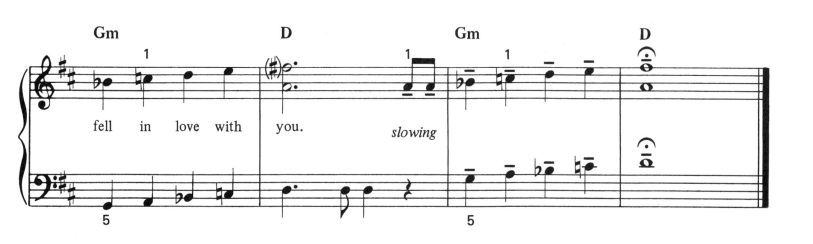

fell   in   love   with   you.   *slowing*

IN MY LIFE

Words and Music by JOHN LENNON
and PAUL McCARTNEY

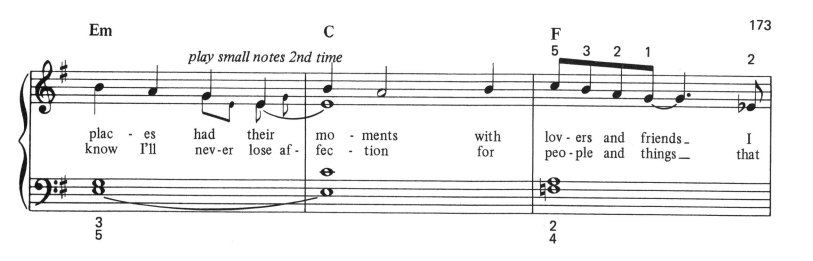

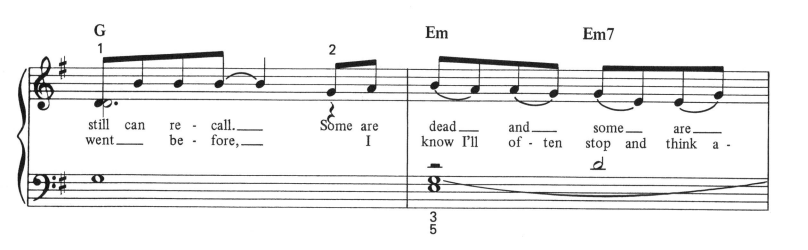

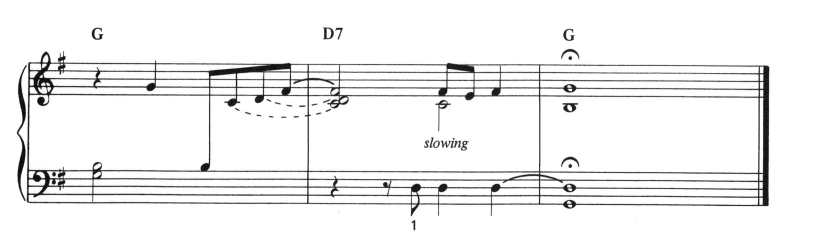

IT WON'T BE LONG

Words and Music by
PAUL McCARTNEY

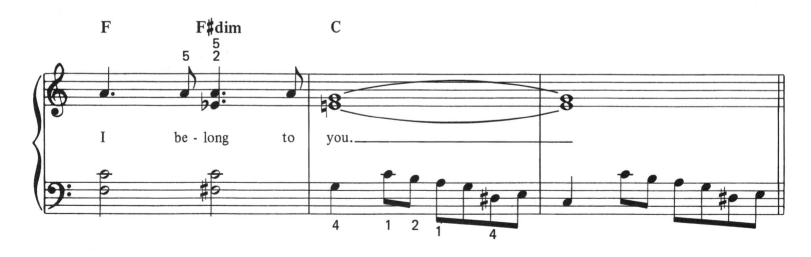

Ev - 'ry night when ev - 'ry-bod - y has fun,
Ev - 'ry night the tears come down from my eyes,
ev - 'ry day we'll be hap - py, I know,

Here am I sit - ting all on my own.
Ev - 'ry day I've done noth - ing but cry.
Now I know that you won't leave me no more.)

It won't be long yeah, yeah, yeah, It won't be long yeah, yeah,

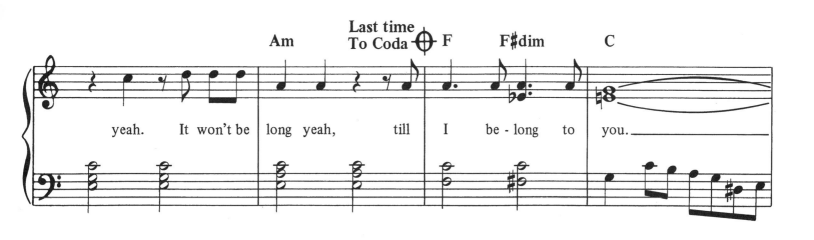

yeah. It won't be long yeah, till I be - long to you.

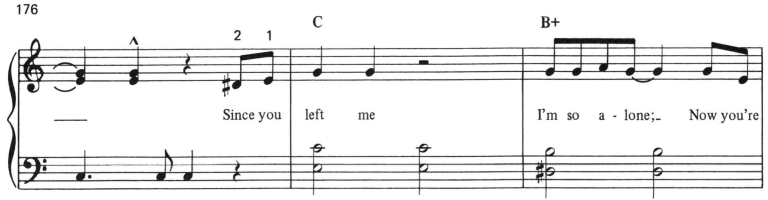

Since you left me I'm so a-lone; Now you're

com-ing, you're com-ing on home. I'll be good like I

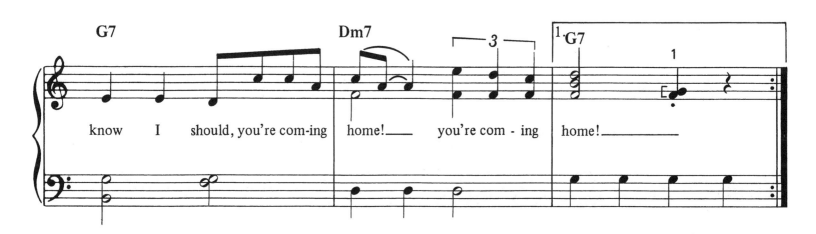

know I should, you're com-ing home! you're com-ing home! you're com-ing home!

home! So

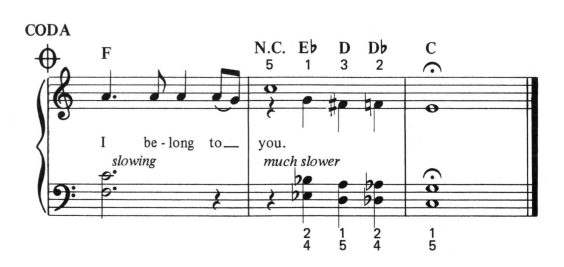

I be-long to you.

slowing   *much slower*

LADY MADONNA

Brightly, with a beat
(in 2, ♩ = 1 beat)

Words and Music by JOHN LENNON
and PAUL McCARTNEY

Lady Ma - don - na, chil - dren at your feet,
Lady Ma - don - na, ba - by at your breast,
Lady Ma - don - na, chil - dren at your feet,

Last time
to Coda

Won - der how you man - age to make ends meet.
won - ders how you man - age to feed the rest.
Won - der how you man - age to make ends meet.

Who finds the mon - ey when you pay the rent?
La - dy Ma - don - na, ly - ing on the bed,

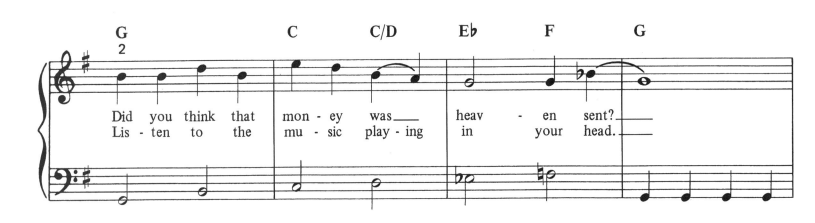

Did you think that mon - ey was__ heav - en sent?__
Lis - ten to the mu - sic play - ing in your head.__

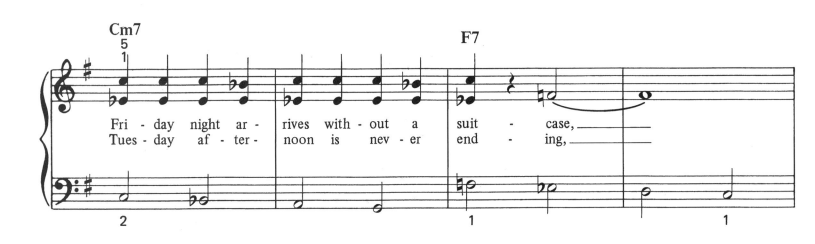

Fri - day night ar - rives with - out a suit - case,__
Tues - day af - ter - noon is nev - er end - ing,__

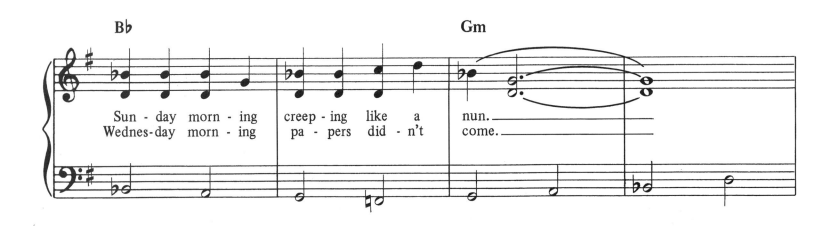

Sun - day morn - ing creep - ing like a nun.__
Wednes - day morn - ing pa - pers did - n't come.__

Cm7   F7

Mon - day's child has   learned to tie his   boot - lace,____

Thurs - day night your   stock - ings need - ed   mend - ing,____

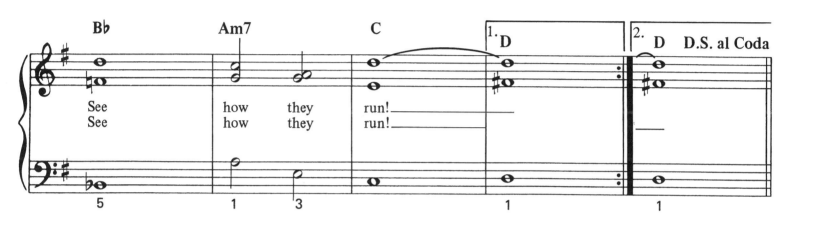

Bb   Am7   C   1. D   2. D   D.S. al Coda

See   how they run!____

See   how they run!____

CODA

G   Am7   Bbdim   Am7   G

p

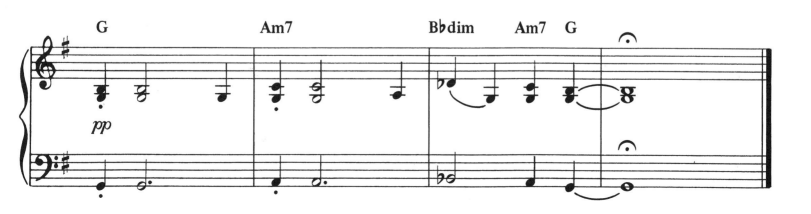

G   Am7   Bbdim   Am7   G

pp

IT'S ONLY LOVE

Words and Music by JOHN LENNON
and PAUL McCARTNEY

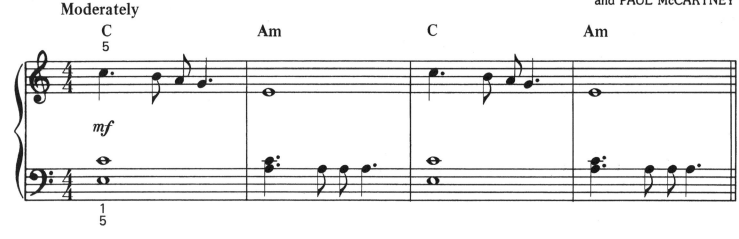

I get high when I see you go by,
Is it right that you and I should fight My oh my.
ev-'ry night?

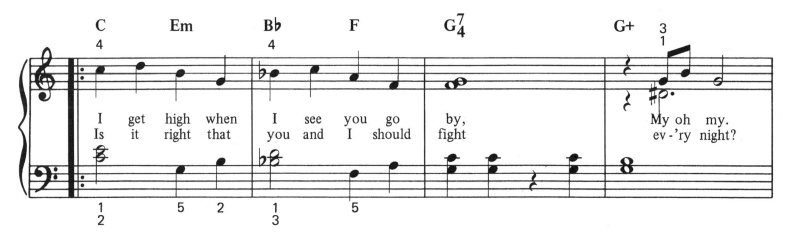

When you sigh, my, my in-side just flies, but-ter-flies.
Just the sight of you makes night-time bright, ver-y bright.

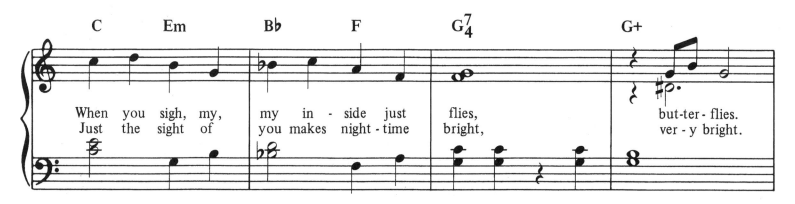

Why am I so shy when I'm be-side you?
Have-n't I the right to make it up girl? It's on-ly

love,   and that is   all,   Why should I   feel   the way I   do?   It's on - ly

love,   and that is   all,   But it's so   hard   lov-ing   you.

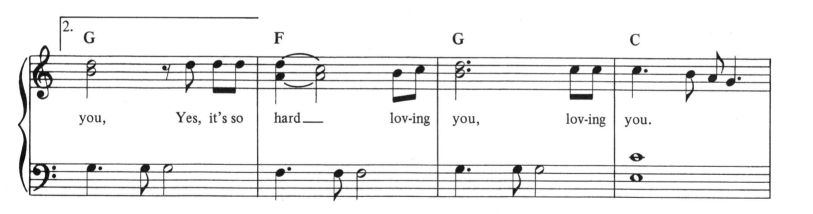

you,   Yes, it's so   hard___   lov-ing   you,   lov-ing   you.

slowing

JULIA

Words and Music by JOHN LENNON
and PAUL McCARTNEY

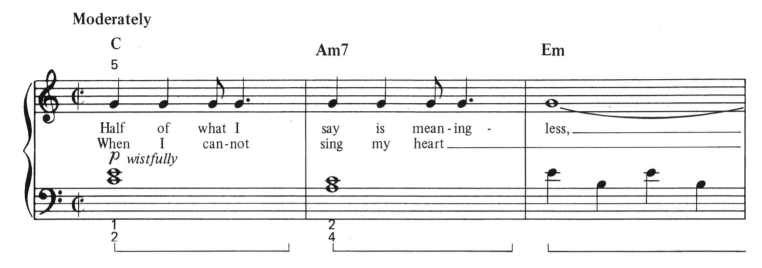

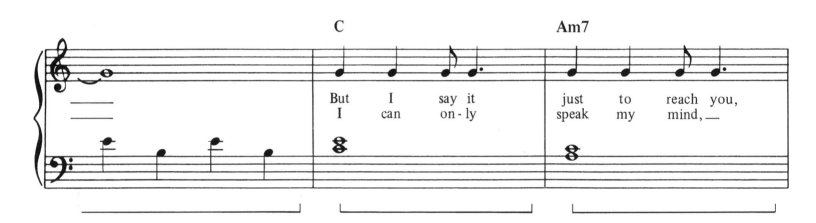

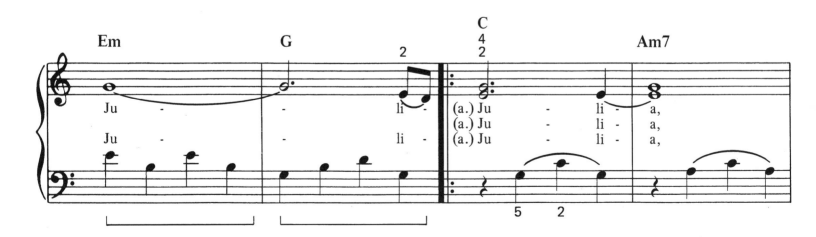

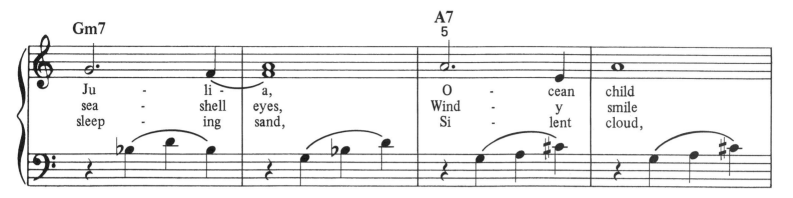

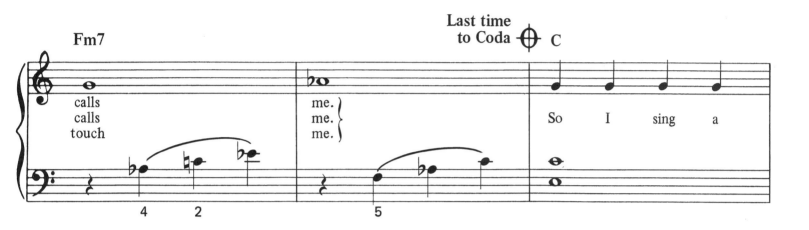

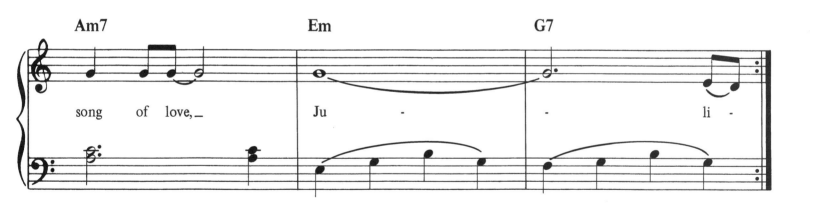

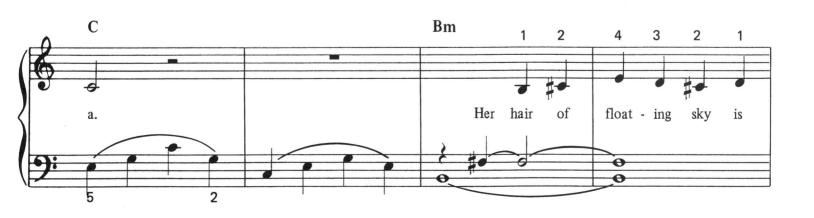

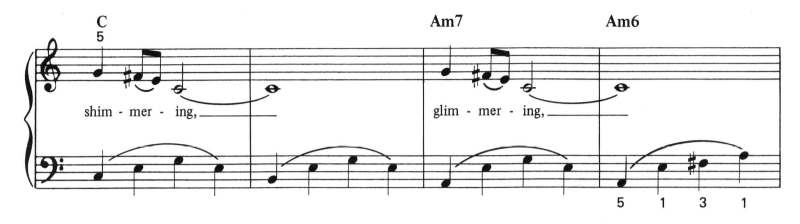

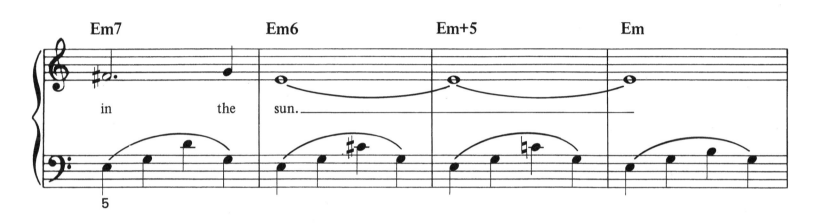

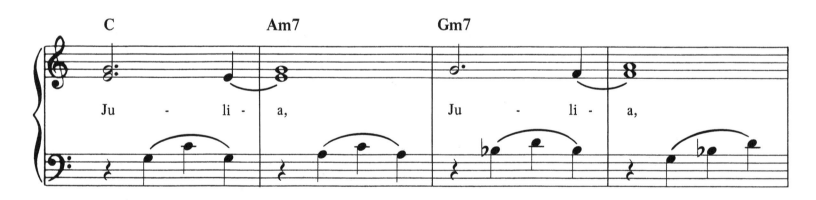

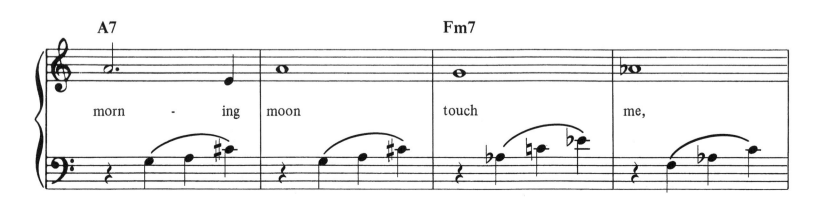

185

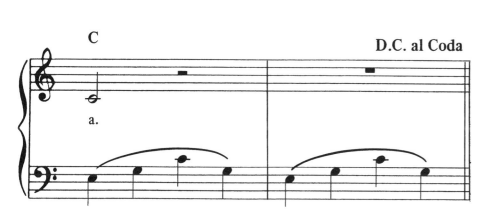

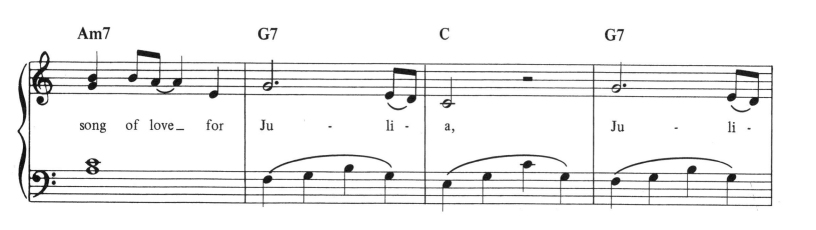

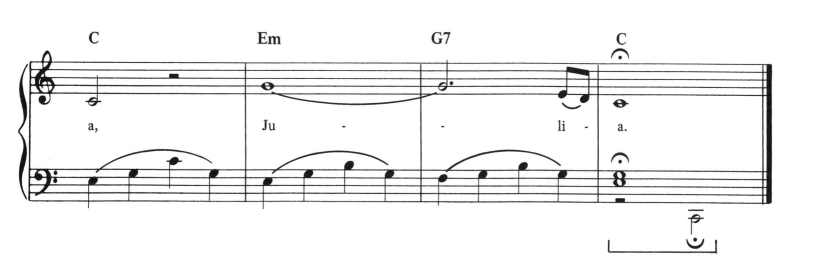

LET IT BE

Words and Music by JOHN LENNON
and PAUL McCARTNEY
Arranged by DAN FOX

Slowly, in 2 (♩ = 1 beat)

When I find my-self in times of trou-ble, Moth-er Ma-ry
(Instrumental)
comes to me Speak-ing words of wis-dom, let it be.
And in my hour of dark-ness she is stand-ing right in
front of me, Speak-ing words of wis-dom, let it be.

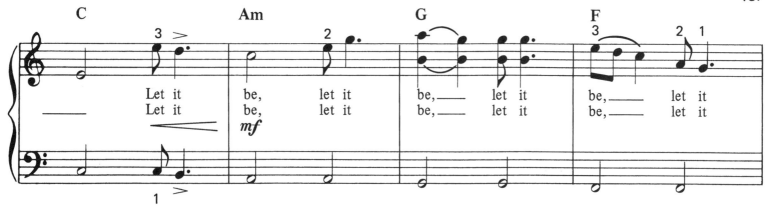

Let it be, let it be, let it be, let it
Let it be, let it be, let it be, let it

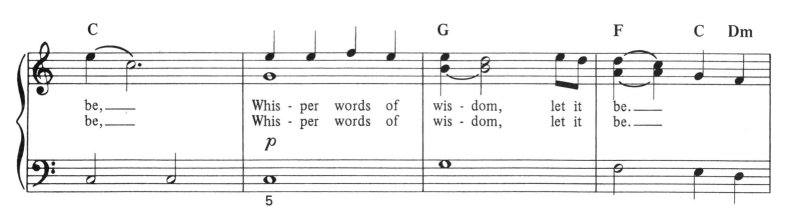

be, Whis - per words of wis - dom, let it be.
be, Whis - per words of wis - dom, let it be.

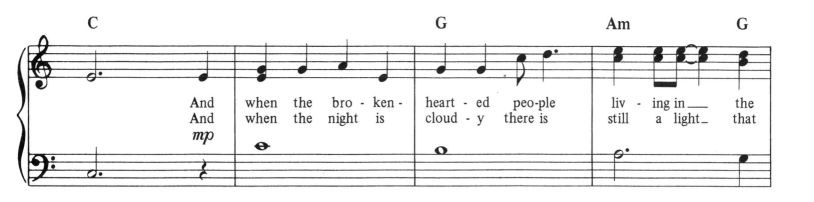

And when the bro - ken - heart - ed peo-ple liv - ing in the
And when the night is cloud - y there is still a light that

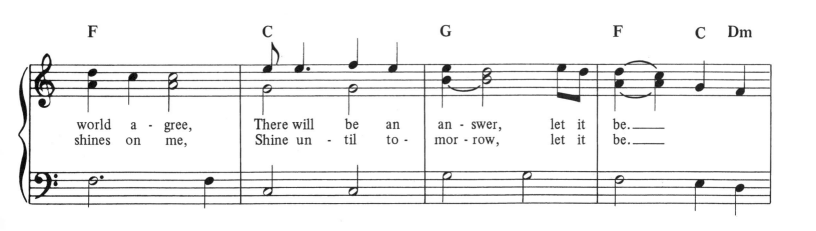

world a - gree, There will be an an - swer, let it be.
shines on me, Shine un - til to - mor - row, let it be.

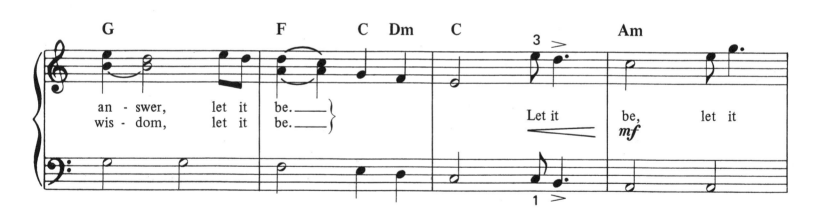

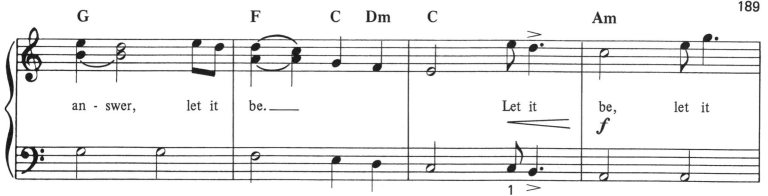

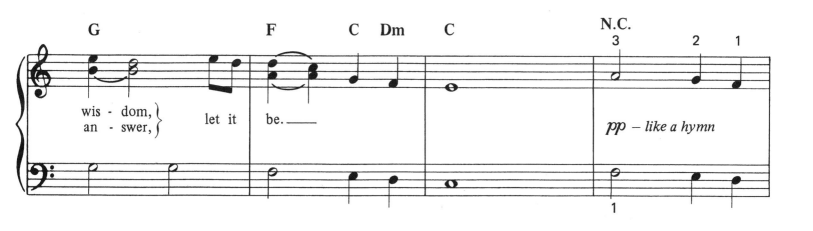

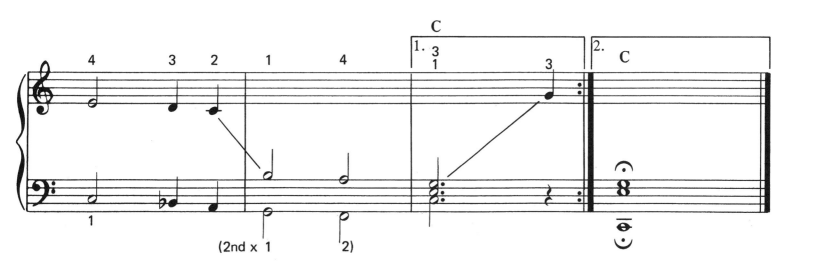

THE LONG AND WINDING ROAD

Words and Music by JOHN LENNON
and PAUL McCARTNEY

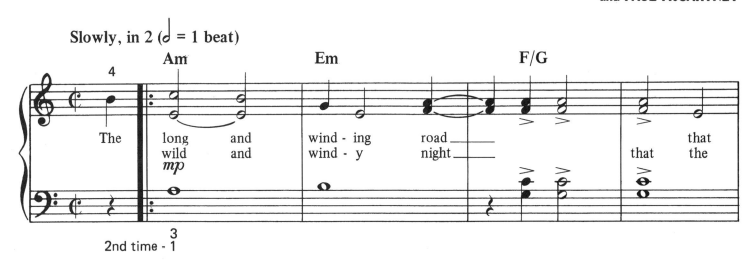

Slowly, in 2 (♩ = 1 beat)

The long and wind-ing road
wild and wind-y night

mp

2nd time - 1

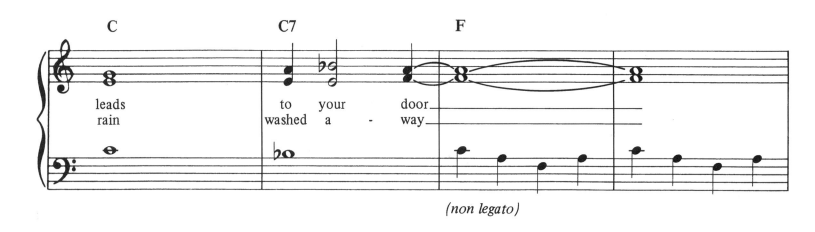

leads to your door
rain washed a - way

(non legato)

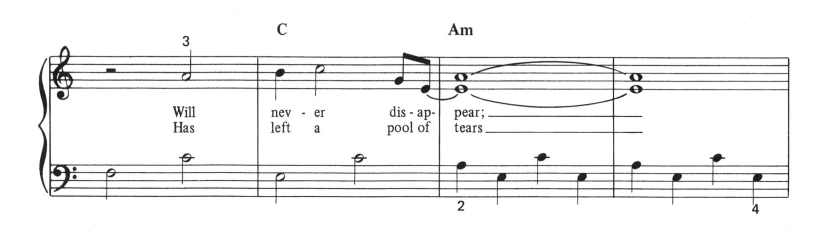

Will nev - er dis-ap-pear;
Has left a pool of tears

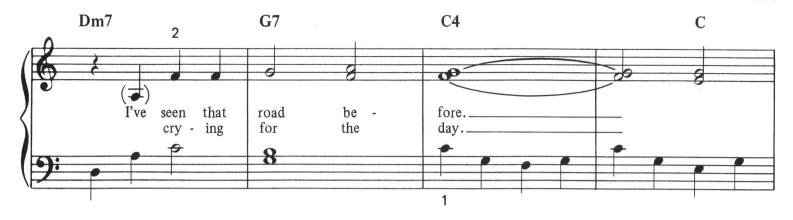

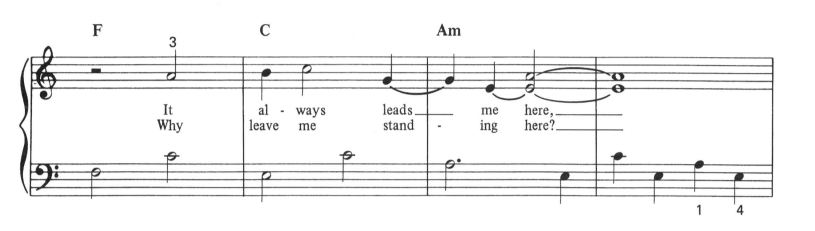

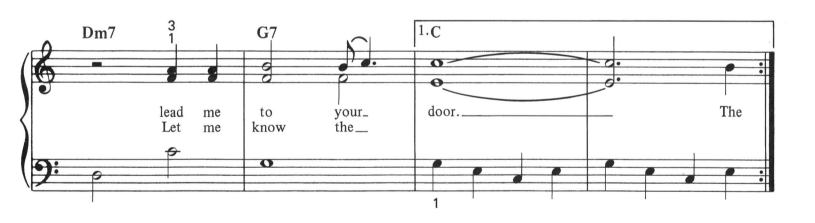

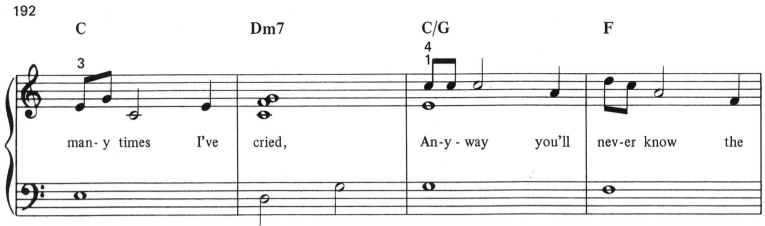

man-y times I've cried, An-y-way you'll nev-er know the

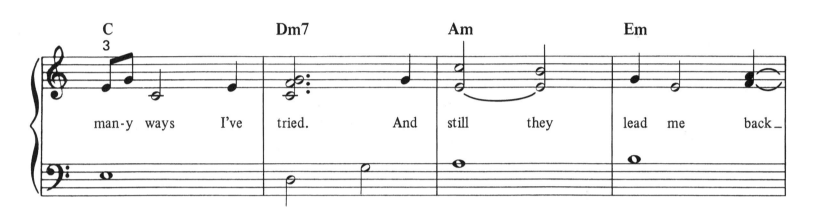

man-y ways I've tried. And still they lead me back

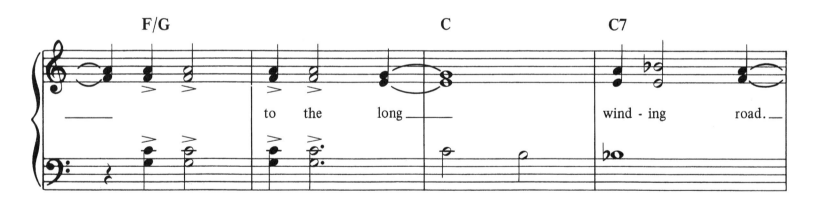

to the long wind-ing road.

You left me stand-ing

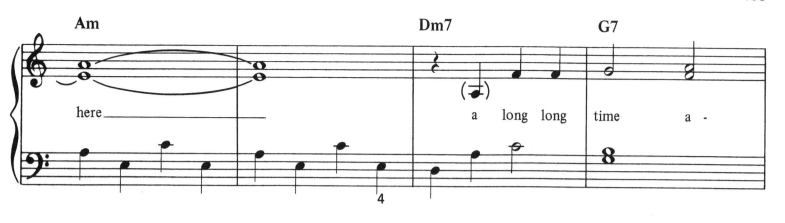

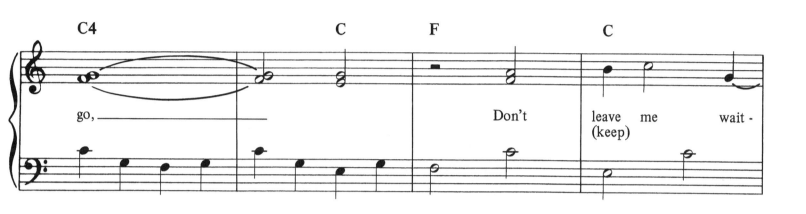

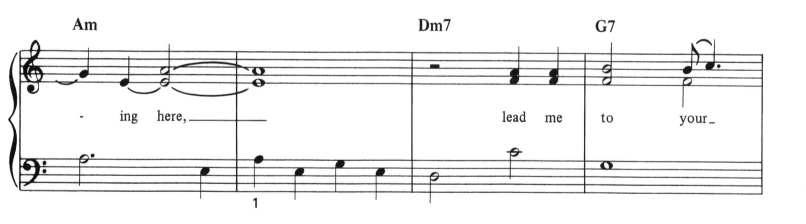

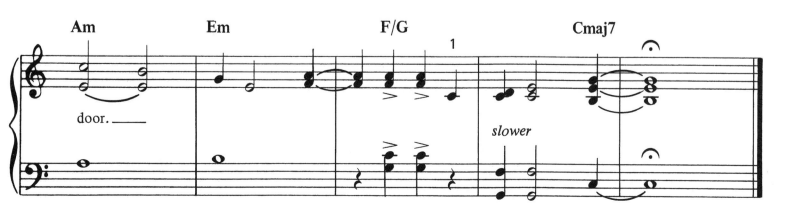

LOVE ME DO

Words and Music by PAUL McCARTNEY
and JOHN LENNON

195

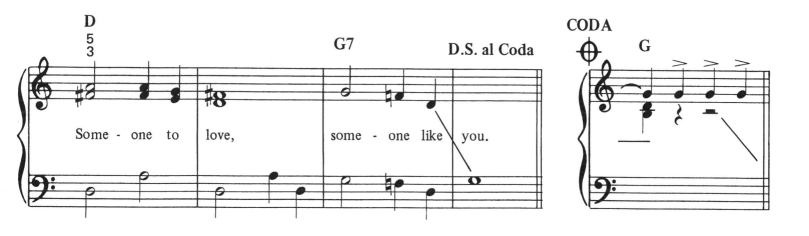

LOVELY RITA

Words and Music by JOHN LENNON
and PAUL McCARTNEY

Moderately, in 2 (♩ = 1 beat)

Love-ly Ri-ta, me-ter maid, noth-ing can come be- tween us;

When it gets dark I tow your heart a- way.

Stand-ing by a park - ing me-ter, when I caught a
Took her out and tried to win her, had a laugh and

glimpse of Ri-ta fill-ing in a tick-et in her lit-tle white book.
o - ver din-ner told her I would real-ly like to see her a - gain.

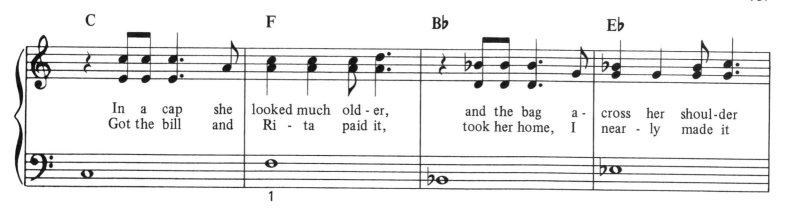

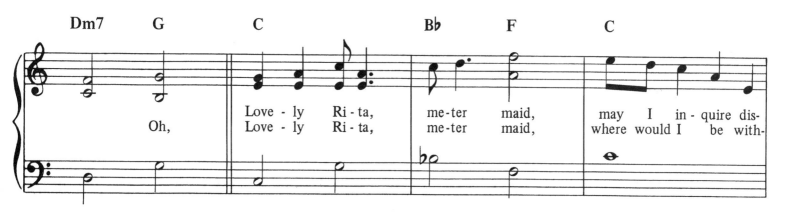

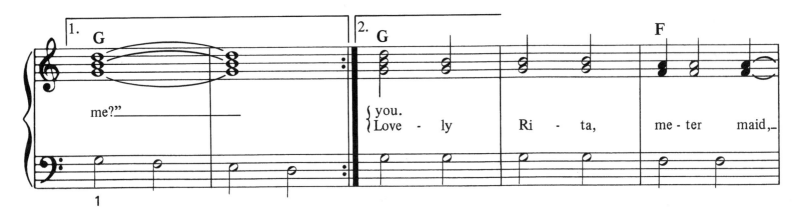

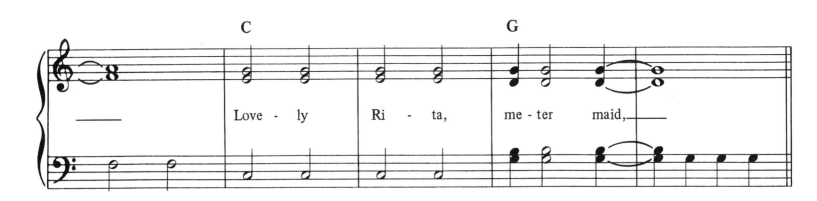

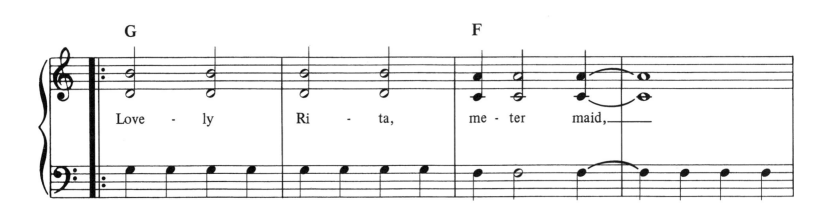

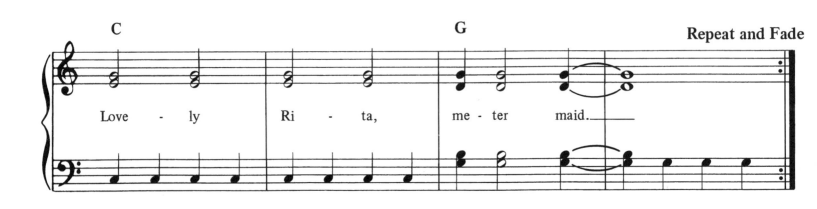

MAGICAL MYSTERY TOUR

Words and Music by JOHN LENNON
and PAUL McCARTNEY

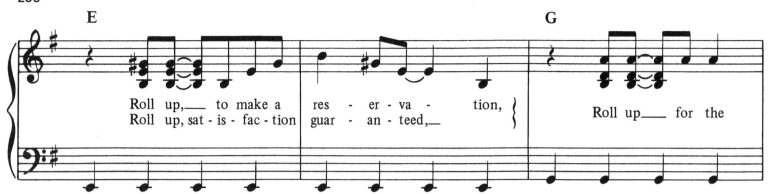

Roll up,____ to make a res - er - va - tion,
Roll up, sat - is - fac - tion guar - an - teed,____
Roll up____ for the

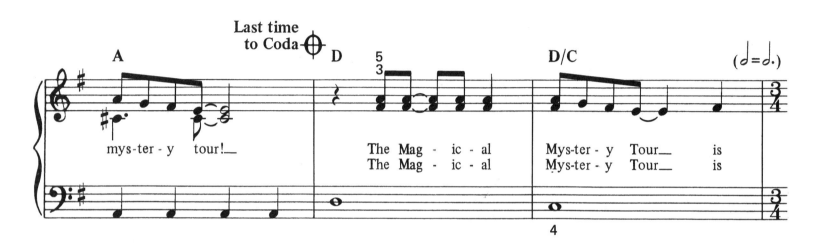

Last time to Coda

mys - ter - y tour!____
The Mag - ic - al Mys - ter - y Tour____ is
The Mag - ic - al Mys - ter - y Tour____ is

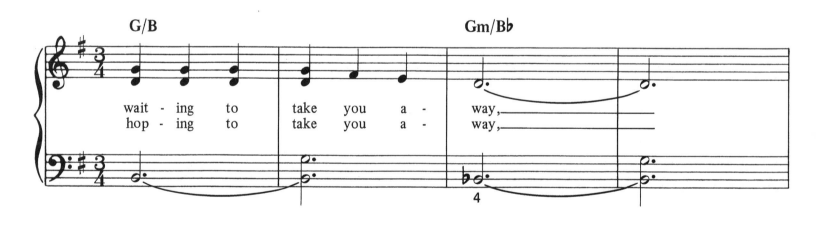

wait - ing to take you a - way,____
hop - ing to take you a - way,____

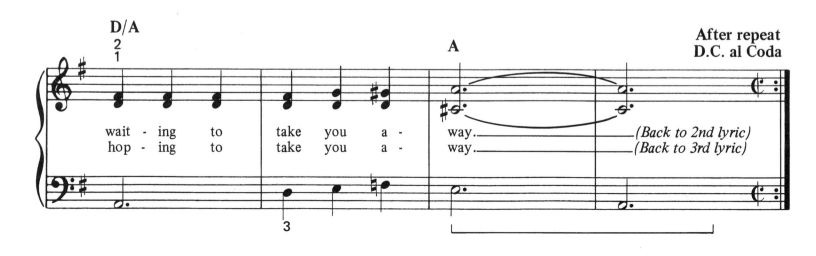

After repeat
D.C. al Coda

wait - ing to take you a - way.____ (Back to 2nd lyric)
hop - ing to take you a - way.____ (Back to 3rd lyric)

CODA

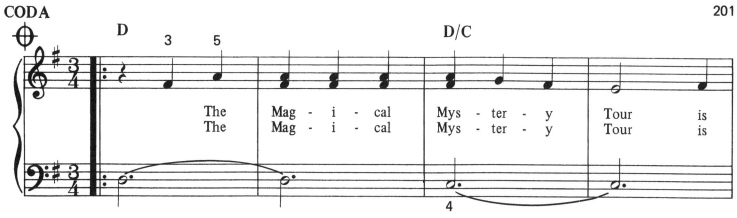

The Mag - i - cal Mys - ter - y Tour is
The Mag - i - cal Mys - ter - y Tour is

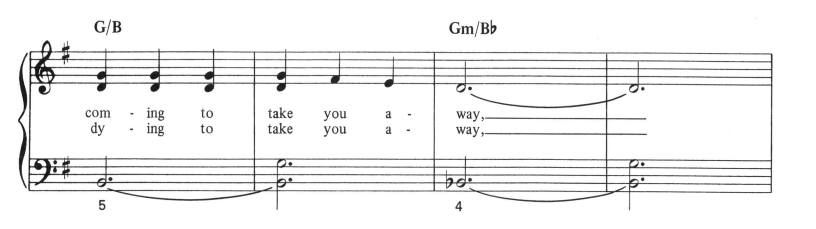

com - ing to take you a - way,
dy - ing to take you a - way,

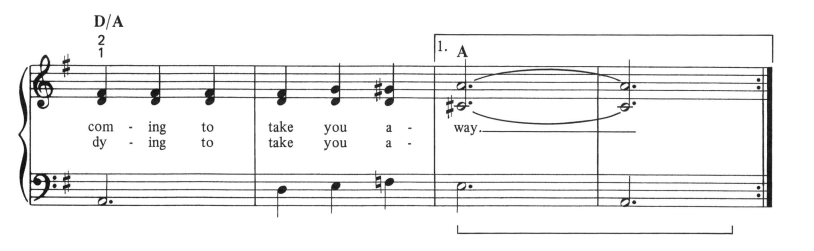

com - ing to take you a - way.
dy - ing to take you a -

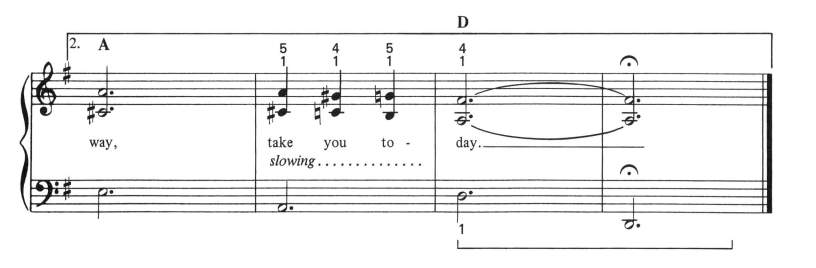

way, take you to - day.

slowing . . . .

LUCY IN THE SKY WITH DIAMONDS

Words and Music by JOHN LENNON
and PAUL McCARTNEY

Moderately flowing

N.C.

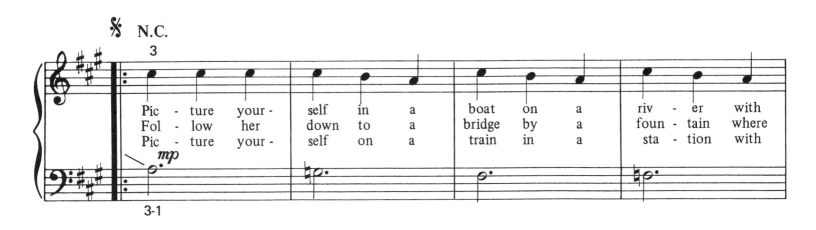

Pic - ture your - self in a boat on a riv - er with
Fol - low her down to a bridge by a foun - tain where
Pic - ture your - self on a train in a sta - tion with

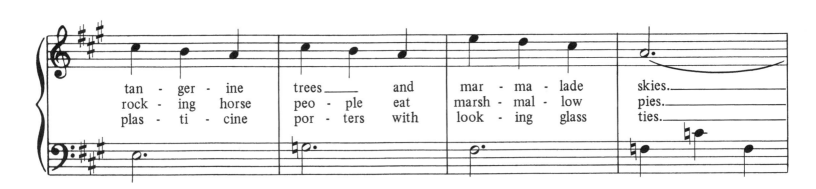

tan - ger - ine trees____ and mar - ma - lade skies.____
rock - ing horse peo - ple eat marsh - mal - low pies.____
plas - ti - cine por - ters with look - ing glass ties.____

203

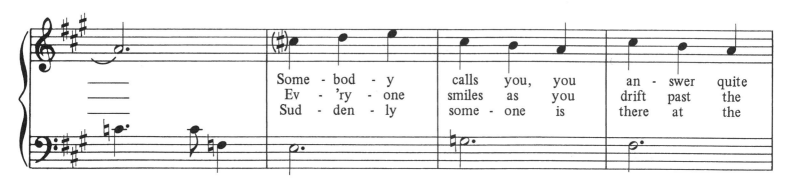

Some - bod - y   calls you, you   an - swer quite
Ev - 'ry - one   smiles as you   drift past the
Sud - den - ly   some - one is   there at the

slow - ly,   a   girl with ka -   lei - do - scope   eyes.
flow - ers   that   grow so in -   cred - i - bly   high.
turn - stile: The   girl with ka -   lei - do - scope   eyes.

Last time to Coda ⊕

(To Coda)   1   4   B♭

Cel - lo - phane
News - pa - per

C7   Dm/F

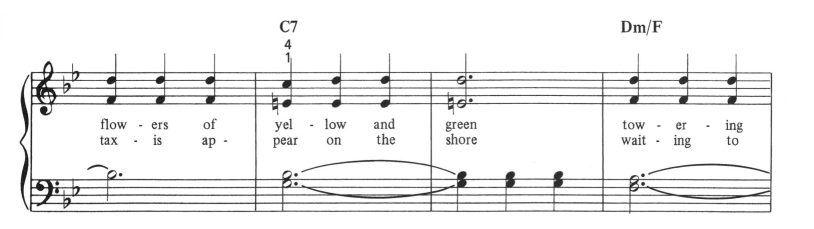

flow - ers   of   yel - low and   green   tow - er - ing
tax - is   ap -   pear on the   shore   wait - ing to

o - ver your head._____
take you a - way._____

Bb

C9

Look for the
Climb in the

G

girl with the sun in her eyes and she's
back with your head in the clouds and you're

Steady 4
D

gone. }
gone. }

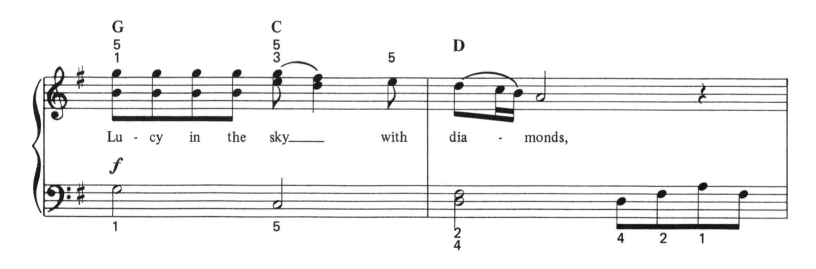

G   **C**   **D**

Lu - cy in the sky_____ with dia - monds,

f

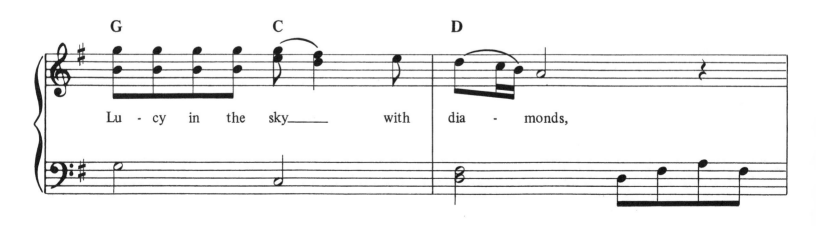

G   **C**   **D**

Lu - cy in the sky_____ with dia - monds,

Lu - cy in the sky___ with dia - monds, Ah!

CODA

Lu - cy in the sky___ with dia - monds,

Lu - cy in the sky with dia - monds, Lu - cy in the sky with

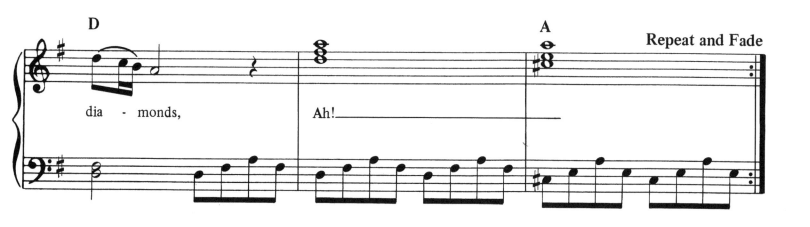

dia - monds, Ah!_____

Repeat and Fade

MARTHA MY DEAR

Words and Music by JOHN LENNON
and PAUL McCARTNEY

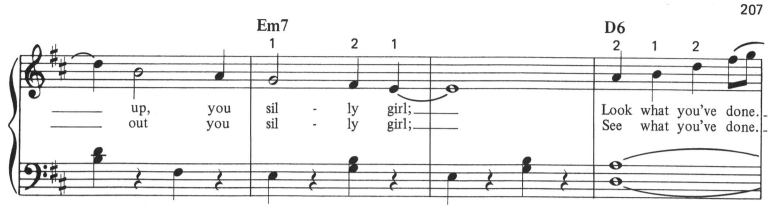

up, you sil - ly girl; Look what you've done.
out you sil - ly girl; See what you've done.

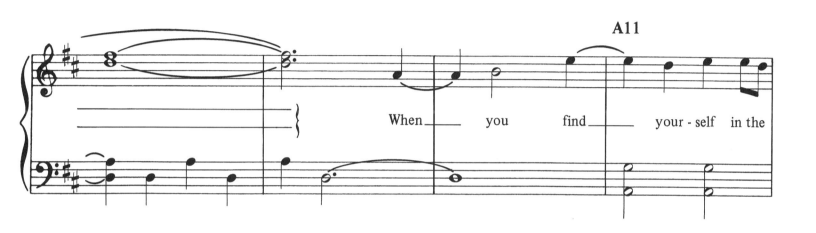

When you find your - self in the

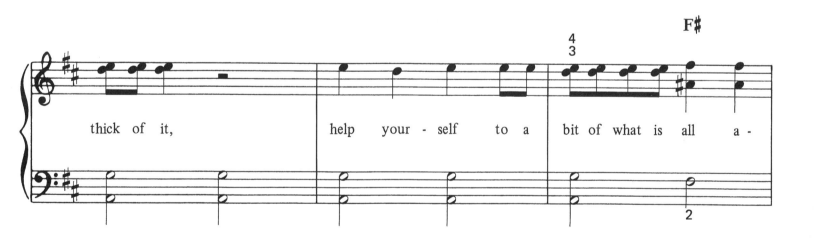

thick of it, help your - self to a bit of what is all a -

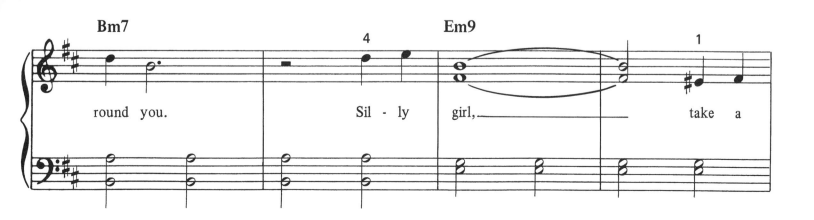

round you. Sil - ly girl, take a

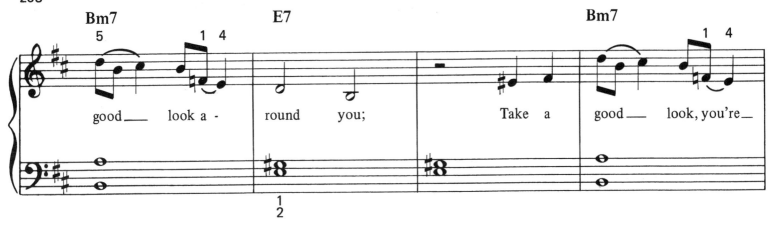

good___ look a - round you; Take a good___ look, you're___

bound to see___ that you and me___ were

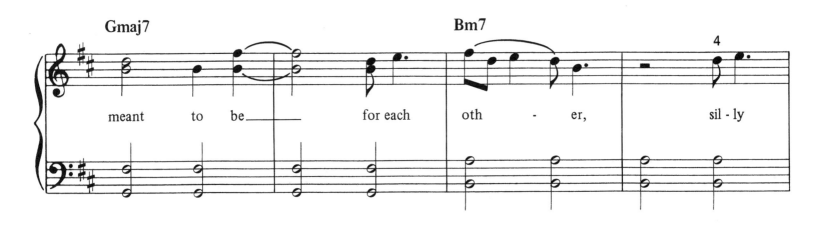

meant to be___ for each oth - er, sil - ly

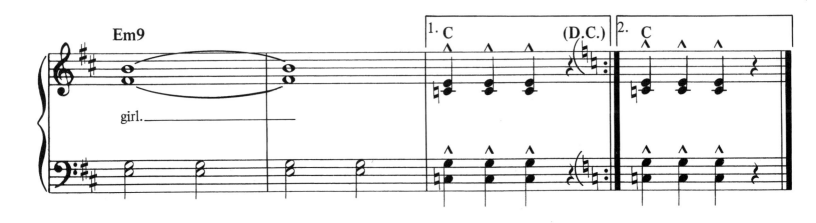

girl.___

MAXWELL'S SILVER HAMMER

Words and Music by JOHN LENNON
and PAUL McCARTNEY

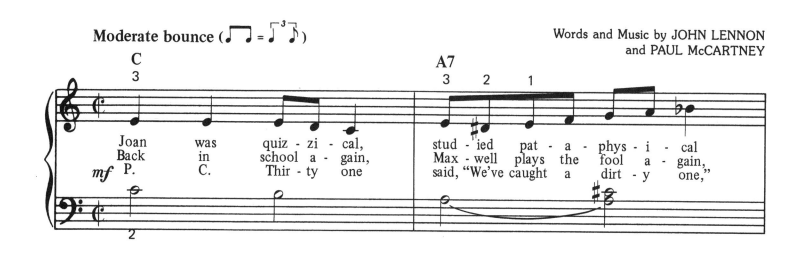

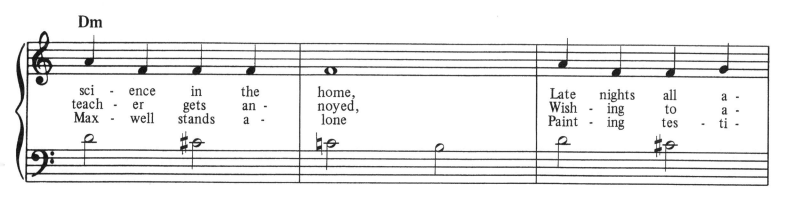

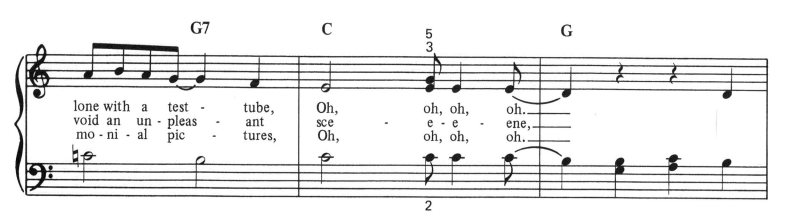

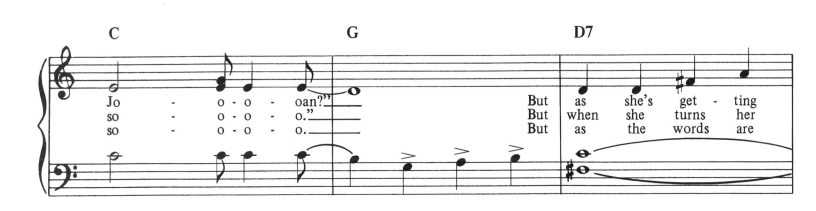

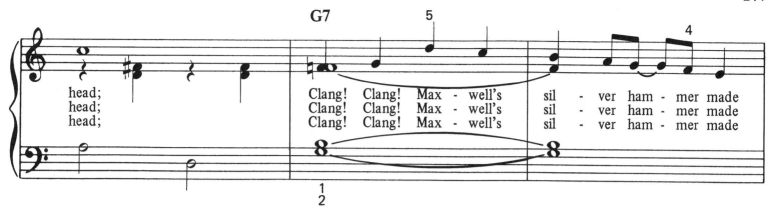

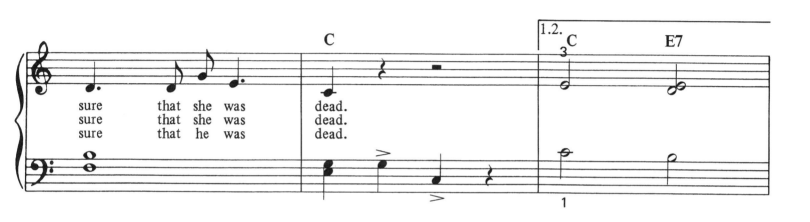

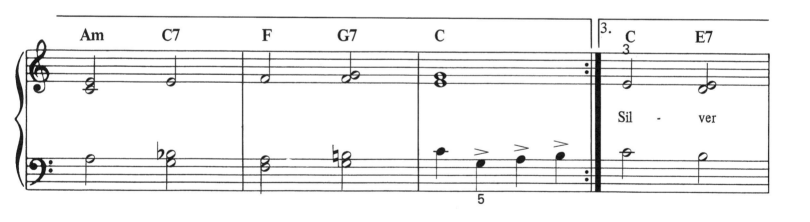

MEAN MR. MUSTARD

Words and Music by JOHN LENNON
and PAUL McCARTNEY

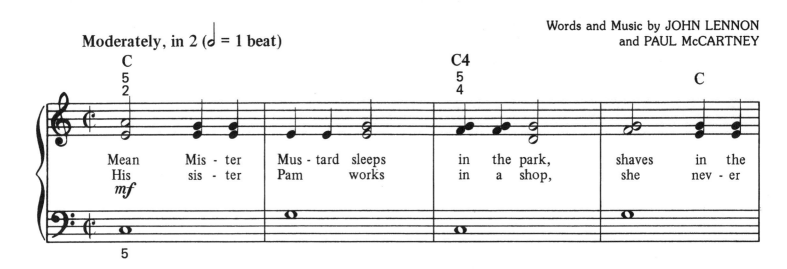

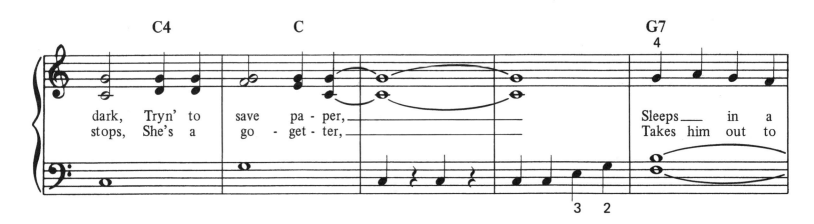

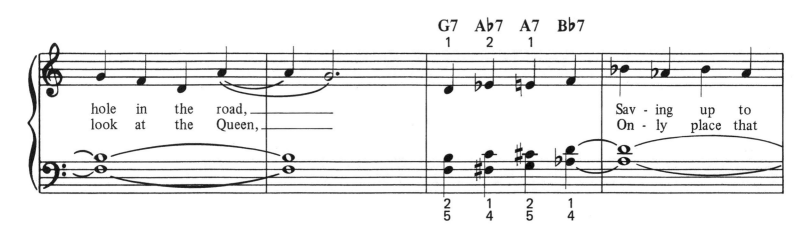

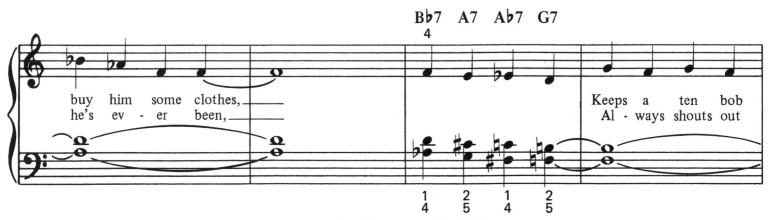

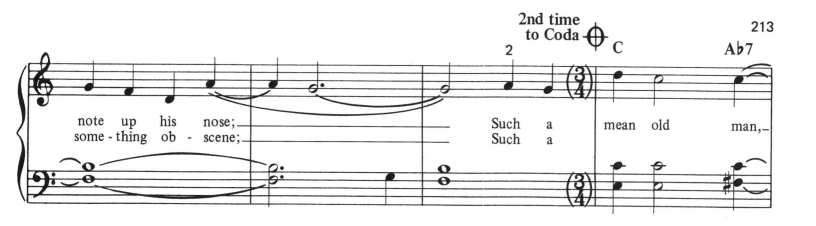

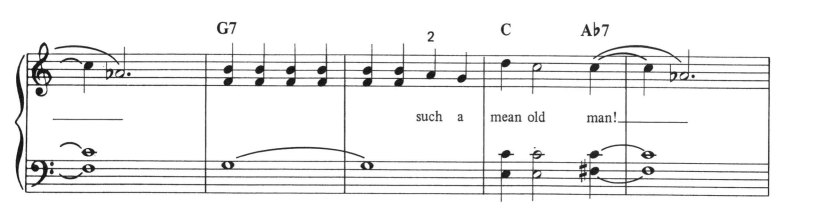

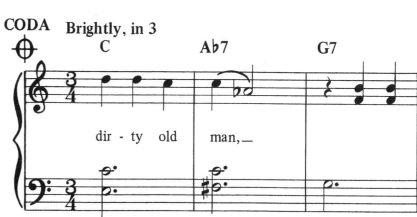

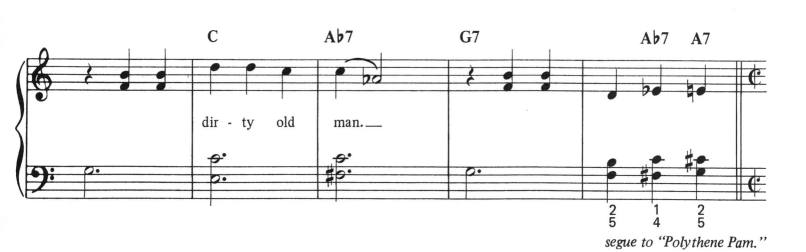

segue to "Polythene Pam."

POLYTHENE PAM

Words and Music by JOHN LENNON
and PAUL McCARTNEY

215

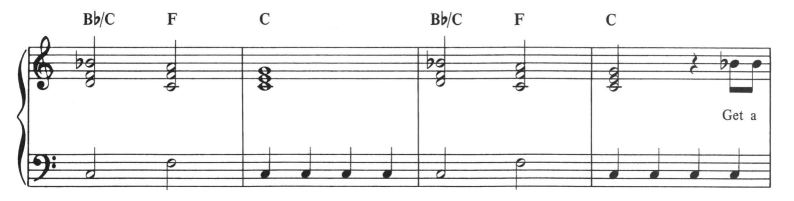

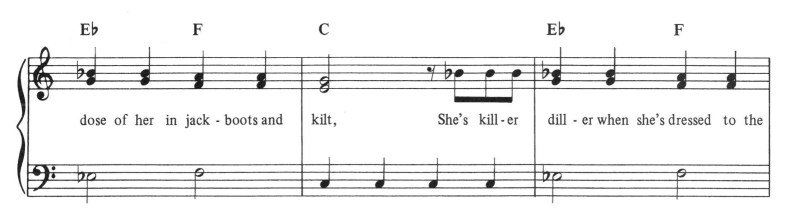

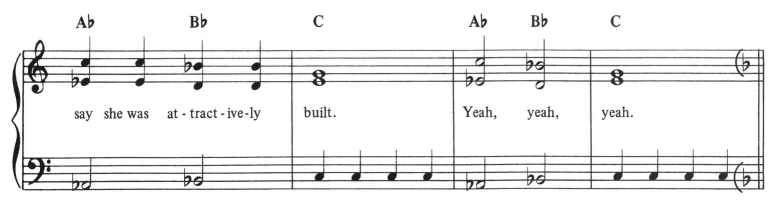

segue to "She Came In Through The Bathroom Window."

SHE CAME IN THROUGH THE BATHROOM WINDOW

Words and Music by JOHN LENNON
and PAUL McCARTNEY

Half the previous tempo

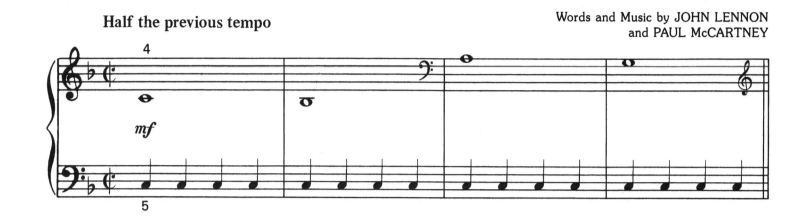

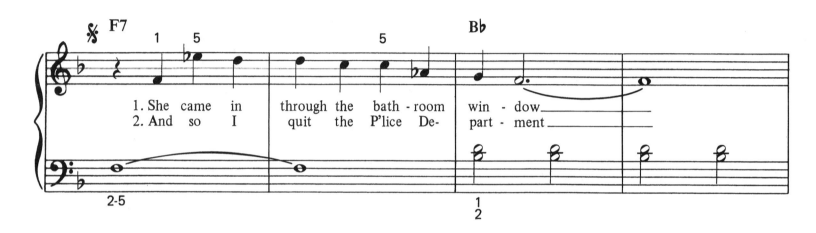

1. She came in through the bath-room win-dow
2. And so I quit the P'lice De-part-ment

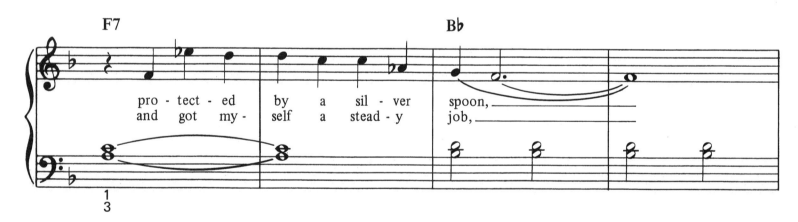

pro-tect-ed by a sil-ver spoon,
and got my-self a stead-y job,

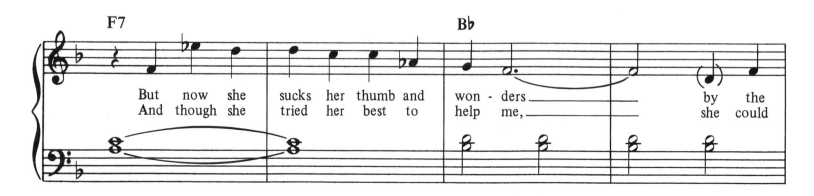

But now she sucks her thumb and won-ders by the
And though she tried her best to help me, she could

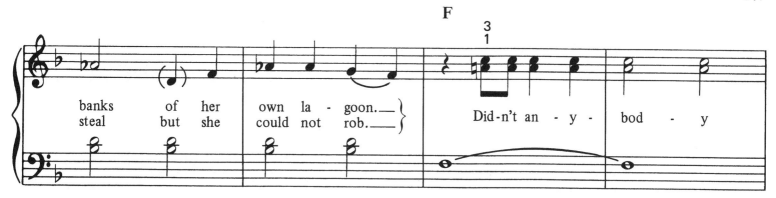

banks of her own la - goon.___
steal but she could not rob.___

Did-n't an - y - bod - y

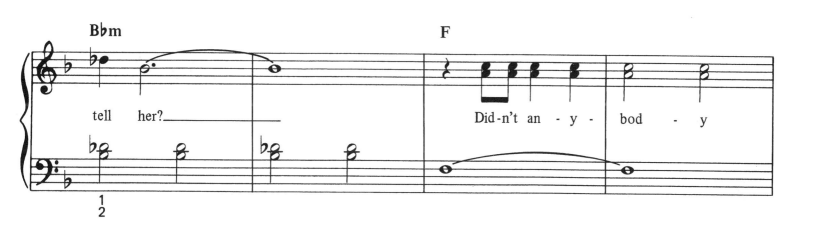

tell her?___

Did-n't an - y - bod - y

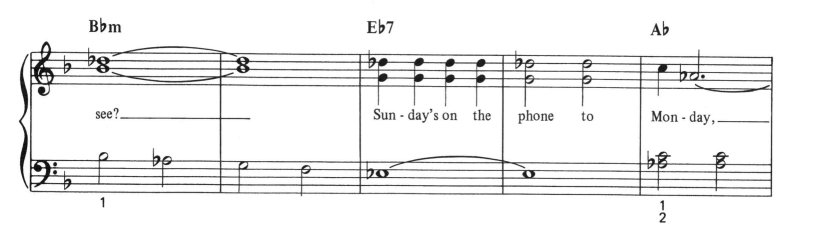

see?___

Sun - day's on the phone to Mon - day,

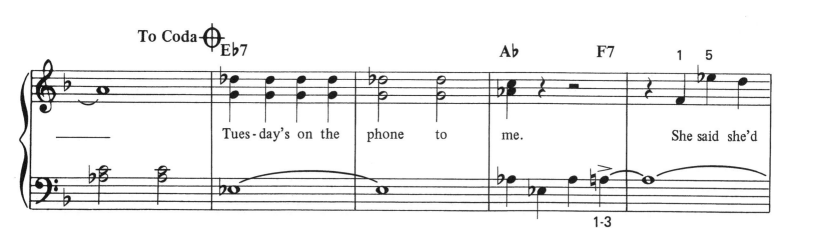

Tues - day's on the phone to me.

She said she'd

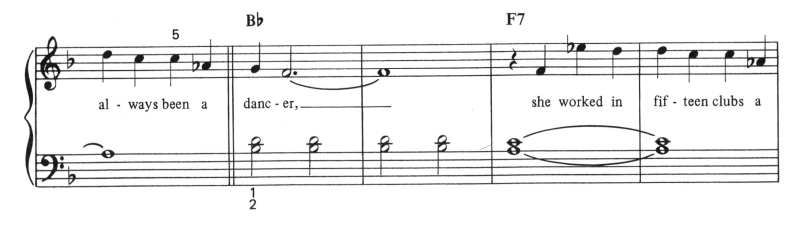

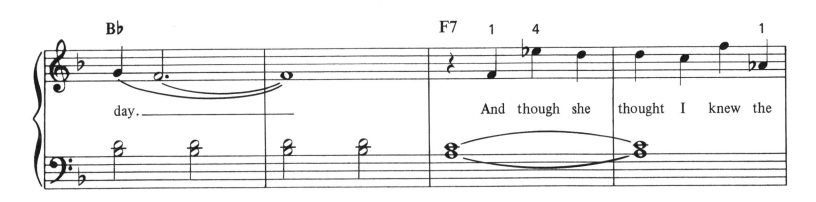

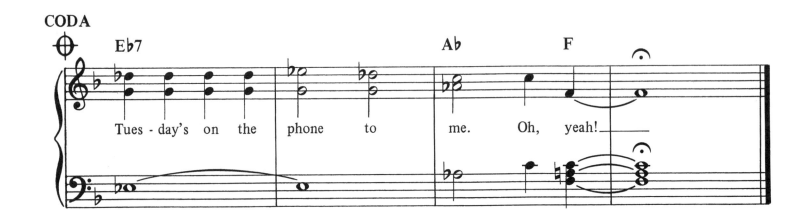

MICHELLE

Words and Music by JOHN LENNON
and PAUL McCARTNEY

Gentle Ballad (but not too slow)

Mi - chelle, ma belle, these are words that go to - geth - er well, my Mi - chelle.

Mi - chelle, I love you......

ma belle, sont des mots qui vont tres bien en -
ma belle, sont des mots qui vont tres bien en -
(Instrumental) _____

220

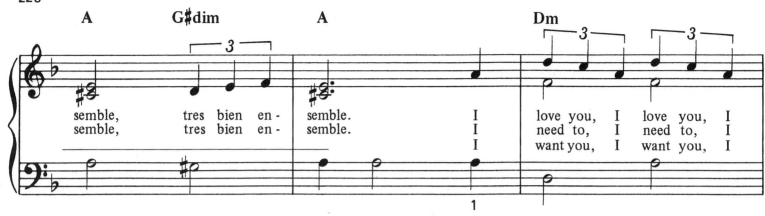

221

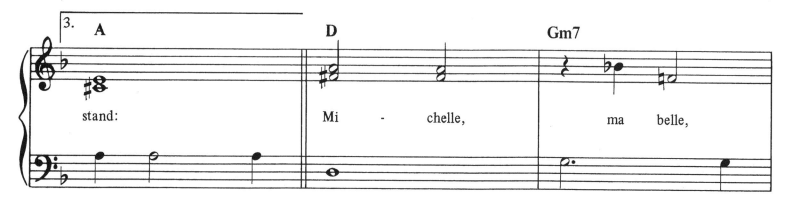

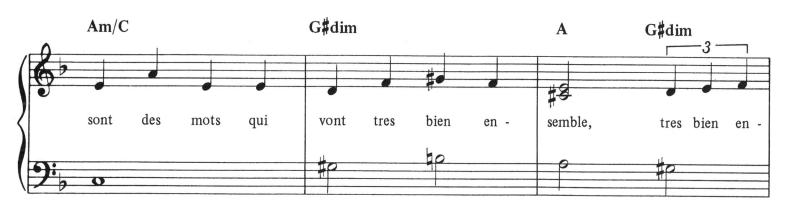

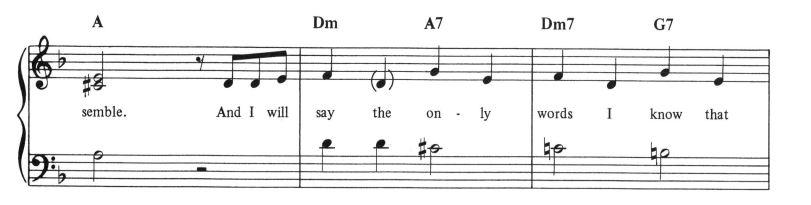

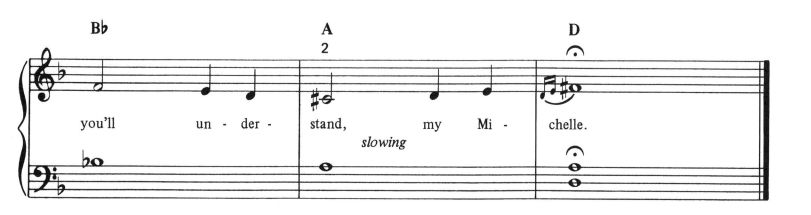

NO REPLY

Words and Music by JOHN LENNON
and PAUL McCARTNEY

Moderate rock

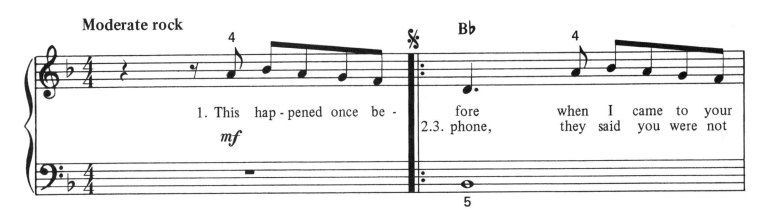

1. This hap-pened once be-fore, when I came to your
2.3. phone, they said you were not

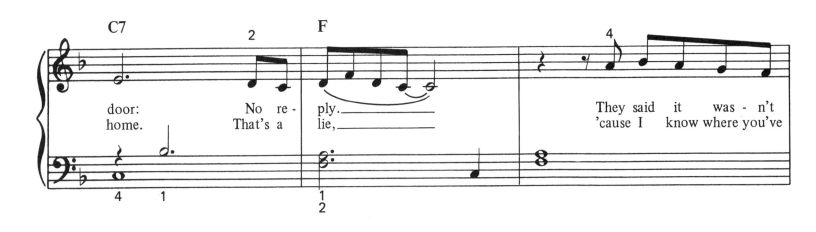

door: No re-ply.
home. That's a lie,

They said it was-n't
'cause I know where you've

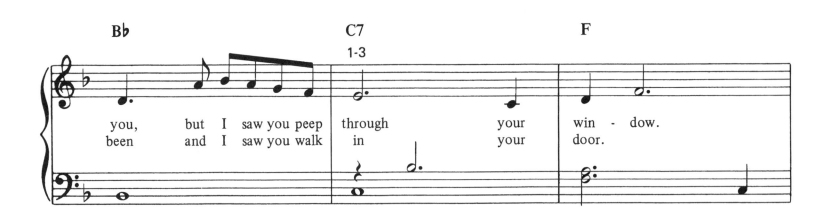

you, but I saw you peep through your win-dow.
been and I saw you walk in your door.

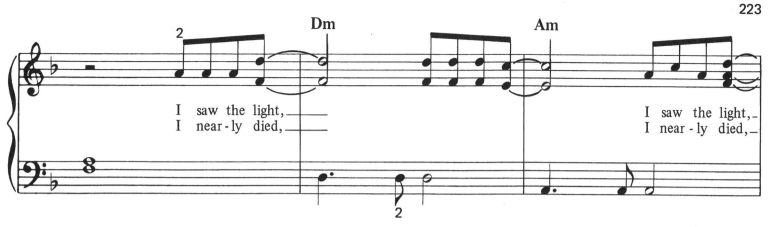

I saw the light,
I near-ly died,

I saw the light,
I near-ly died,

I know that you saw me 'cause I looked up to
'cause you walked hand in hand with an-oth-er

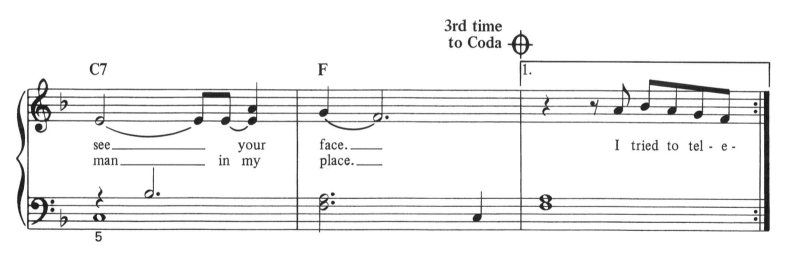

3rd time
to Coda

see your face.
man in my place.

I tried to tel-e-

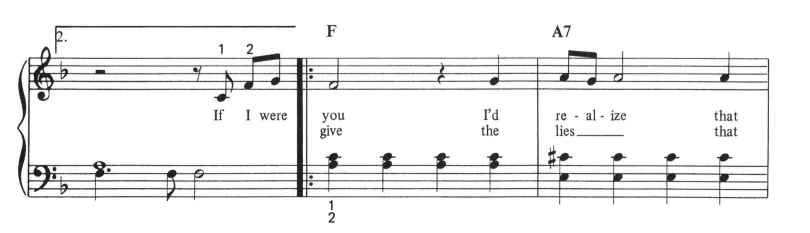

If I were you I'd give the re-al-ize that lies that

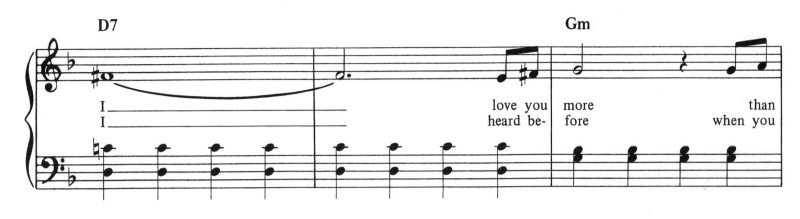

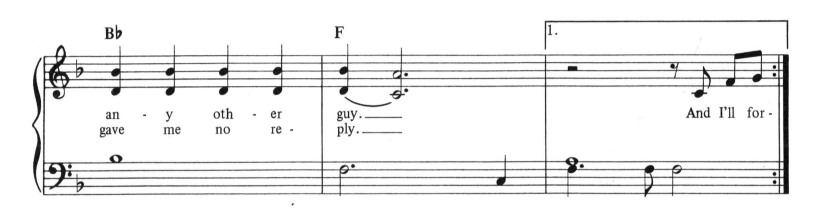

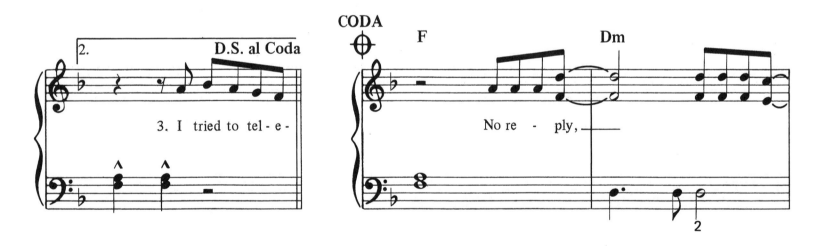

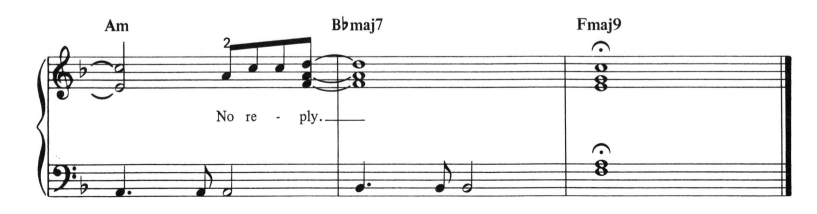

NORWEGIAN WOOD
(This Bird Has Flown)

Moderately flowing, in 1 (Each measure = 1 beat)

Words and Music by JOHN LENNON
and PAUL McCARTNEY

asked me to stay and she told me to sit an - y-
told me she worked in the morn - ing and start - ed to

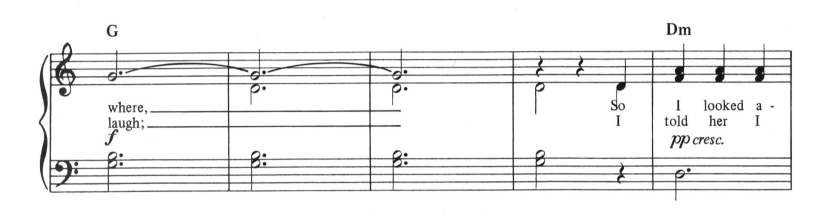

where, So I looked a -
laugh; I told her I

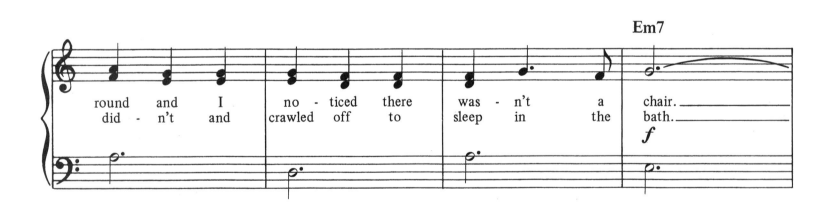

round and I no - ticed there was - n't a chair.
did - n't I and crawled off there to sleep in the bath.

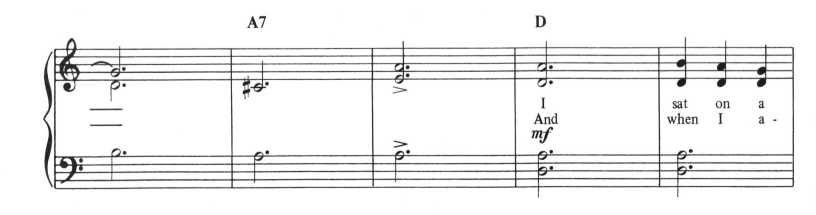

I sat on a
And when I a -

rug, / woke,   bid - ing my / I was a -   time, / lone,   **Am7/D** drink - ing her / this bird her   **G/D**

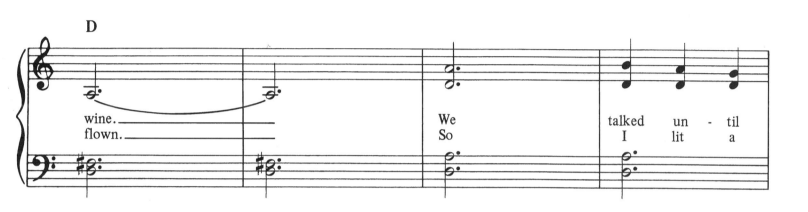

D   wine. / flown.   We / So   talked un - til / I lit a

two, / fire;   and then she / Is - n't it   said, / good   **Am7/D** "It's time for / Nor - we - gian   **G/D** / *2nd time, much slower*

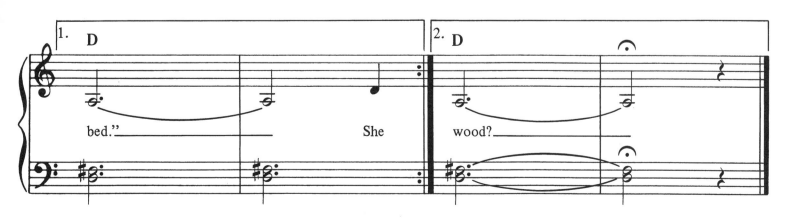

1. **D**   bed."   She   2. **D**   wood?

NOWHERE MAN

Moderate Rock Ballad

Words and Music by JOHN LENNON
and PAUL McCARTNEY

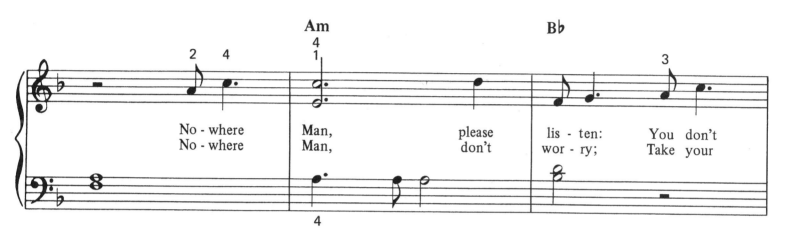

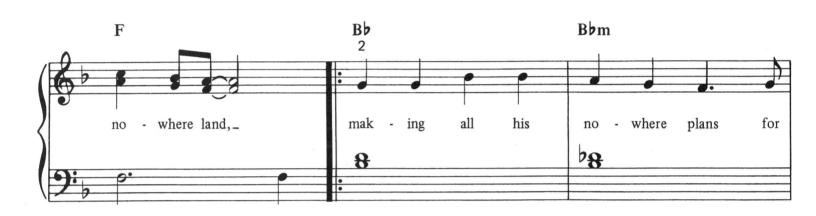

OB-LA-DI, OB-LA-DA

Words and Music by JOHN LENNON
and PAUL McCARTNEY

Bright ska tempo

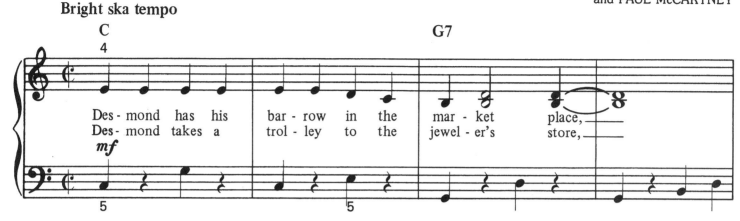

Des - mond has his / bar - row in the / mar - ket place, /
Des - mond takes a / trol - ley to the / jewel - er's store,

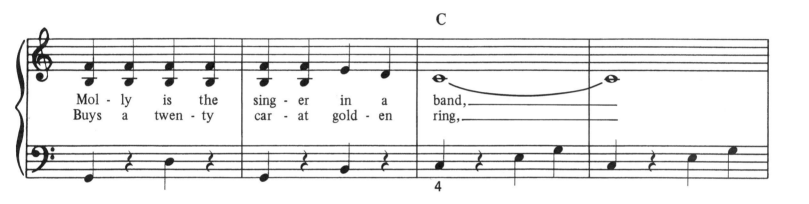

Mol - ly is the / sing - er in a / band, /
Buys a twen - ty / car - at gold - en / ring,

Des - mond says to / Mol - ly "Girl, I / like your face." ___ And Mol - ly /
Takes it back to / Mol - ly wait - ing / at the door, ___ And as he

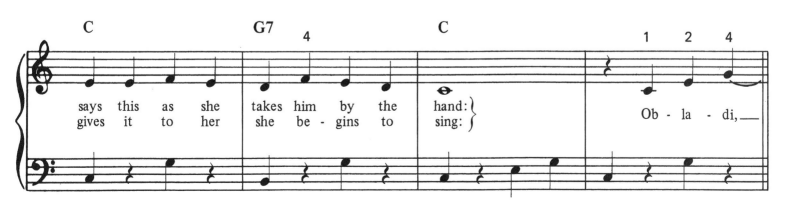

says this as she / takes him by the / hand: } / Ob - la - di, ___
gives it to her / she be - gins to / sing:

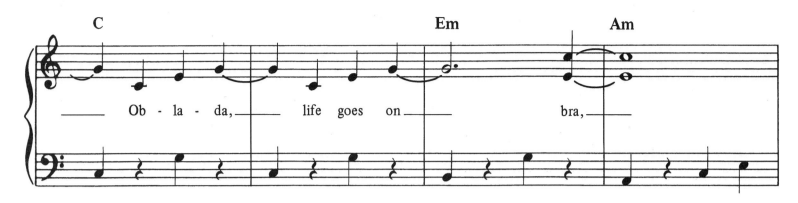

Ob - la - da, life goes on bra,

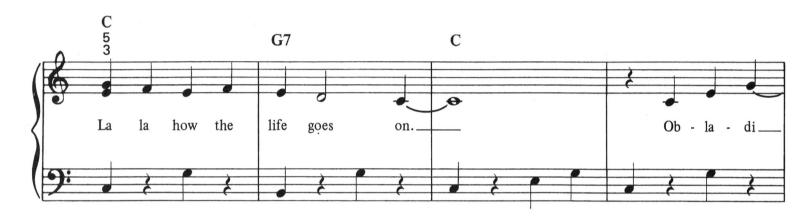

La la how the life goes on. Ob - la - di

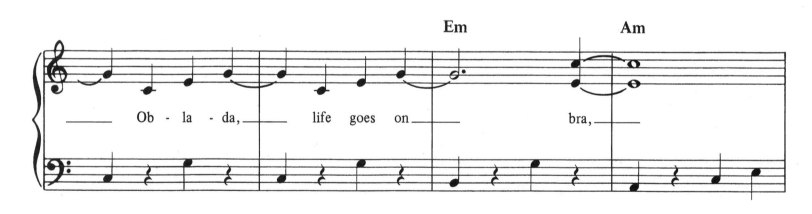

Ob - la - da, life goes on bra,

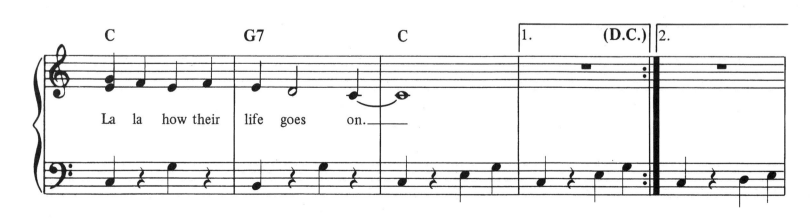

La la how their life goes on.

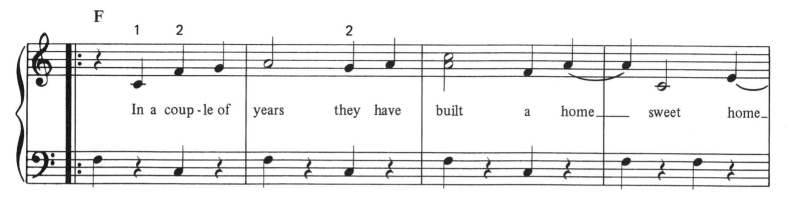

In a coup-le of years they have built a home___ sweet home___

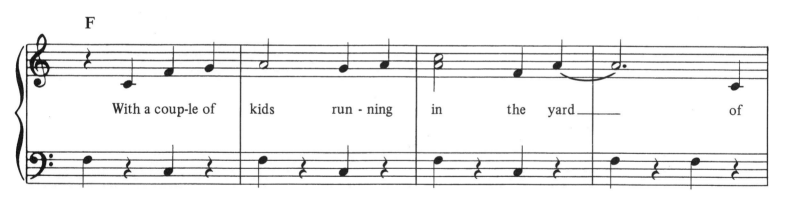

With a coup-le of kids run - ning in the yard___ of

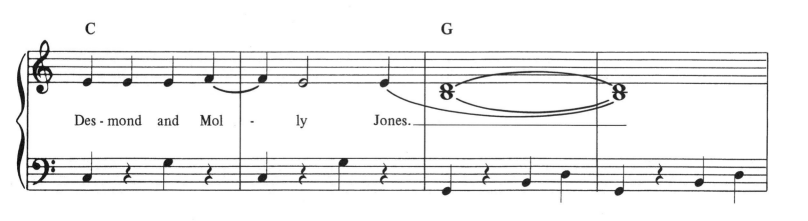

Des - mond and Mol - ly Jones.___

234

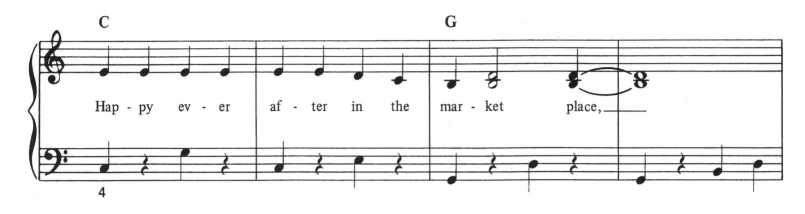

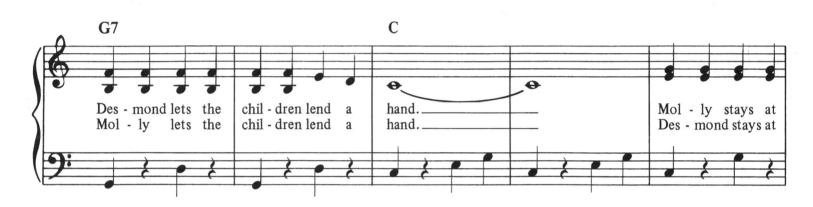

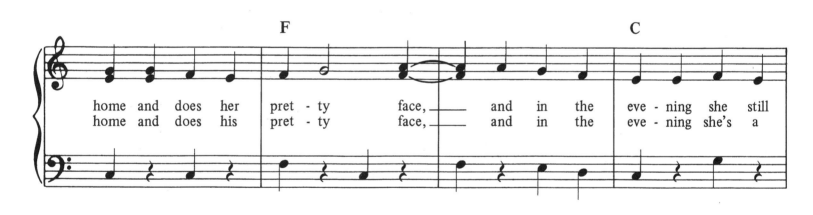

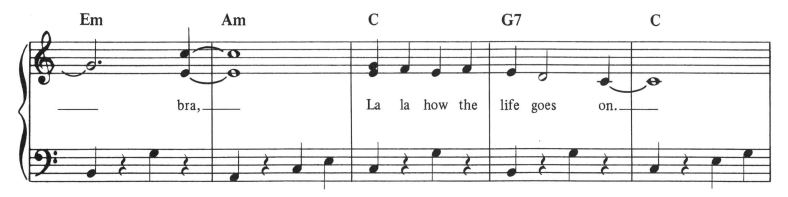

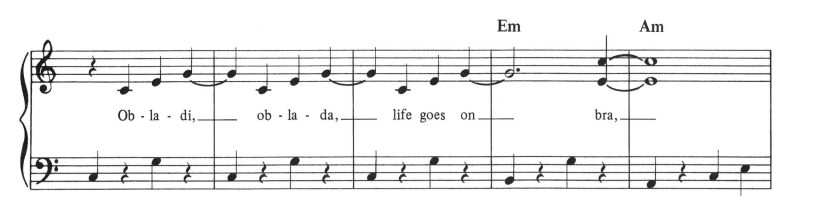

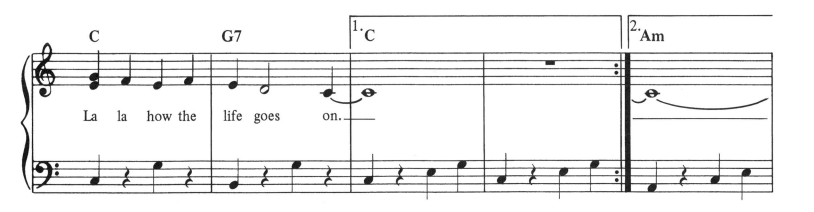

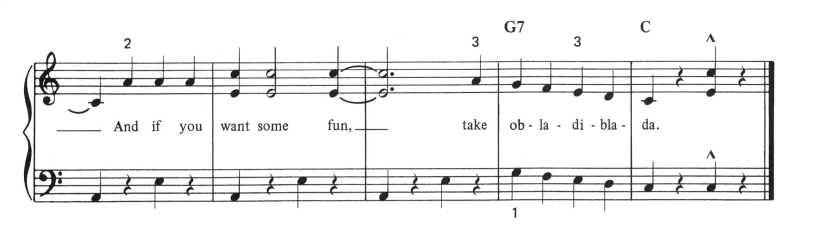

OCTOPUS'S GARDEN

Words and Music by
RICHARD STARKEY

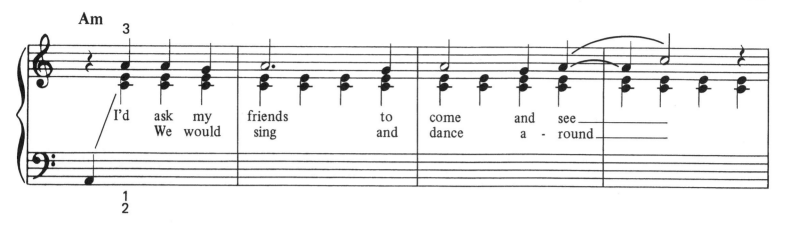

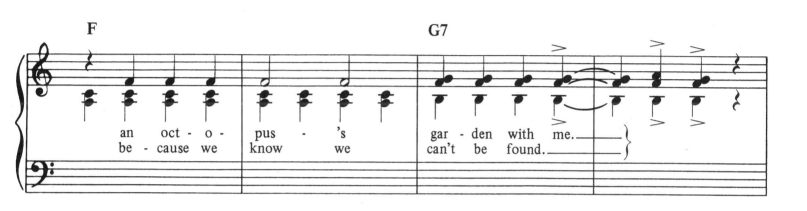

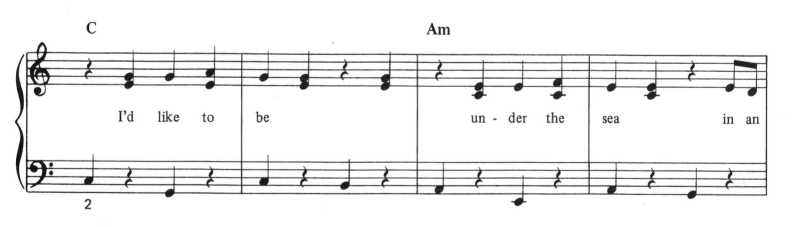

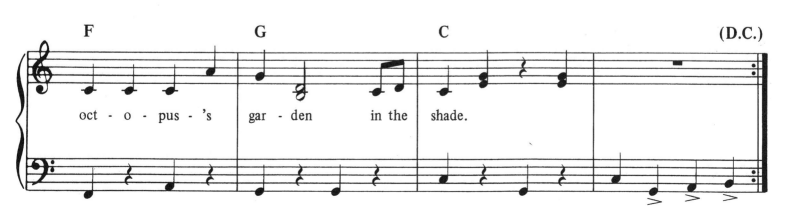

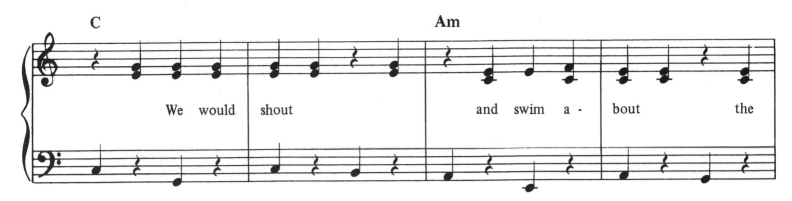

We would shout and swim a - bout the

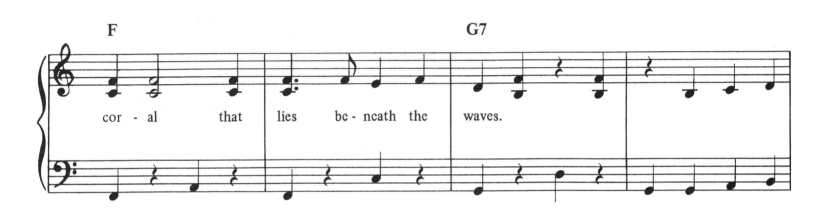

cor - al that lies be - neath the waves.

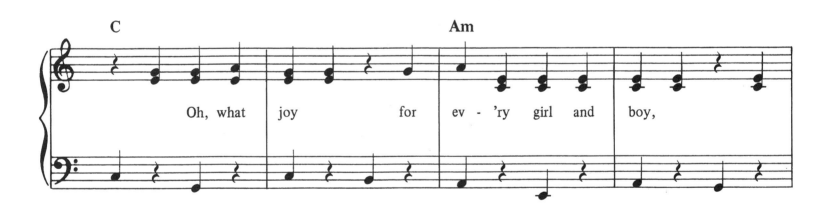

Oh, what joy for ev - 'ry girl and boy,

know - ing they're hap - py and they're safe.

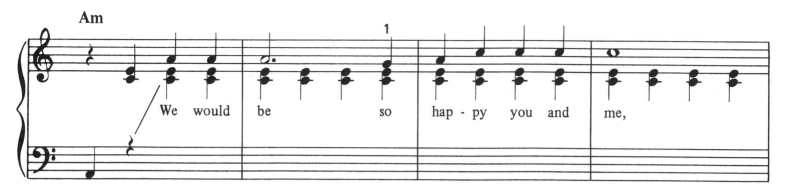

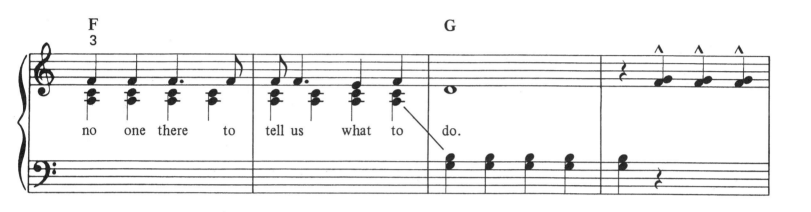

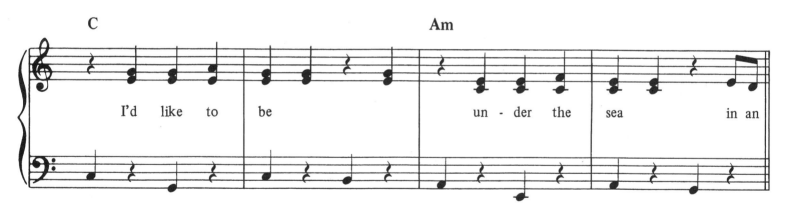

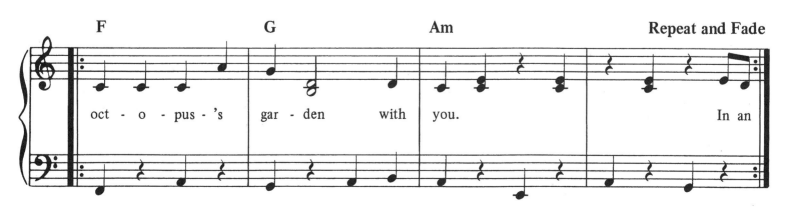

OH! DARLING

Words and Music by JOHN LENNON
and PAUL McCARTNEY

Slowly, in 2 (♩. = 1 beat)

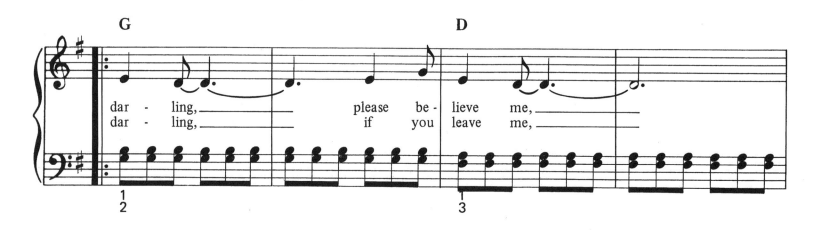

dar - ling,_____ please be - lieve me,_____
dar - ling,_____ if you leave me,_____

I'll nev - er do you_____ no harm; Be-
I'll nev - er make it_____ a - lone; Be-

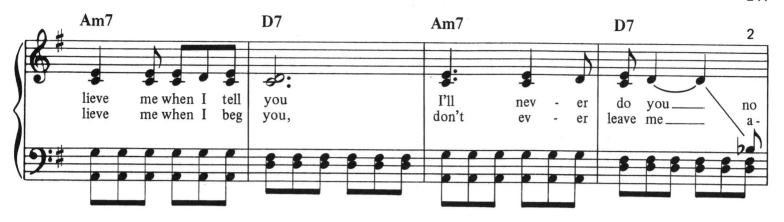

cried.

When you told me _____ you did-n't

need me ___ an - y - more, _____ well you know I near - ly fell down and

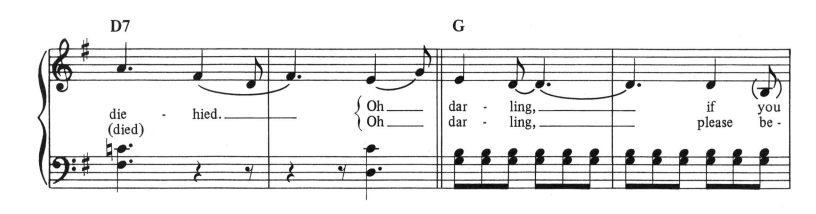

die - hied. _____
(died)

Oh ___ dar - ling, _____ if you
Oh ___ dar - ling, _____ please be-

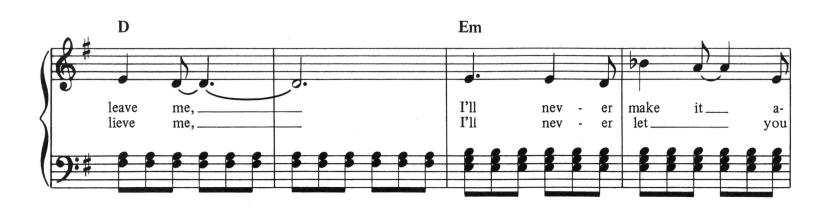

leave me, _____
lieve me, _____

I'll nev - er make it ___ a-
I'll nev - er let _____ you

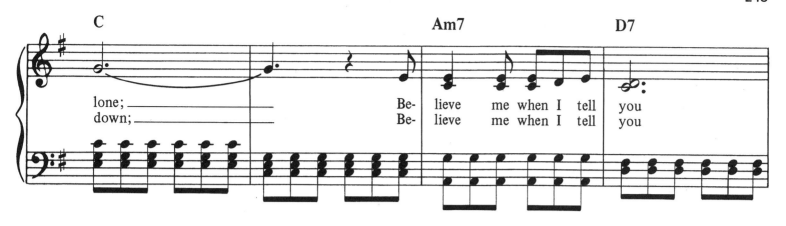

C   Am7   D7

lone; _____ Be- lieve me when I tell you
down; _____ Be- lieve me when I tell you

1. Am7   D7   G   C

I'll nev - er do you _____ no harm.

G   G7   2. Am7   D7

When you   I'll nev - er do you ___ no

5   2 1 4   3   2

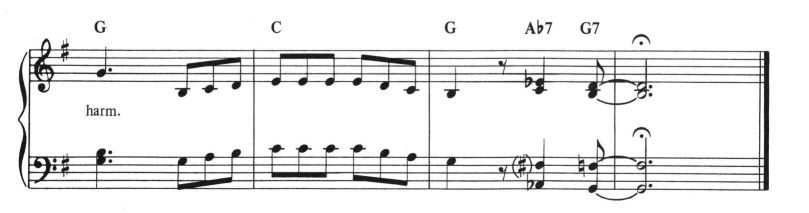

G   C   G   A♭7   G7

harm.

P.S. I LOVE YOU

Words and Music by JOHN LENNON
and PAUL McCARTNEY

Moderate Rock

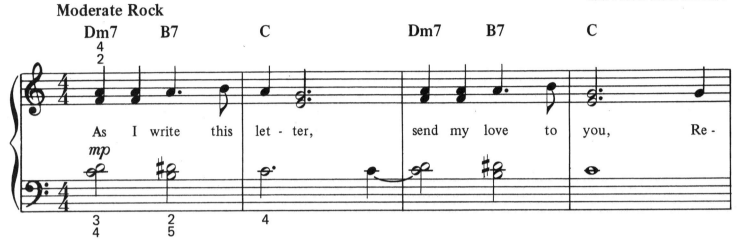

As I write this let- ter, send my love to you, Re-

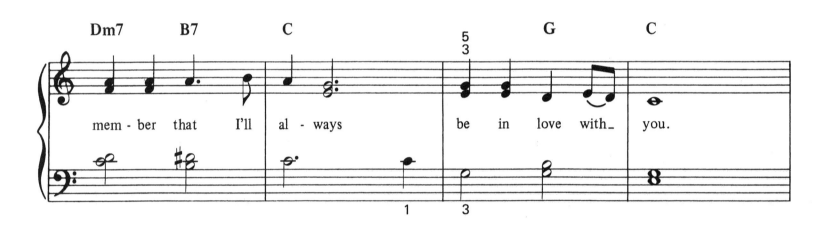

mem- ber that I'll al- ways be in love with_ you.

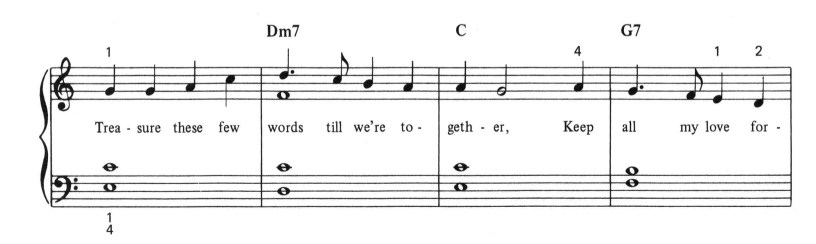

Trea- sure these few words till we're to- geth- er, Keep all my love for-

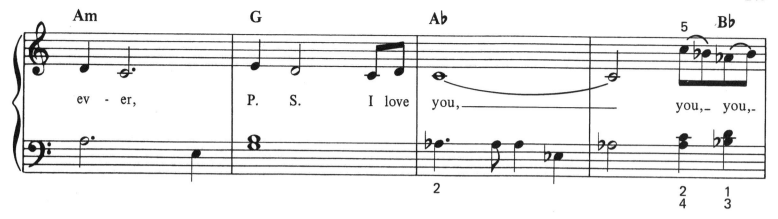

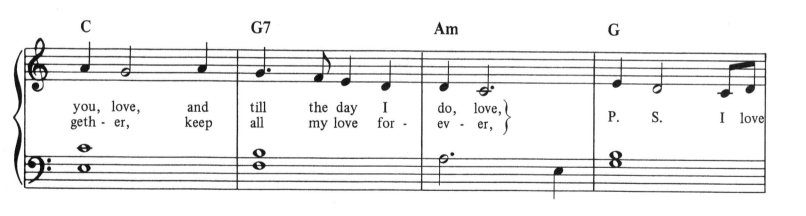

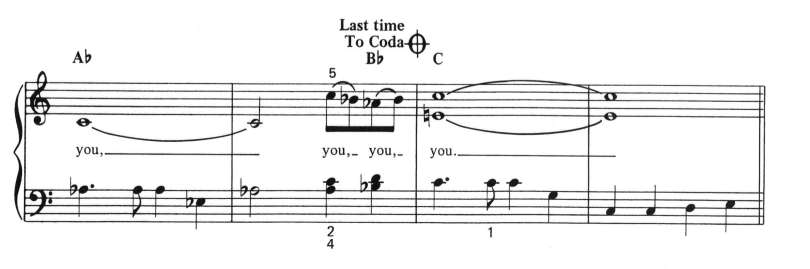

As I write this let-ter, send my love to you, Re-

mem-ber that I'll al-ways be in love with_ you.

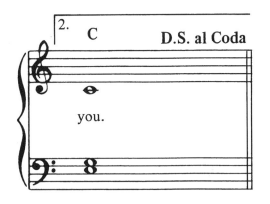

2. C D.S. al Coda

you.

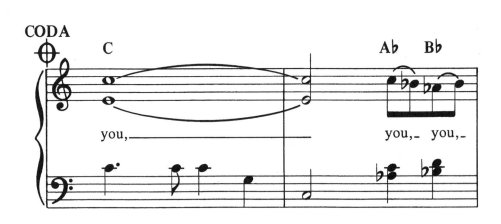

CODA

you,_____ you,_ you,_

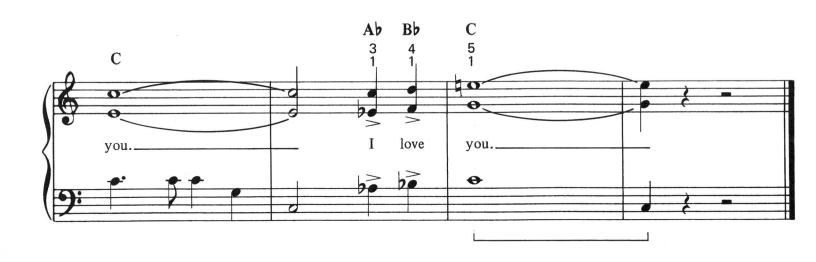

you._____ I love you._____

PAPERBACK WRITER

Words and Music by JOHN LENNON
and PAUL McCARTNEY

Bright rock beat

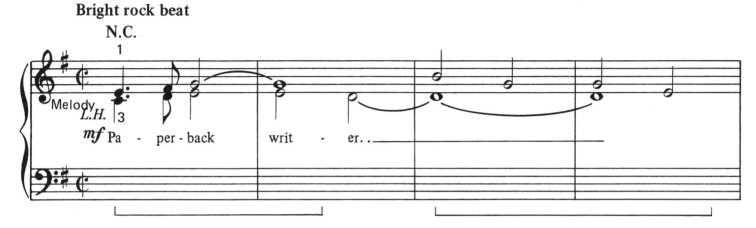

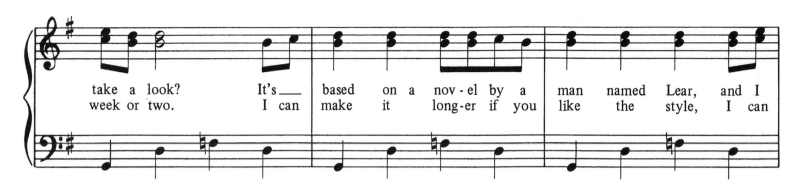

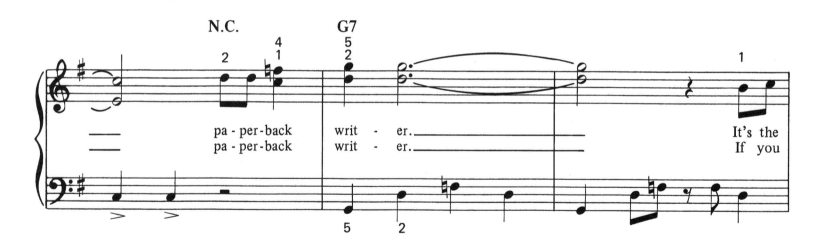

un-der-stand. His son is work-ing for the Dai - ly Mail;__ It's a
o - ver - night. If you must re - turn it, you can send it here,__ But I

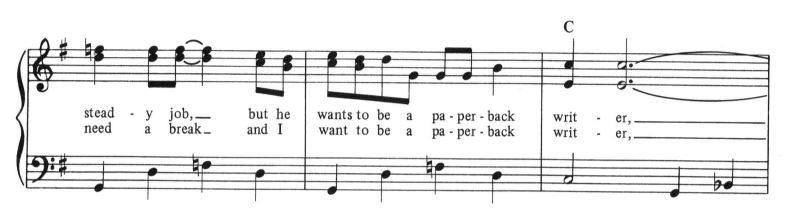

C

stead - y job,__ but he wants to be a pa-per-back writ - er,_____
need a break__ and I want to be a pa-per-back writ - er,_____

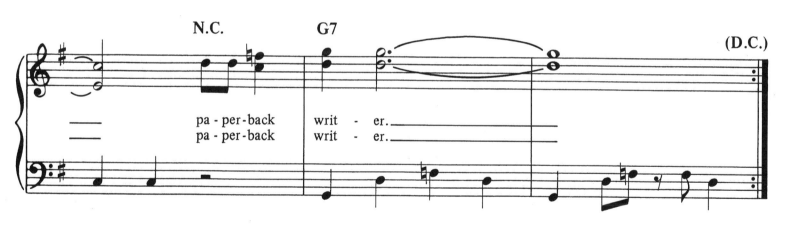

N.C.   G7   (D.C.)

__ pa - per - back writ - er._____
__ pa - per - back writ - er._____

G7   Repeat and Fade

Pa - per - back writ - er..._____

PENNY LANE

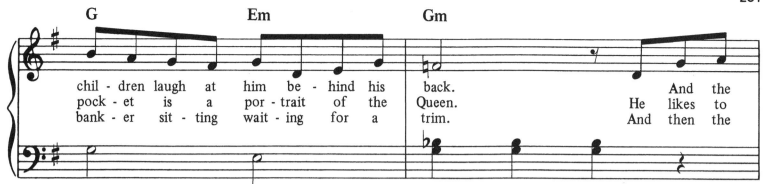

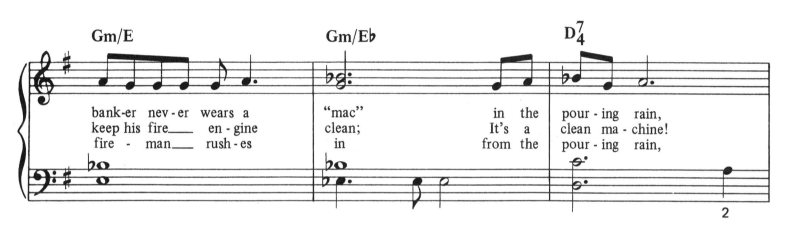

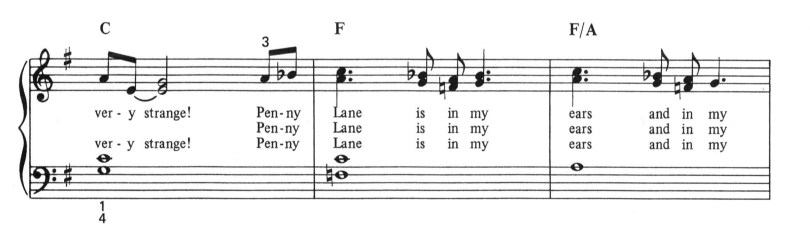

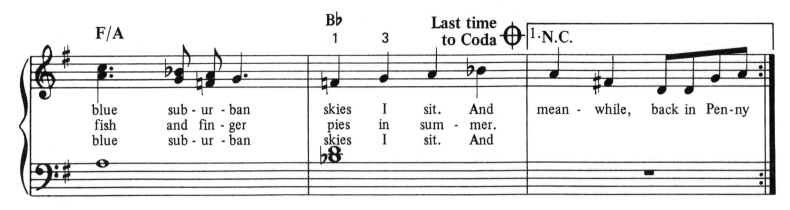

blue sub-ur-ban
fish and fin-ger
blue sub-ur-ban

skies I sit. And
pies in sum - mer.
skies I sit. And

mean - while, back in Pen-ny

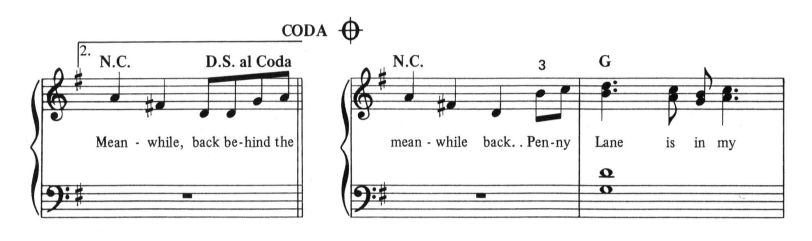

Mean - while, back be-hind the

mean - while back. . Pen-ny Lane is in my

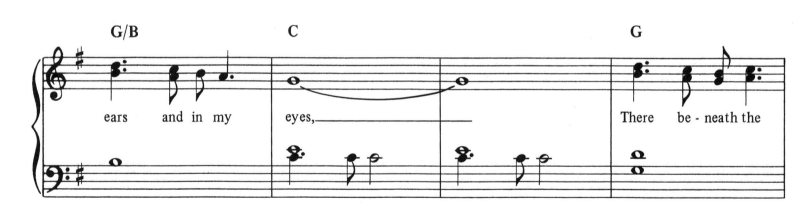

ears and in my eyes,_____

There be - neath the

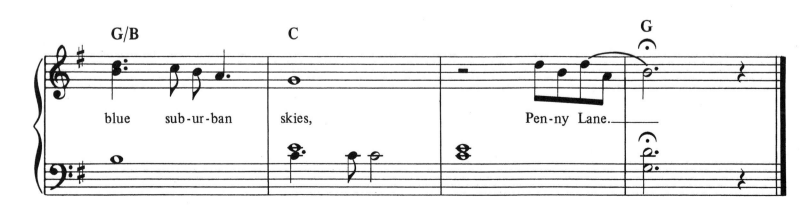

blue sub-ur-ban skies,

Pen-ny Lane._____

PLEASE PLEASE ME

Words and Music by JOHN LENNON
and PAUL McCARTNEY

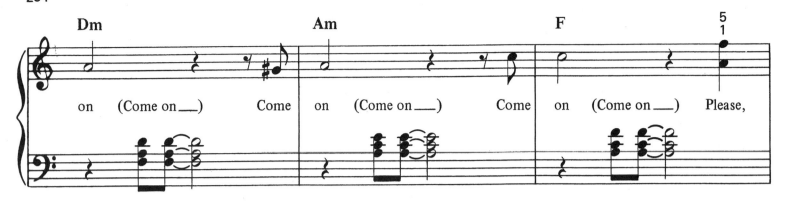

on (Come on ___) Come on (Come on ___) Come on (Come on ___) Please,

please me, wo yeah, like I please you.

I don't want to sound com-plain-ing

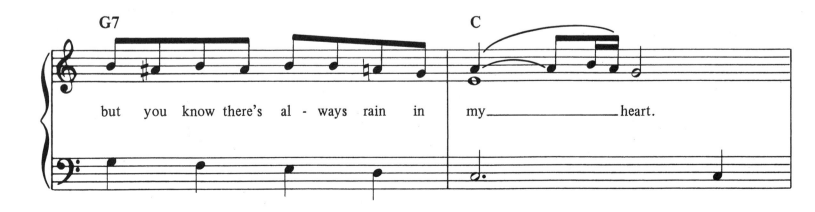

but you know there's al - ways rain in my _____ heart.

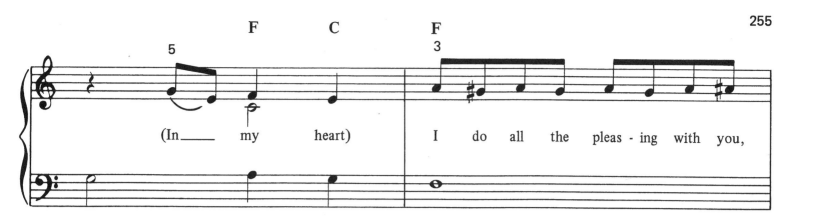

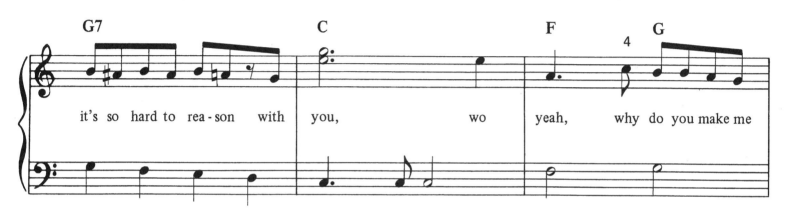

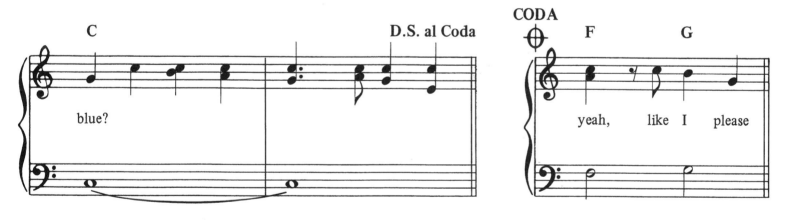

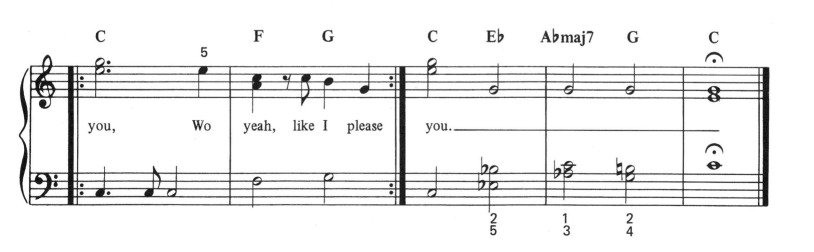

RAIN

Words and Music by JOHN LENNON
and PAUL McCARTNEY

Moderate Rock

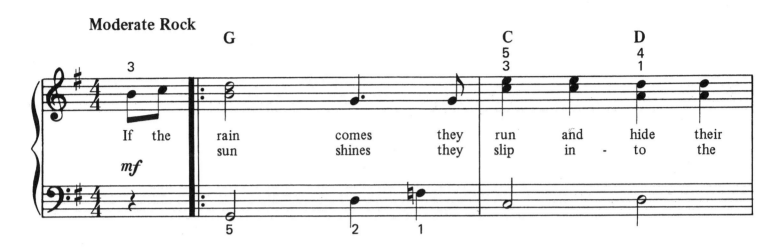

If the rain comes they run and hide their
sun shines they slip in - to the

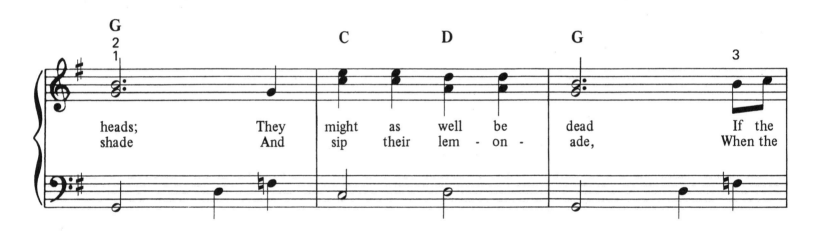

heads; They And might as well be dead ade, If the
shade sip their lem - on - When the

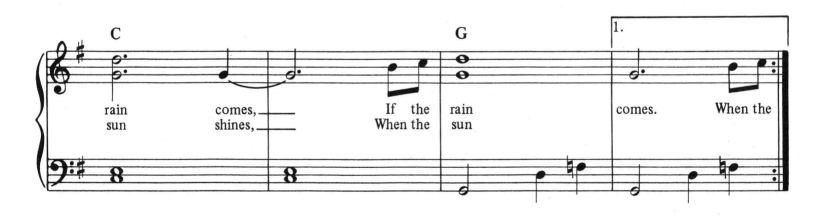

rain comes,_____ If the rain comes. When the
sun shines,_____ When the sun

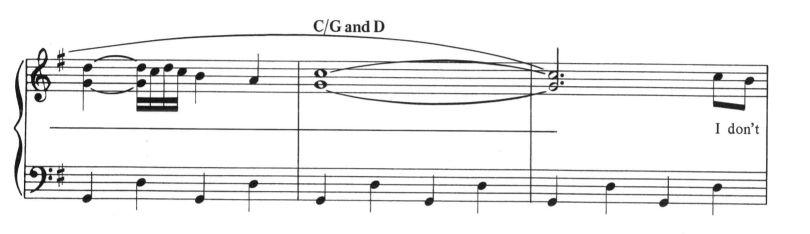

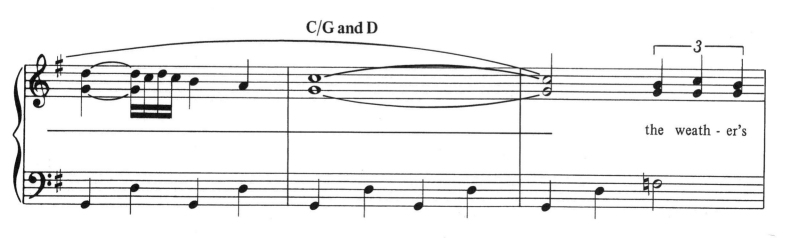

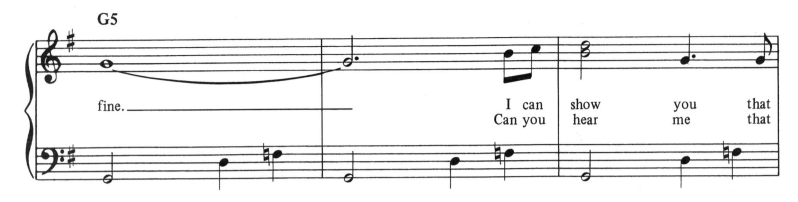

fine. _____

I can   show   you   that
Can you   hear   me   that

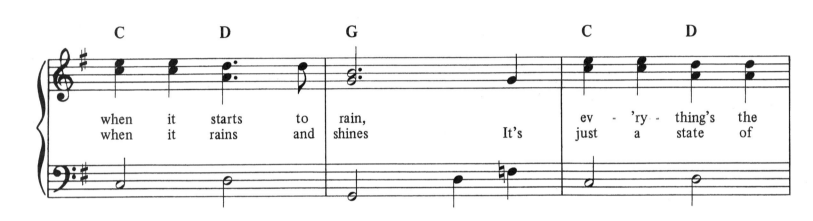

when   it   starts   to   rain,   It's   ev - 'ry - thing's the
when   it   rains   and   shines   just   a   state   of

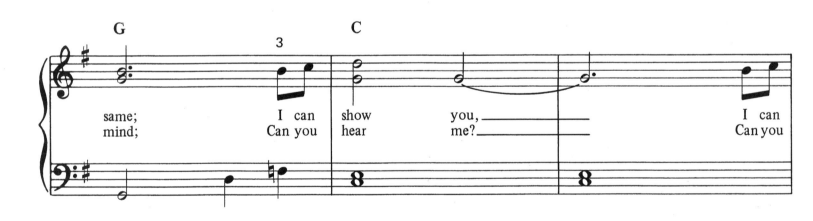

same;   I can   show   you, _____   I can
mind;   Can you hear   me? _____   Can you

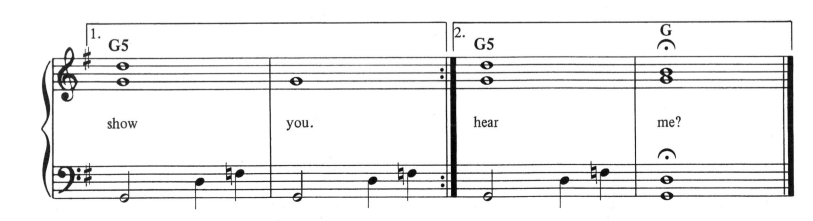

1.   show   you.   2.   hear   me?

REVOLUTION

Words and Music by JOHN LENNON
and PAUL McCARTNEY

you know, _____ we all want to change the
you know, _____ we're all do-ing what we
you know, _____ you bet-ter free your mind in-

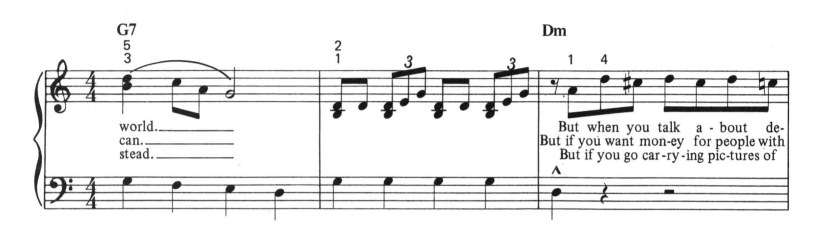

world. _____
can. _____
stead. _____

But when you talk a-bout de-
But if you want mon-ey for people with
But if you go car-ry-ing pic-tures of

struc-tion, _____ don't you know that you can count me out!
minds that hate, _____ all I can tell you is broth-er, you have to wait!
Chair-man Mao, _____ you ain't gon-na make it with an-y-one an-y-how!

Don't you know it's gon-na be al- right,

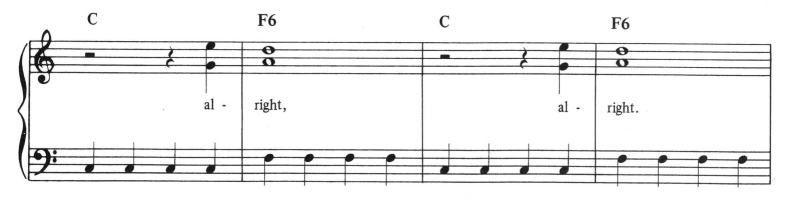

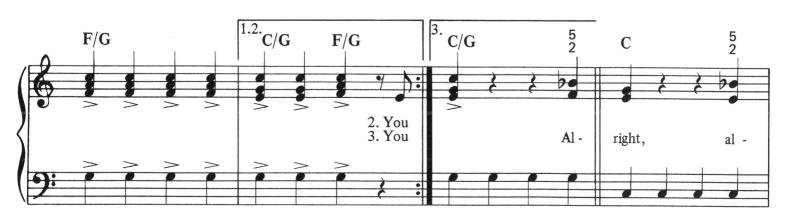

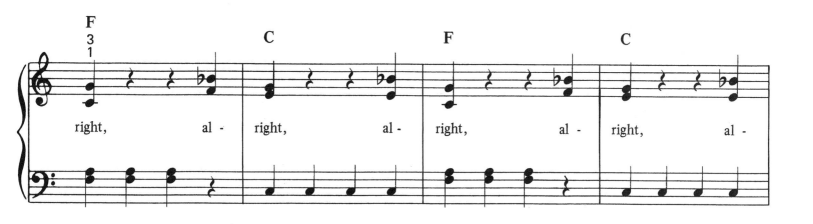

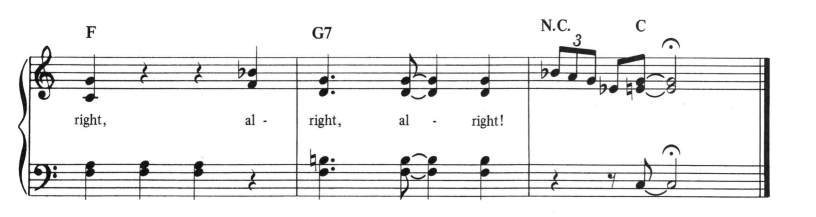

RUN FOR YOUR LIFE

Words and Music by JOHN LENNON
and PAUL McCARTNEY

Bright Country Rock

1.4. Well I'd rath - er see you dead, lit - tle girl, than to
know that I'm a wick - ed guy and I was
Let this be a ser - mon, I mean

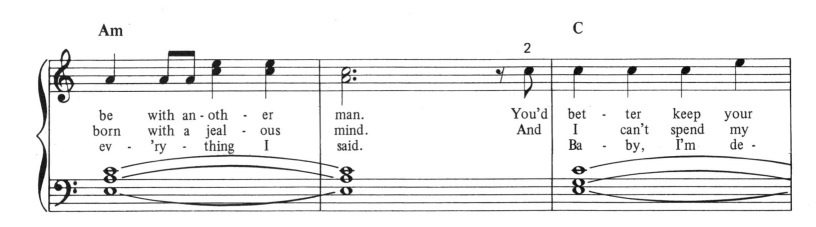

be with an - oth - er man. You'd bet - ter keep your
born with a jeal - ous mind. And I can't spend my
ev - 'ry - thing I said. Ba - by, I'm de -

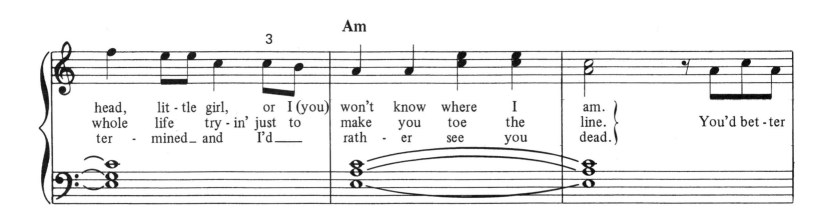

head, lit - tle girl, or I (you) won't know where I am.
whole life try - in' just to make you toe the line. You'd bet - ter
ter - mined and I'd rath - er see you dead.

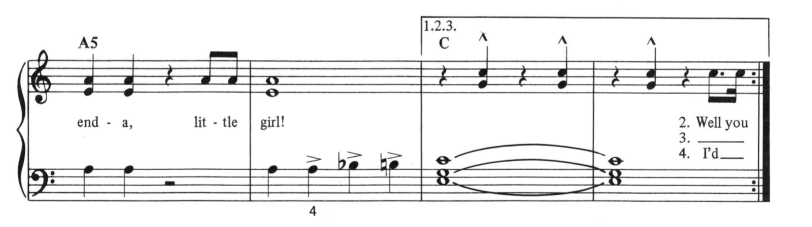

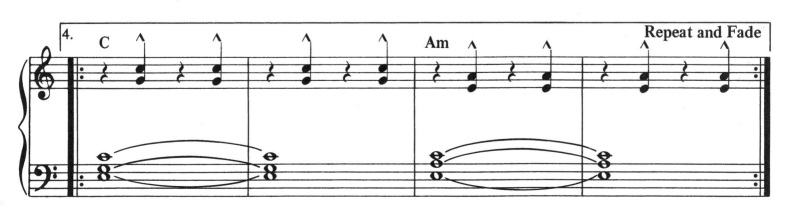

ROCKY RACCOON

Words and Music by JOHN LENNON
and PAUL McCARTNEY

Moderate two-beat style

Rock - y had come, _____ e - quipped with a gun, _____ to he said,
Rock - y burst in, _____ and grin - ning a grin, _____

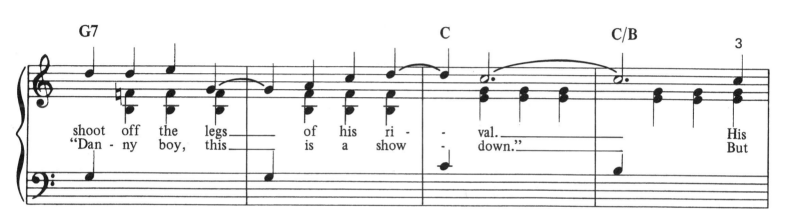

shoot off the legs _____ of his ri - val. _____ His
"Dan - ny boy, this _____ is a show - down." _____ But

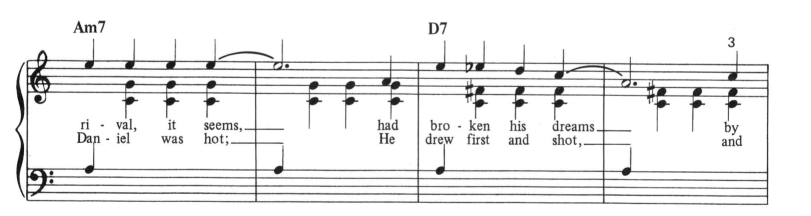

ri - val, it seems, _____ had bro - ken his dreams _____ by
Dan - iel was hot; _____ He drew first and shot, _____ and

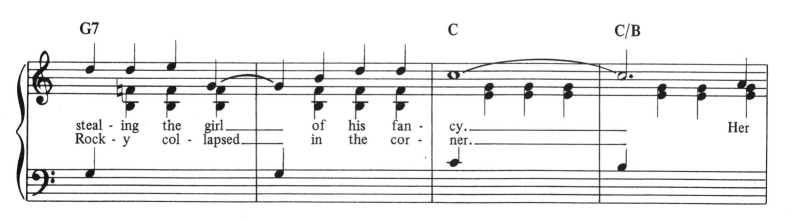

steal - ing the girl _____ of his fan - cy. _____ Her
Rock - y col - lapsed _____ in the cor - ner. _____

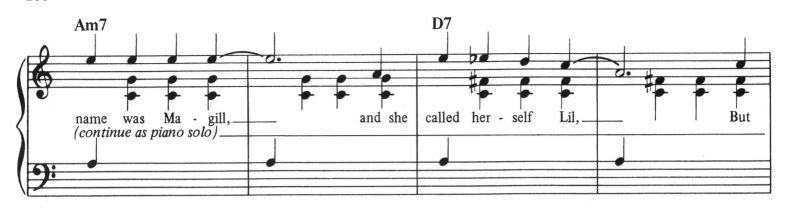

name was Ma - gill, and she called her - self Lil, But
(continue as piano solo)

ev - 'ry - one knew her as Nan - cy. Now

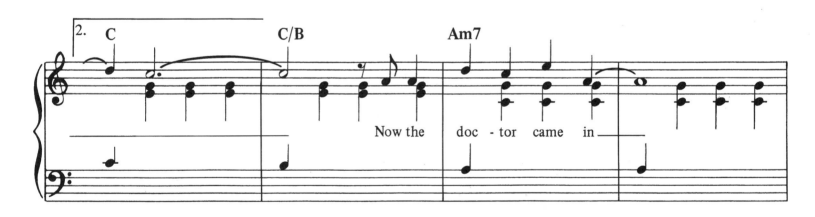

Now the doc - tor came in

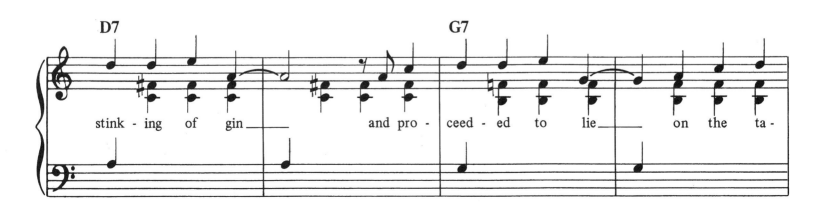

stink - ing of gin and pro - ceed - ed to lie on the ta -

ble. He said, "Rock-y, you met___ your match."

And Rock-y said, "Doc, it's on-ly a scratch, and I'll be

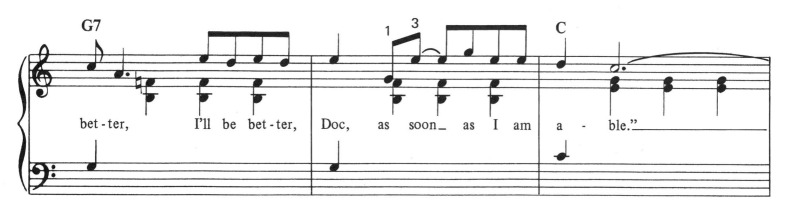

bet-ter, I'll be bet-ter, Doc, as soon___ as I am a- ble."___

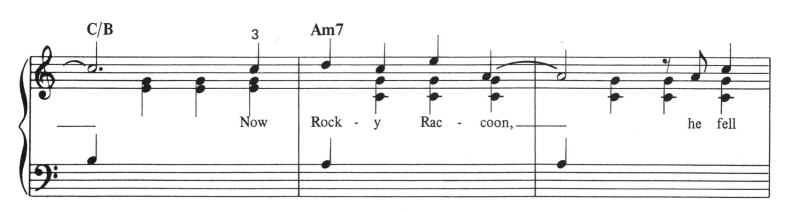

Now Rock-y Rac-coon,___ he fell

back in his room ____ on - ly to find ____

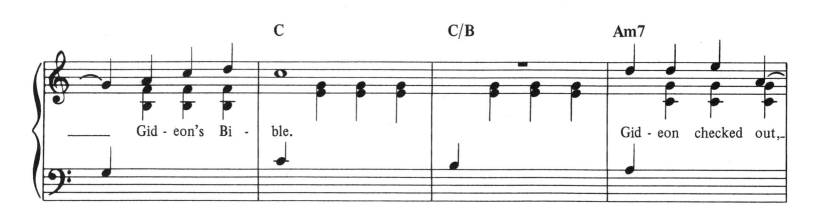

____ Gid - eon's Bi - ble. Gid - eon checked out, ____

____ and he left it, no doubt, ____ to help with good Rock-

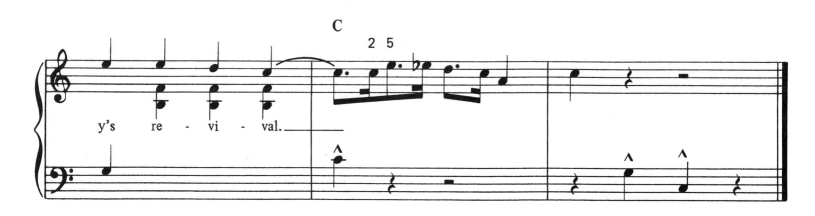

y's re - vi - val. ____

SEXY SADIE

Words and Music by JOHN LENNON
and PAUL McCARTNEY

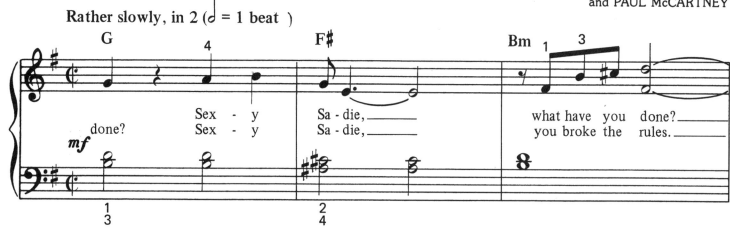

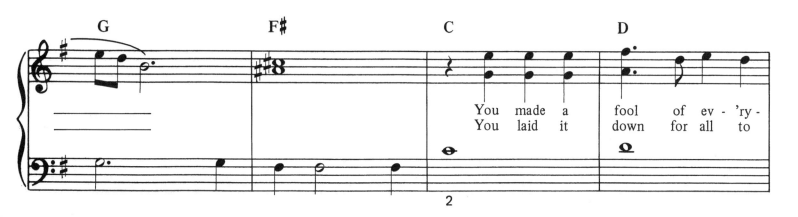

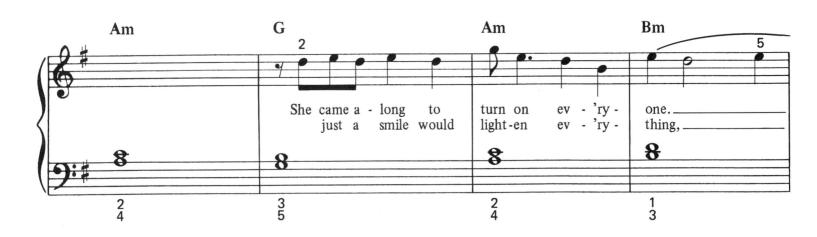

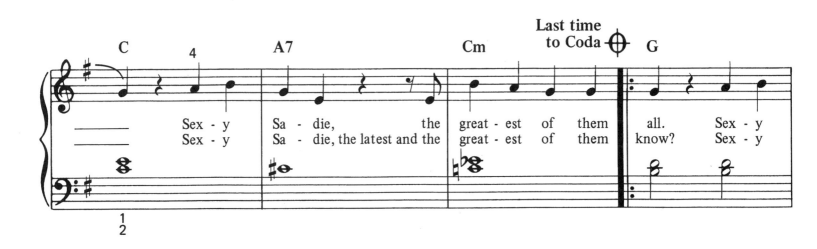

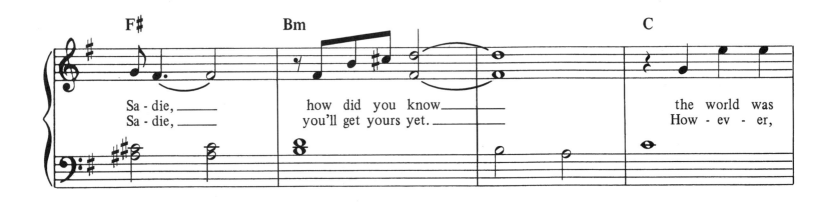

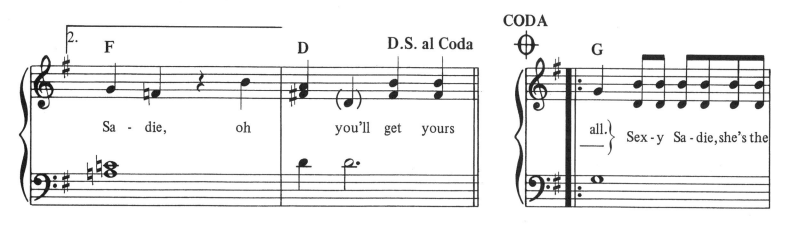

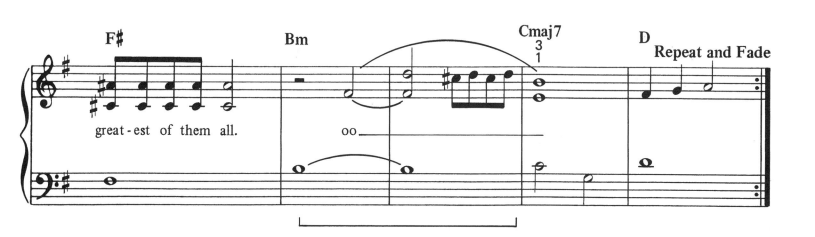

SGT. PEPPER'S LONELY HEARTS CLUB BAND

Words and Music by JOHN LENNON
and PAUL McCARTNEY

Slowly, with a beat

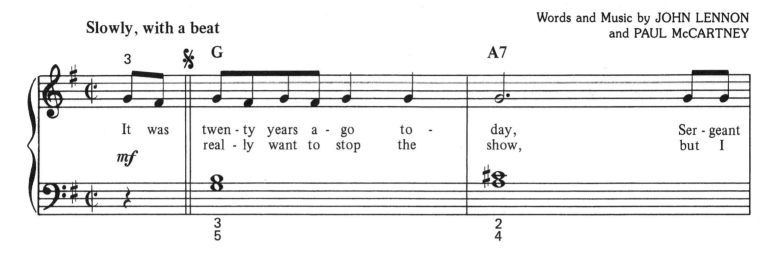

It was twen-ty years a-go to-day, Ser-geant
real-ly want to stop the show, but I

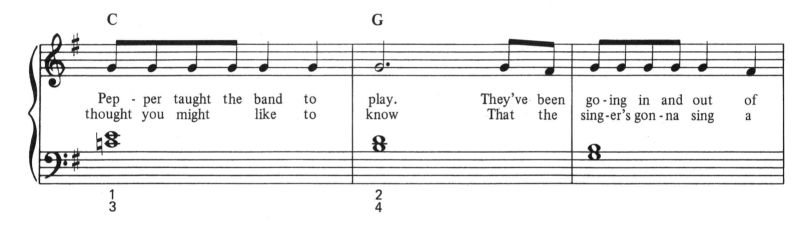

Pep - per taught the band to play. They've been go-ing in and out of
thought you might like to know That the sing-er's gon-na sing a

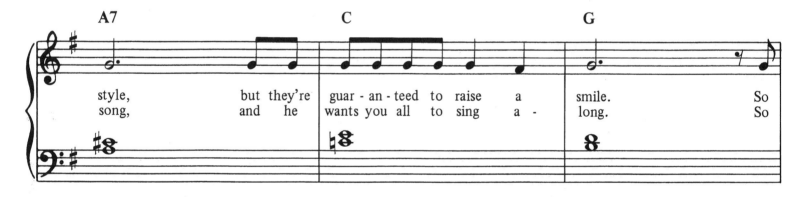

style, but they're guar-an-teed to raise a smile. So
song, and he wants you all to sing a - long. So

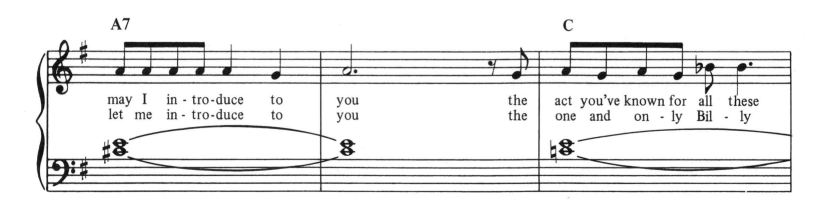

may I in-tro-duce to you the act you've known for all these
let me in-tro-duce to you the one and on-ly Bil - ly

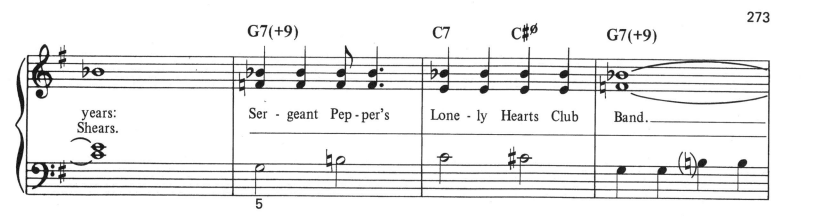

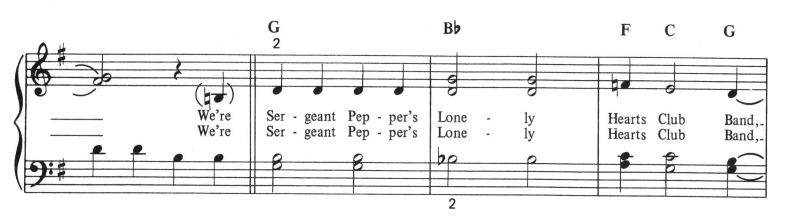

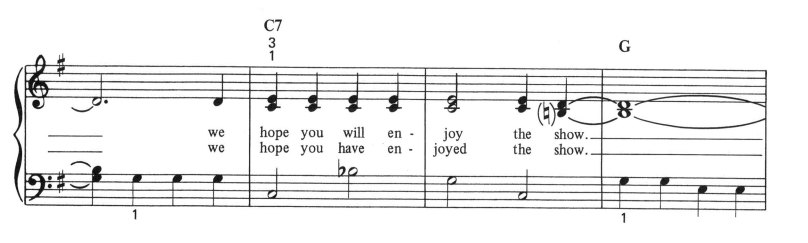

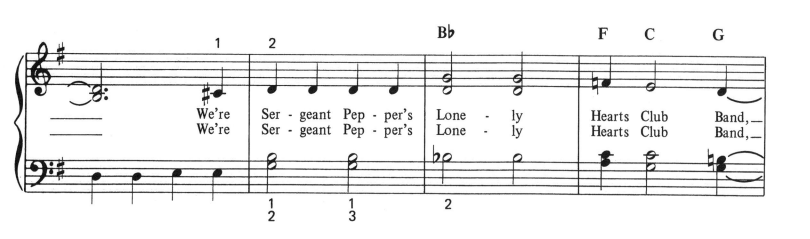

A7   **D7**

sit   back and   let the   eve - ning   go. _____
we're   sor - ry   but it's   time   to   go. _____

1

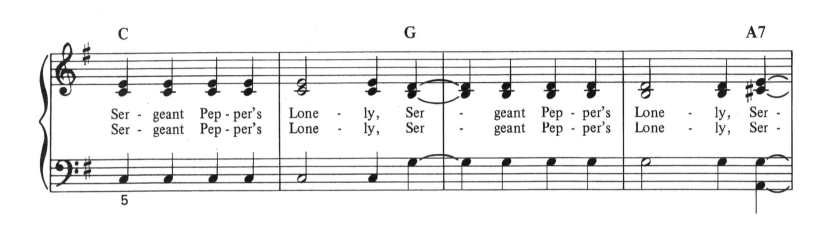

C   **G**   **A7**

Ser - geant Pep - per's   Lone - ly, Ser   -   geant Pep - per's   Lone - ly, Ser -
Ser - geant Pep - per's   Lone - ly, Ser   -   geant Pep - per's   Lone - ly, Ser -

5

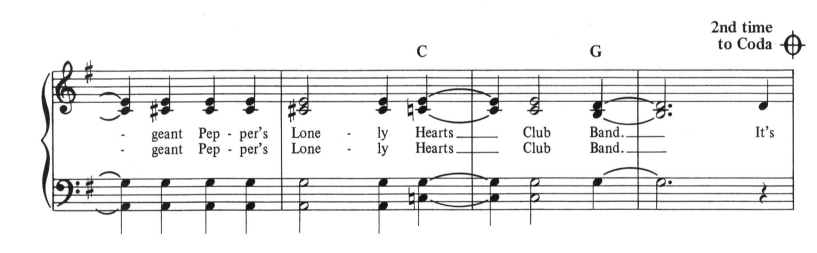

**2nd time
to Coda** ⊕

           C   **G**

- geant Pep - per's   Lone   -   ly Hearts ____ Club   Band. ____   It's
- geant Pep - per's   Lone   -   ly Hearts ____ Club   Band. ____

C7   5   **F7**
                  4
                  1   3

won - der - ful to   be here,   it's   cer - tain - ly a   thrill;   You're

1

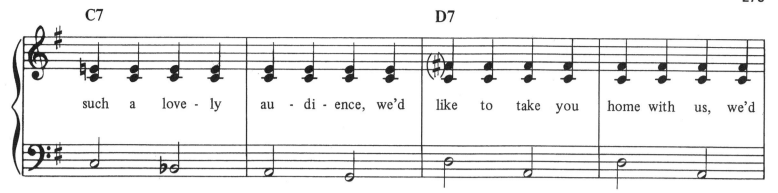

C7 such a love-ly au-di-ence, we'd **D7** like to take you home with us, we'd

D.S. al Coda love to take you home. I don't

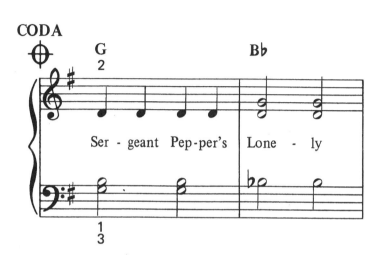

CODA **G** Ser-geant Pep-per's **Bb** Lone-ly

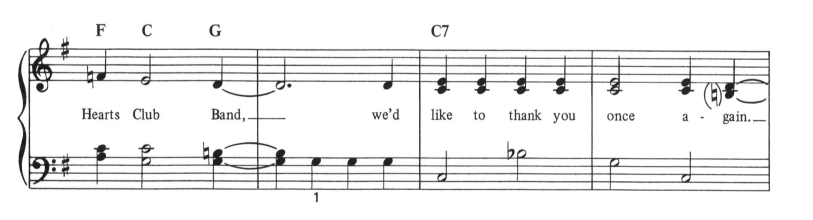

F **C** **G** Hearts Club Band, we'd **C7** like to thank you once a-gain.

G Ser-geant Pep-per's **Bb** one and on-ly

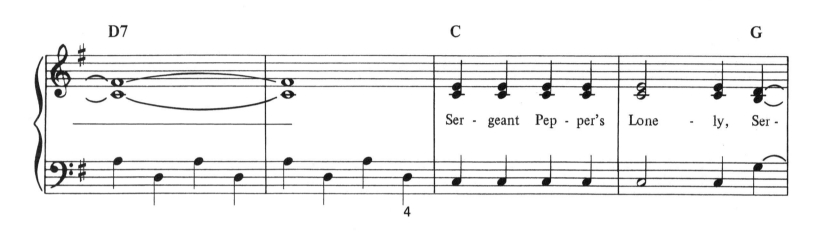

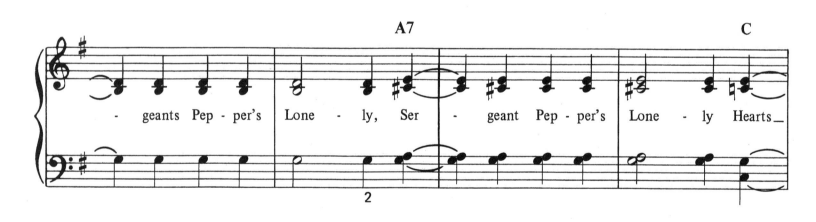

SOMETHING

Words and Music by
GEORGE HARRISON

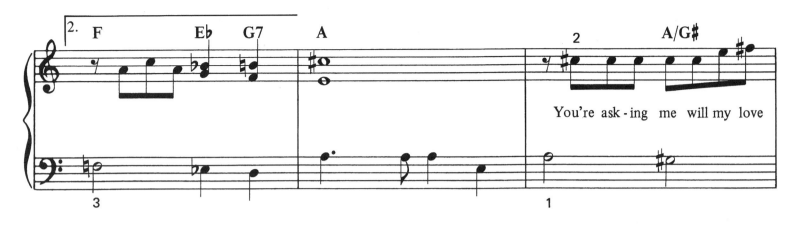

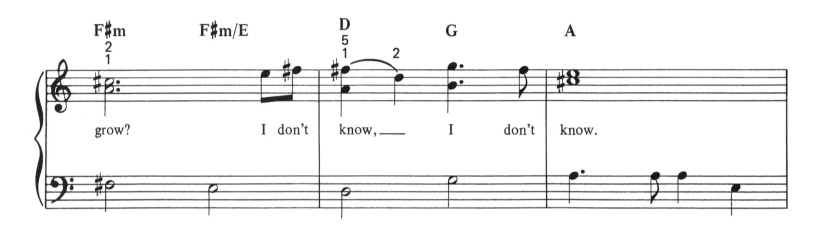

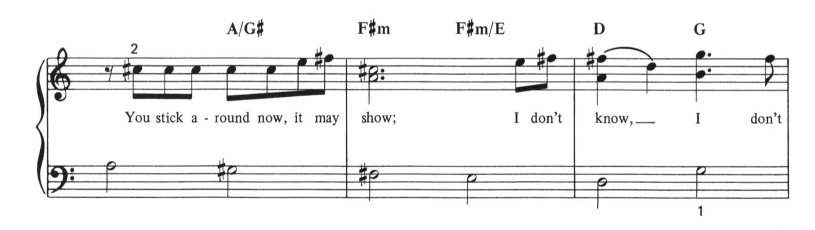

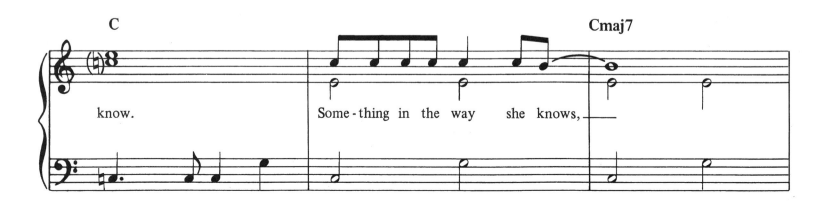

and all I have to do is think of her. Some-thing in the things she

shows___ me, I don't want to leave___ her now, you

know I be-lieve___ and how.__

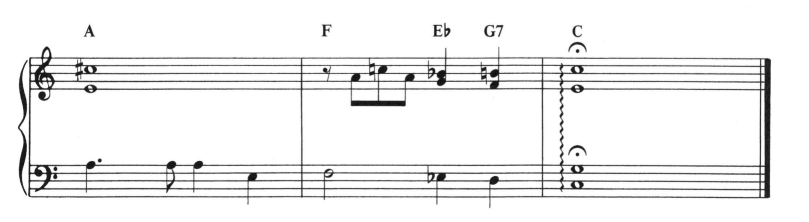

SHE LOVES YOU

Words and Music by JOHN LENNON
and PAUL McCARTNEY

She loves you yeah, yeah, yeah, She loves you, yeah,

yeah, yeah, She loves you, yeah, yeah, yeah, yeah.

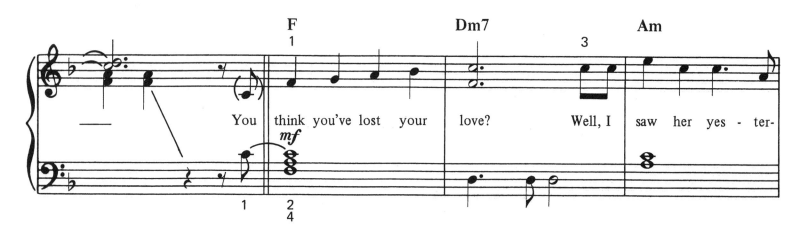

You think you've lost your love? Well, I saw her yes-ter-

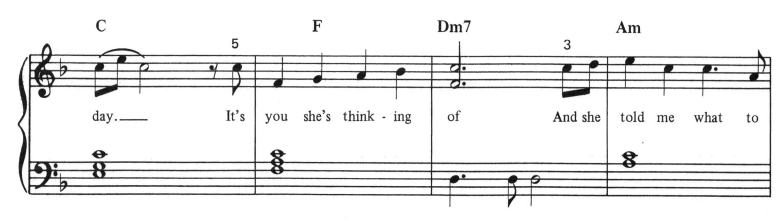

day. It's you she's think-ing of And she told me what to

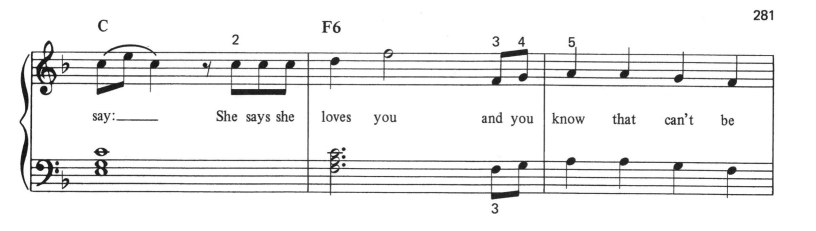

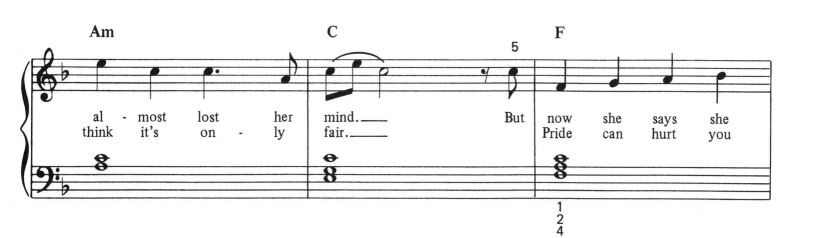

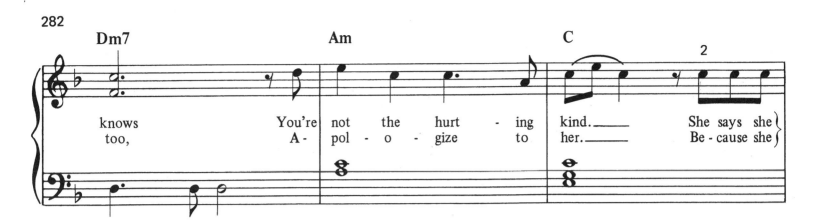

knows   You're not the hurt - ing   kind.____   She says she

too,   A - pol - o - gize to   her.____   Be - cause she

loves you   and you   know that can't be   bad.   Yes, she

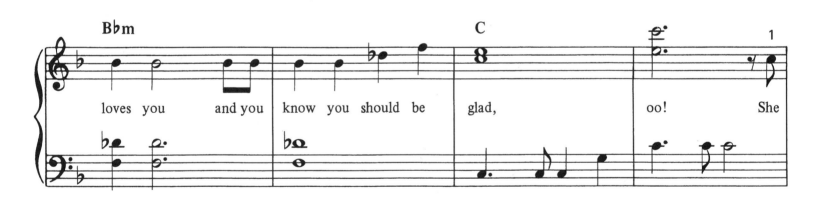

loves you   and you   know you should be   glad,   oo!   She

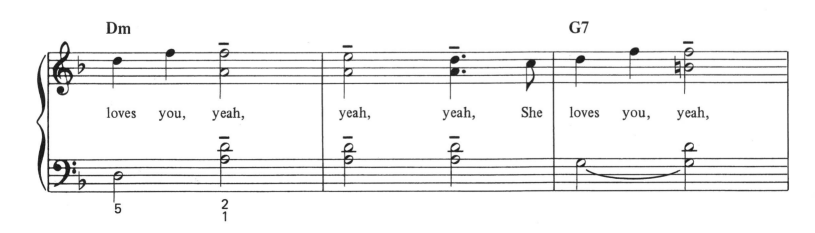

loves you, yeah,   yeah,   yeah,   She loves you, yeah,

283

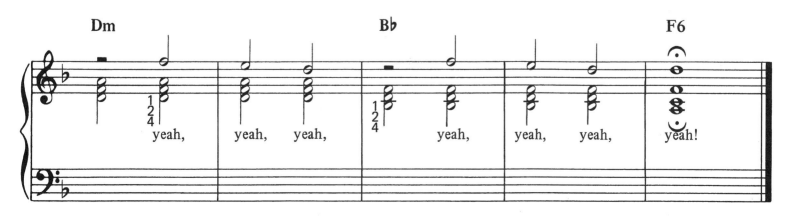

SHE'S A WOMAN

Words and Music by JOHN LENNON
and PAUL McCARTNEY

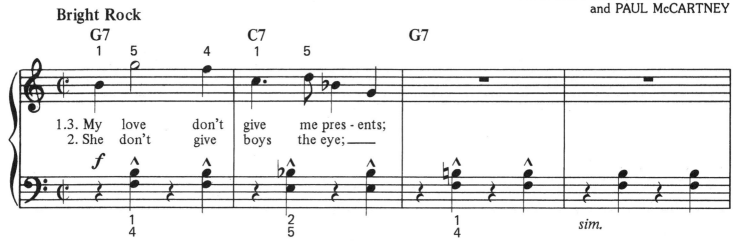

1.3. My love don't give me pres - ents;
2. She don't give boys the eye;____

I know that she's no peas - ant.
She hates that to see me cry.____

On - ly ev - er has to give me love for - ev - er and for - ev - er;
She is hap - py just to hear me say that I will nev - er leave her;

My love don't give me pres - ents.
She don't give boys the eye.____

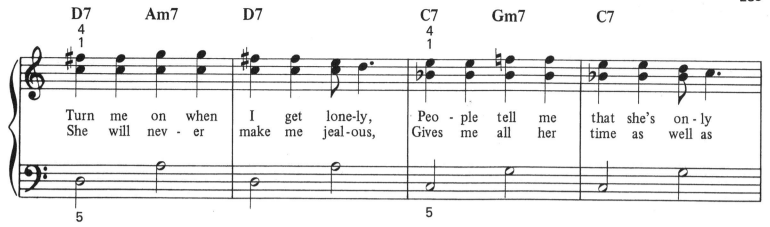

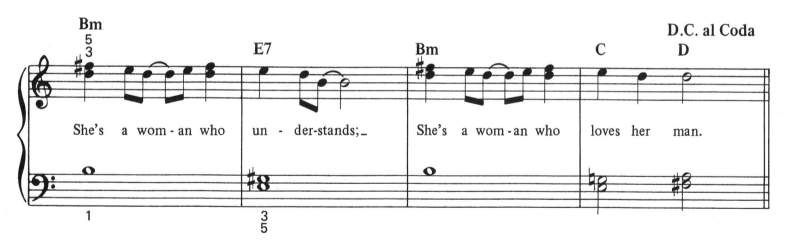

SHE'S LEAVING HOME

Words and Music by JOHN LENNON
and PAUL McCARTNEY

Moderately

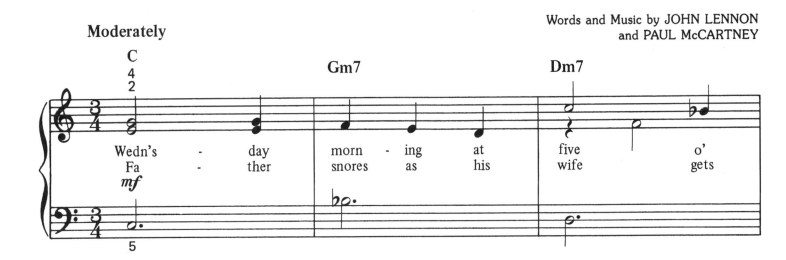

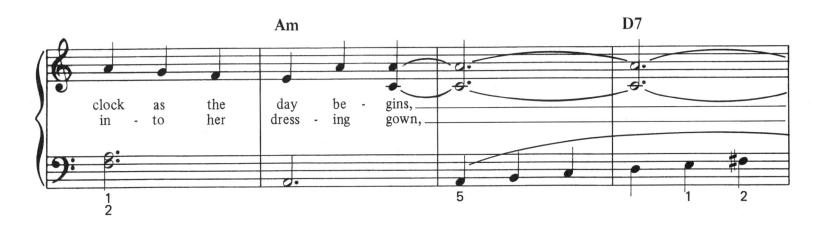

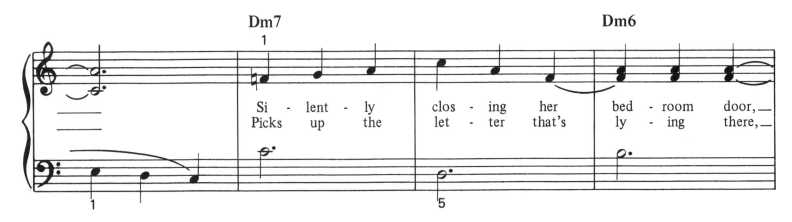

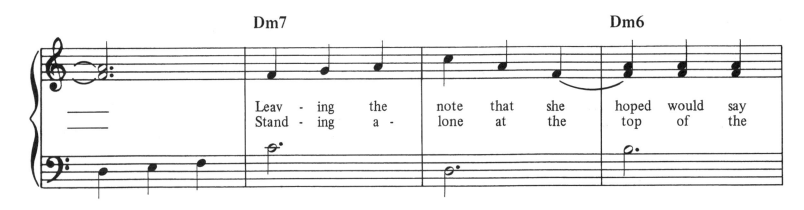

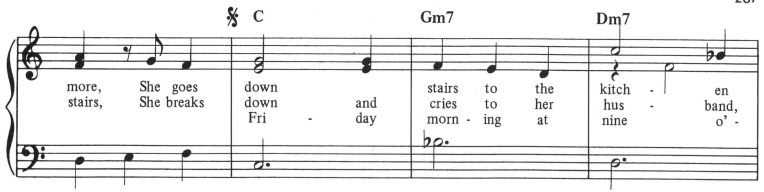

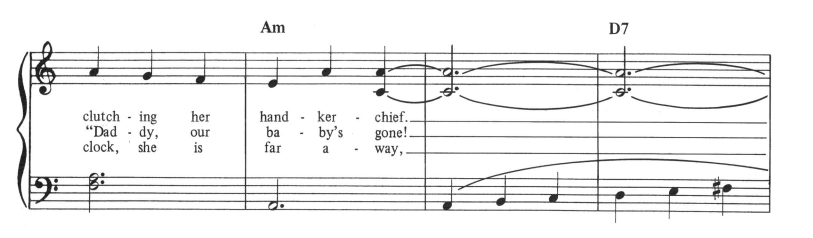

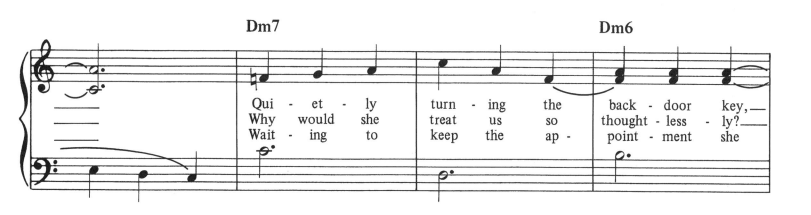

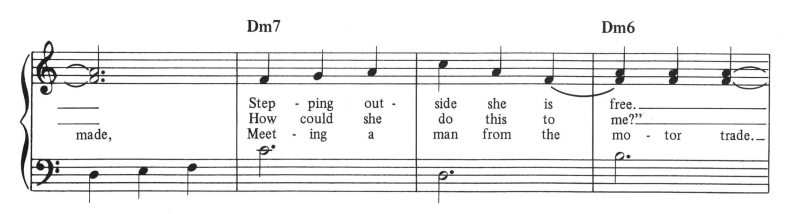

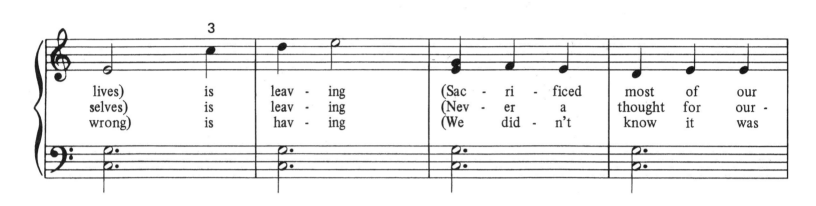

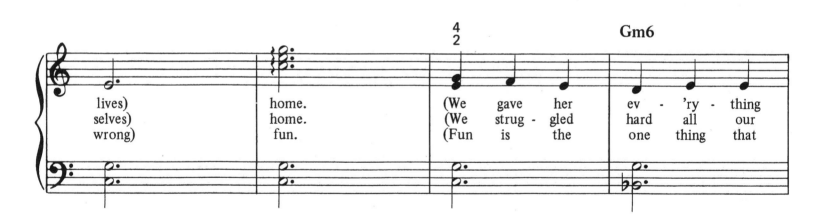

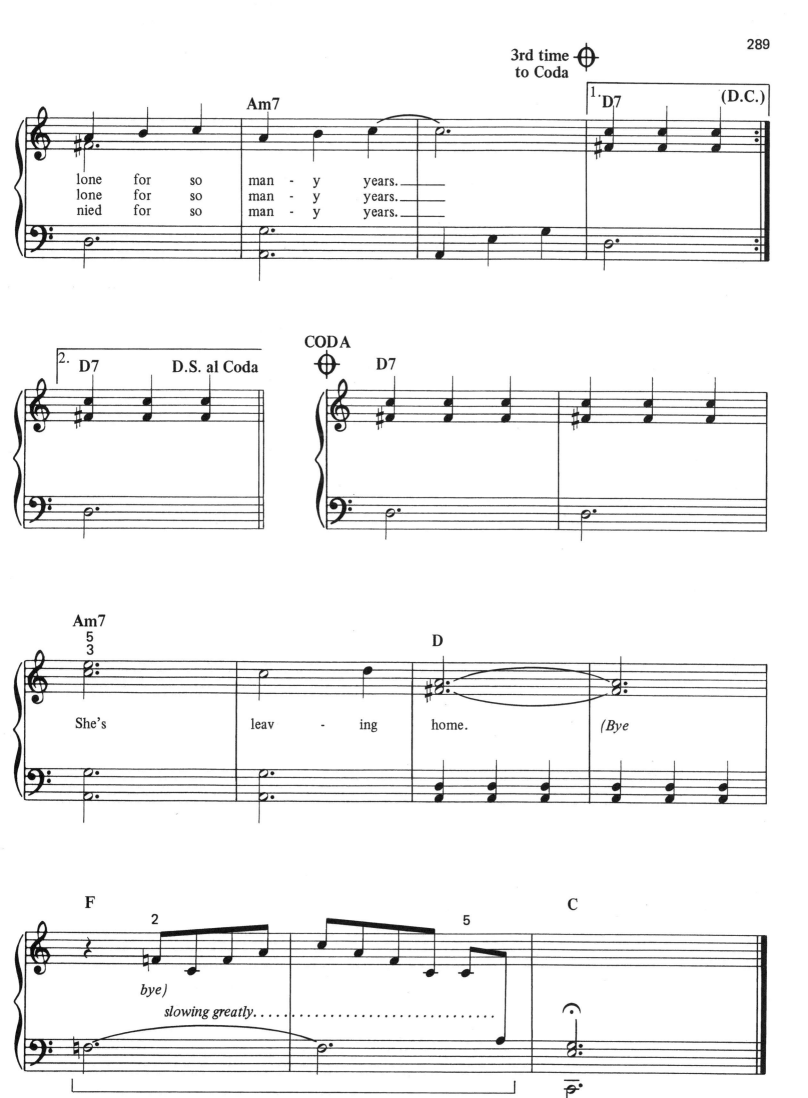

STRAWBERRY FIELDS FOREVER

Words and Music by JOHN LENNON
and PAUL McCARTNEY

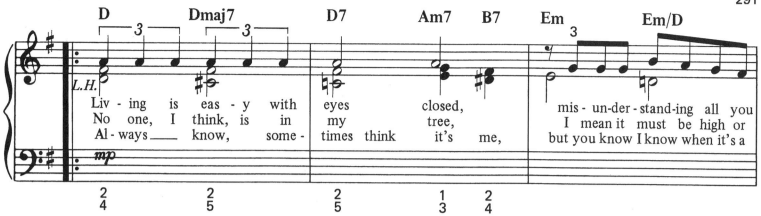

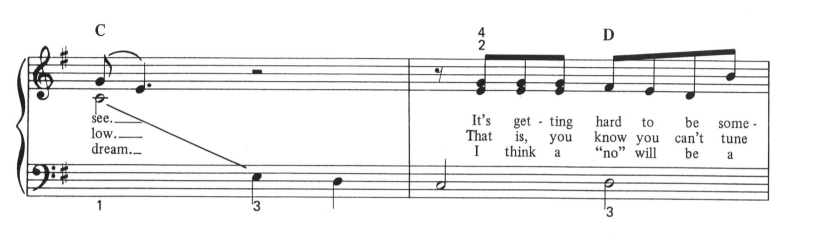

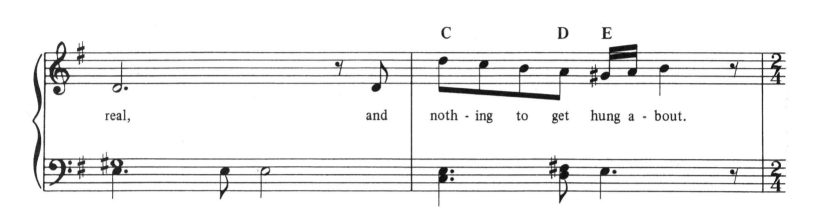

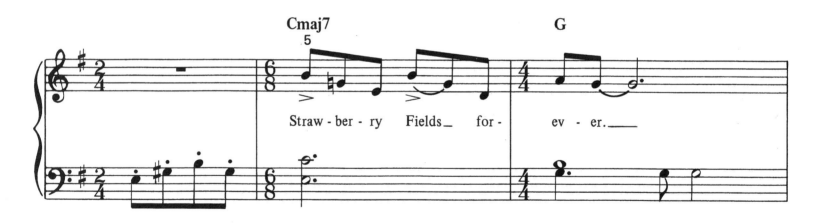

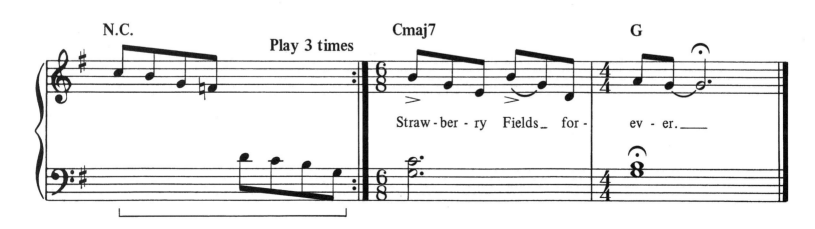

THERE'S A PLACE

Words and Music by JOHN LENNON
and PAUL McCARTNEY

time____ when I'm a - lone.____ I____

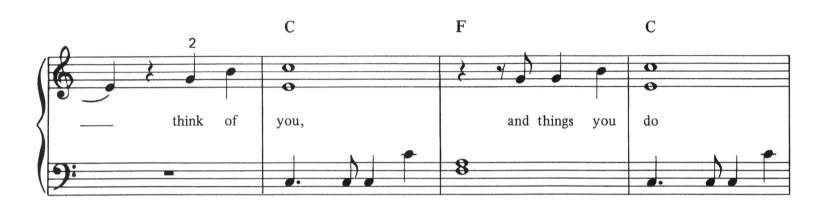

____ think of you, and things you do

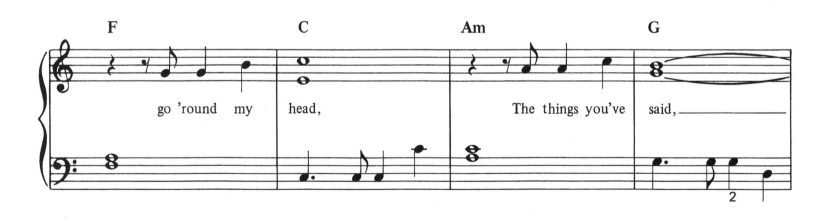

go 'round my head, The things you've said,____

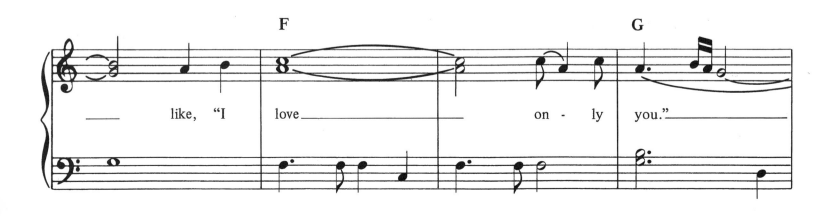

____ like, "I love_____ on - ly you."_____

295

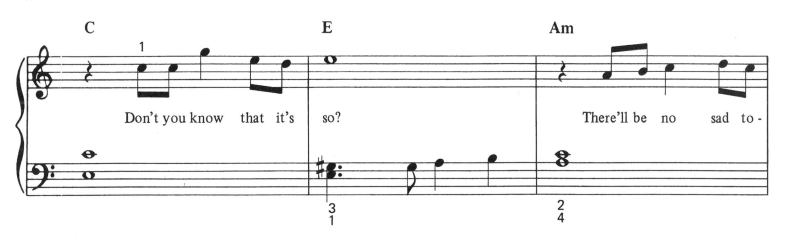

CODA

SUN KING

Words and Music by JOHN LENNON
and PAUL McCARTNEY

Here come the Sun King, Ev-'ry-bod-y's laugh-ing, ev-'ry-bod-y's hap-py, Here come the Sun King.

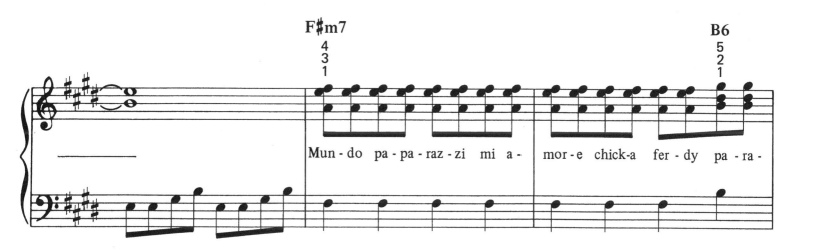

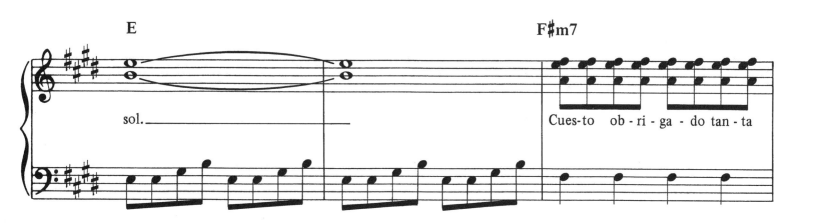

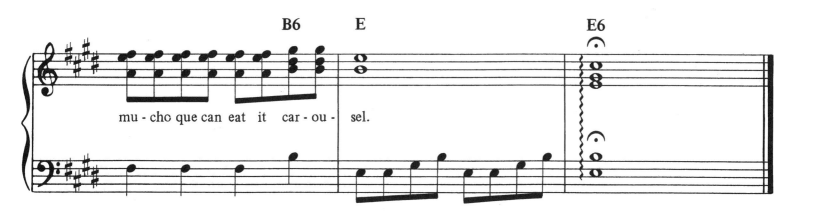

TAXMAN

Words and Music by
GEORGE HARRISON

tax - man, Yeah,___ I'm the tax - man.___

Should five___ per - cent___ ap - pear___
Now my___ ad - vice___ for those.

___ too small,___ Be thank
___ who die: De-clare___

- ful I___ don't take___ it all,___
___ the pen - nies on___ your eyes,___

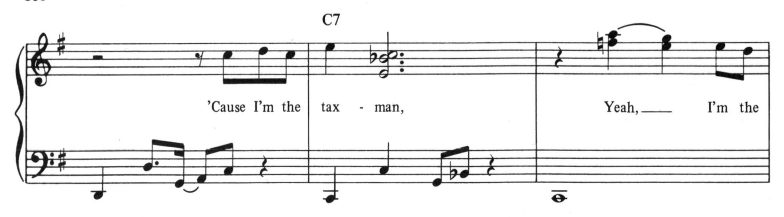

'Cause I'm the tax - man, Yeah,____ I'm the

tax - man.____ If you drive____

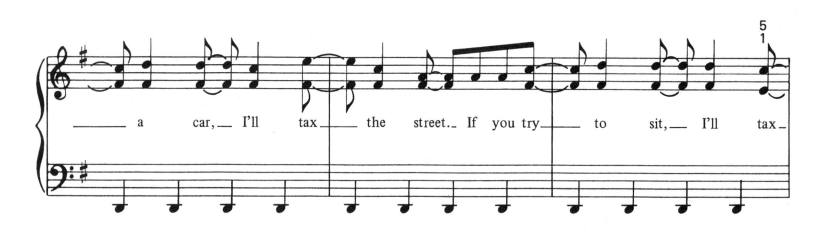

____ a car,_ I'll tax____ the street.._ If you try____ to sit,_ I'll tax_

____ your seat._ If you get____ too cold,_ I'll tax____ the heat.._ If you take_

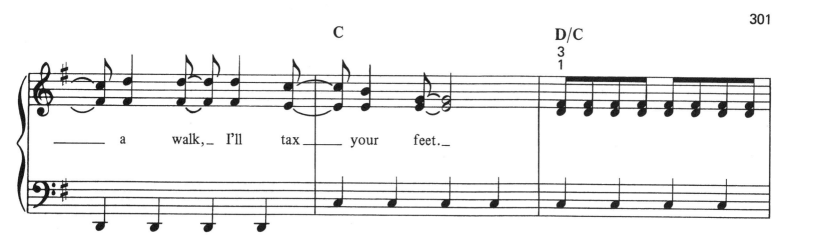

a walk,__ I'll tax__ your feet.__

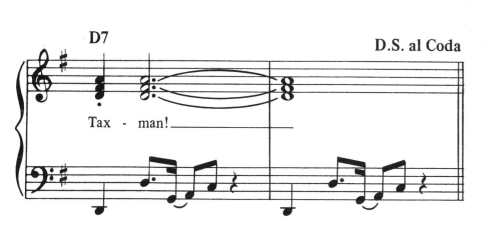

Tax - man!__

D.S. al Coda

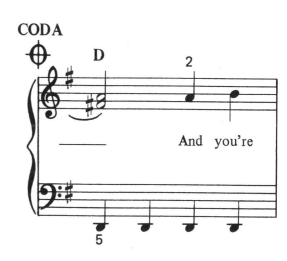

CODA

And you're

work - ing for no one but me.__

Repeat and Fade

TELL ME WHY

Words and Music by JOHN LENNON
and PAUL McCARTNEY

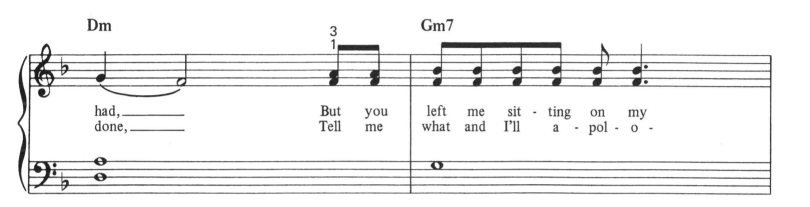

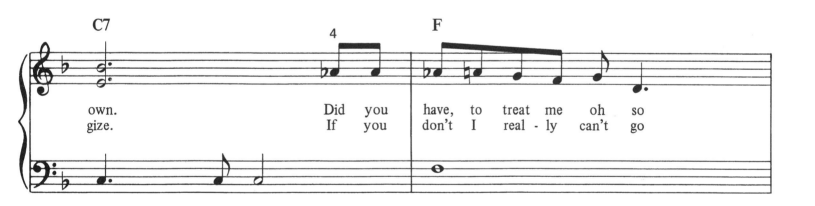

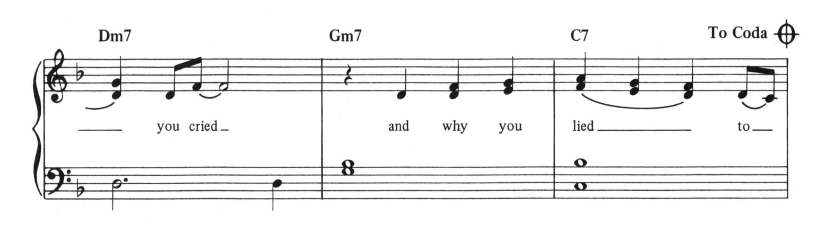

knees____ If you'll on-ly lis-ten to my pleas. Is there

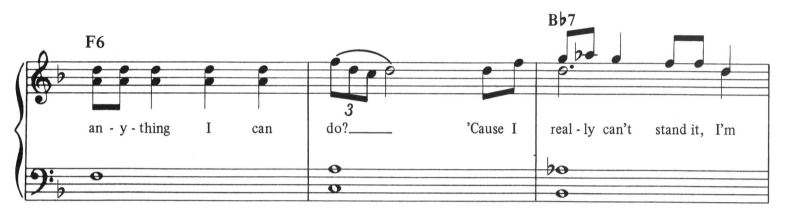

an-y-thing I can do?____ 'Cause I real-ly can't stand it, I'm

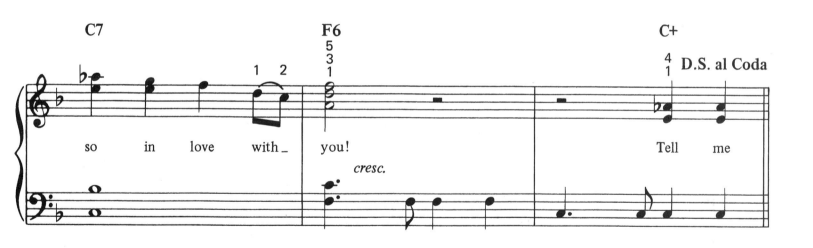

so in love with_ you! Tell me

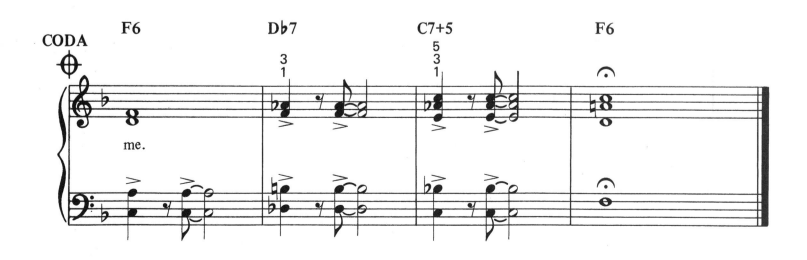

me.

THANK YOU GIRL

Words and Music by JOHN LENNON
and PAUL McCARTNEY

thank you, girl.___   Thank you, girl, for lov - in' me the

way that you do;   That's the kind of love that is too

good to be true.   And all I got-ta do is

thank you, girl,___   thank you, girl.___

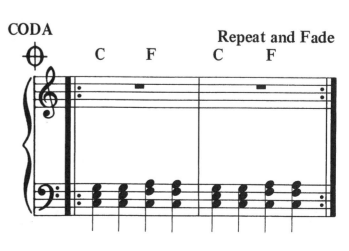

THINGS WE SAID TODAY

Words and Music by JOHN LENNON
and PAUL McCARTNEY

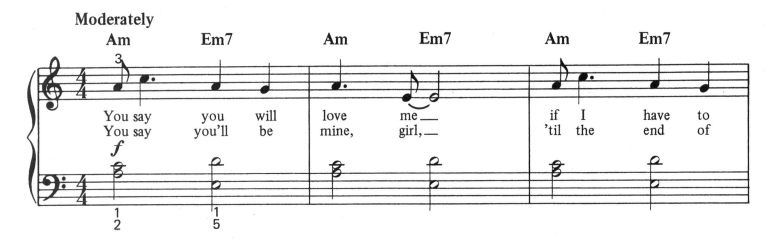

You say you will love me if I have to
You say you'll be mine, girl, 'til the end of

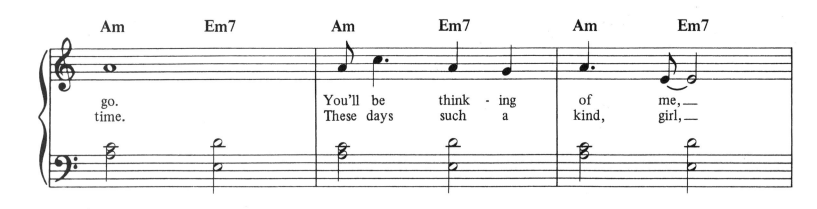

go. You'll be think - ing of me, —
time. These days such a kind, girl, —

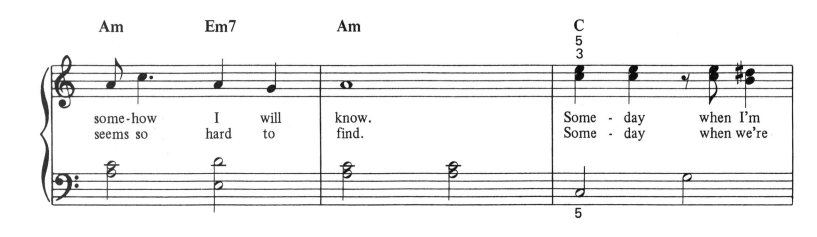

some-how I will know.
seems so hard to find.

Some - day when I'm
Some - day when we're

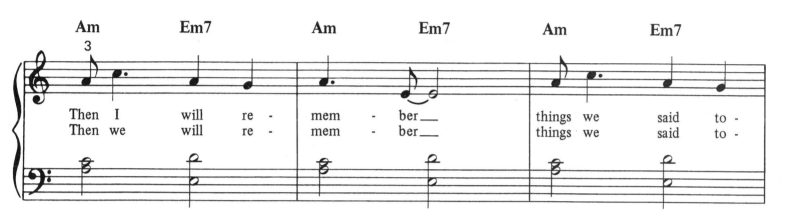

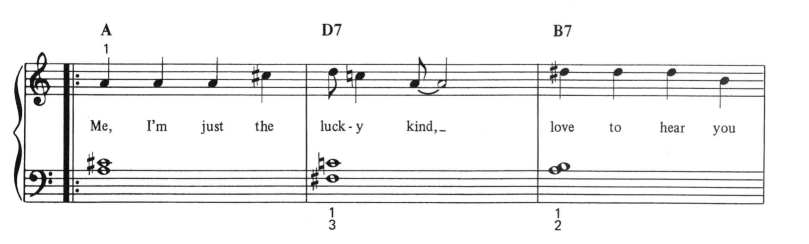

say that love is love, And though we may be blind,—

love is here to stay and that's e-nough to make you

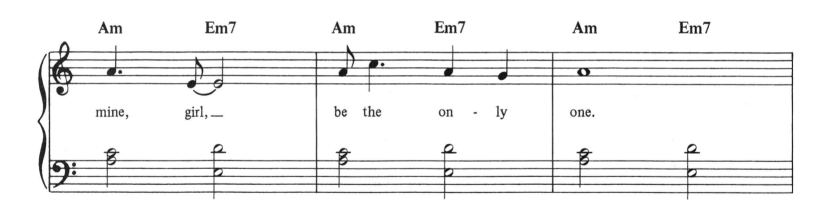

mine, girl,— be the on-ly one.

Love me all the time, girl,— we'll go on and

on. Some - day when we're dream - ing, —

deep in love, — not a lot to say, — Then we will re -

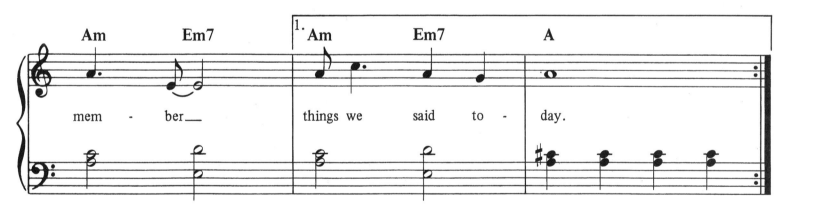

mem - ber — things we said to - day.

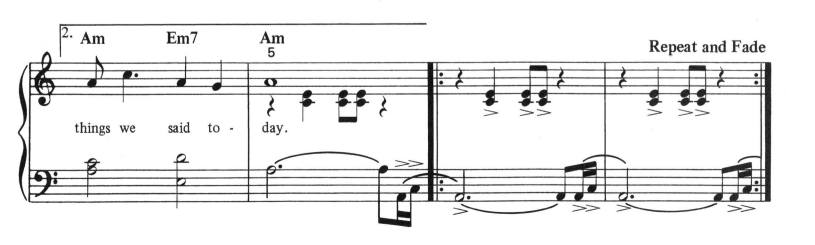

things we said to - day.

Repeat and Fade

THIS BOY
(Ringo's Theme)

Words and Music by JOHN LENNON
and PAUL McCARTNEY

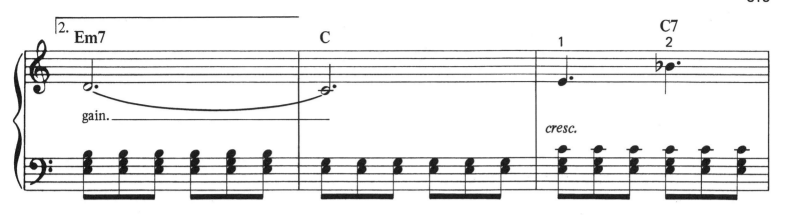

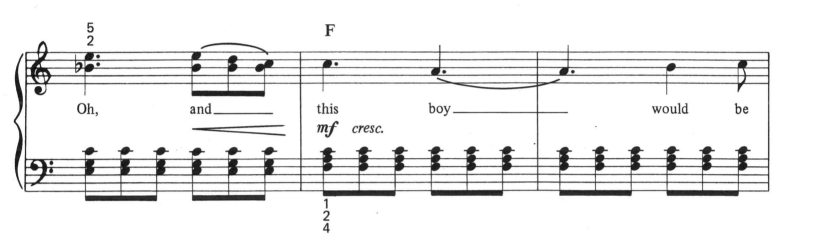

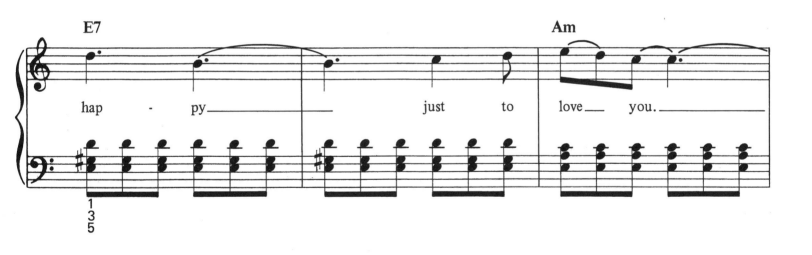

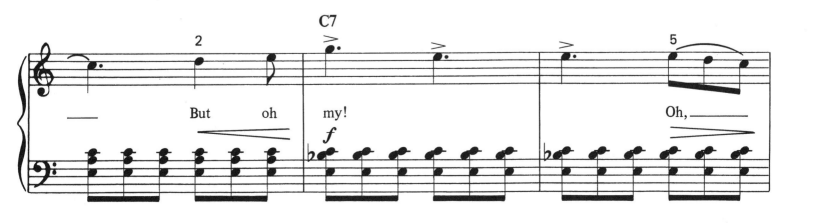

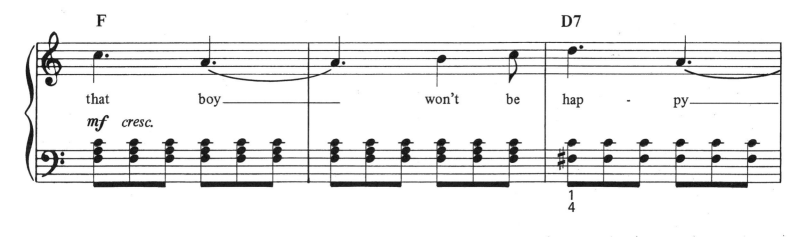

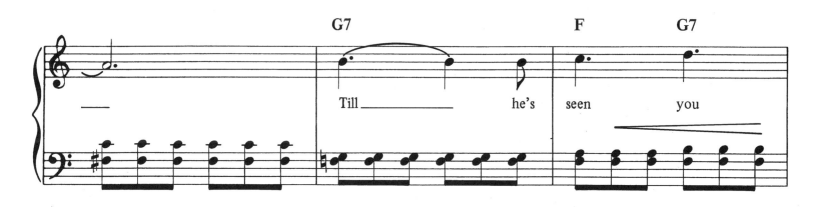

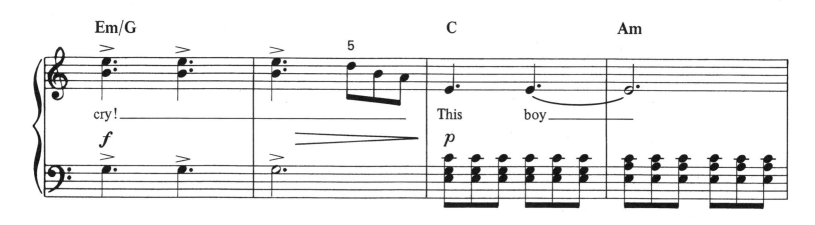

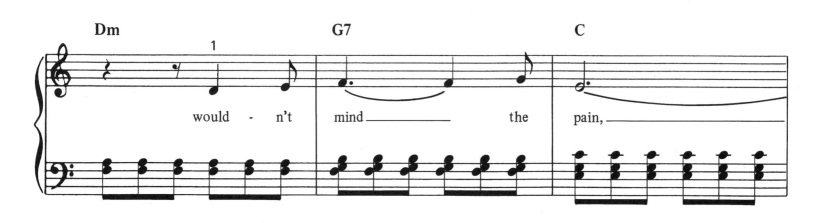

315

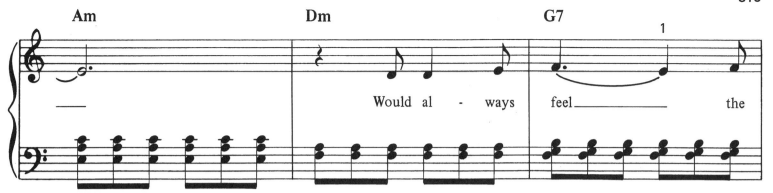

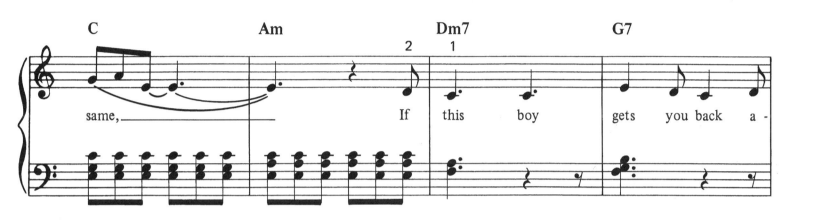

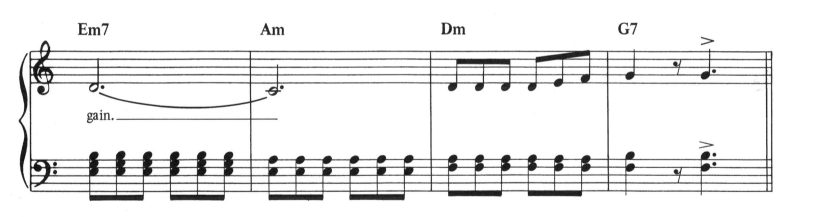

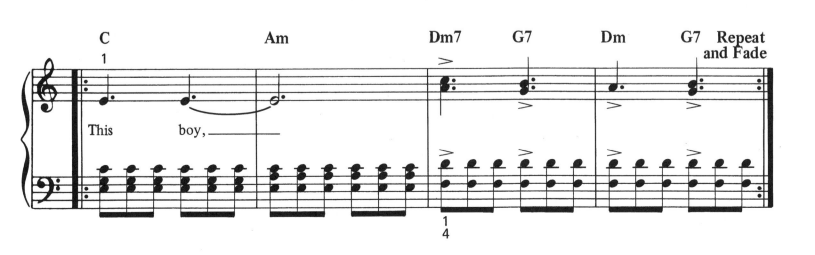

TICKET TO RIDE

Words and Music by JOHN LENNON
and PAUL McCARTNEY

Moderate Rock

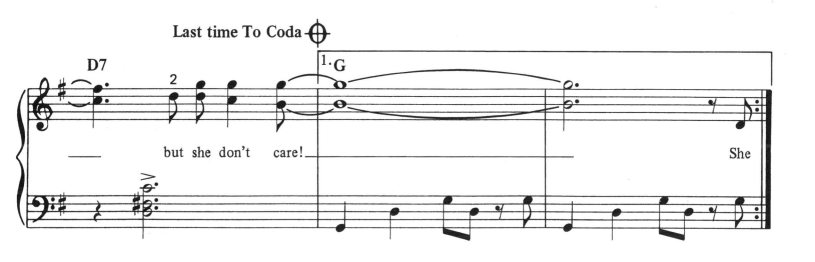

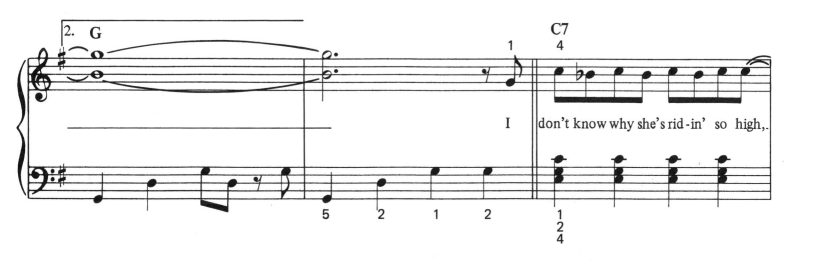

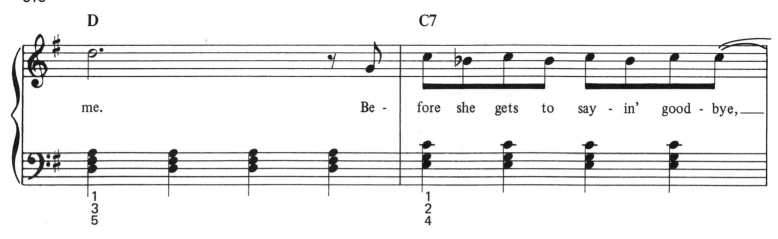

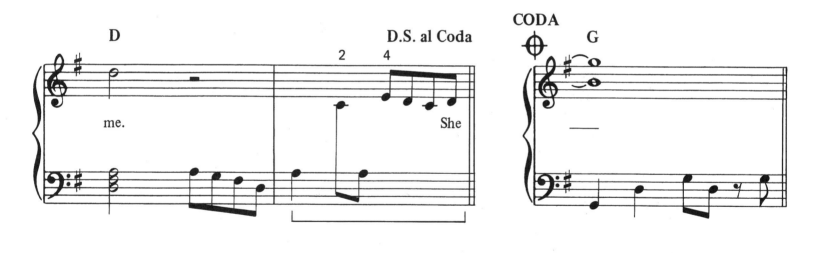

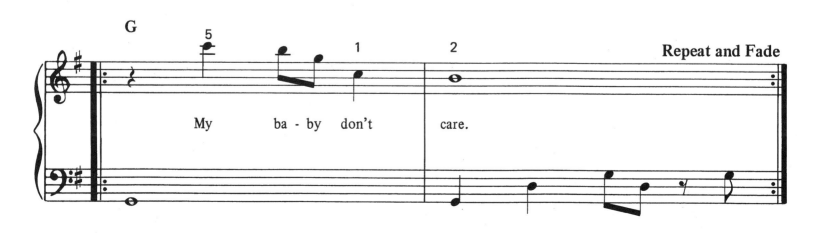

TWO OF US

Brightly, in 2 (♩ = 1 beat)

Words and Music by JOHN LENNON
and PAUL McCARTNEY

Two of us, rid - ing no - where, spend - ing some -
Two of us, send - ing post - cards, writ - ing let -
Two of us, wear - ing rain - coats, stand - ing so -

- one's hard - earned pay.
- ters on my wall.
- lo in the sun.

MCA MUSIC PUBLISHING

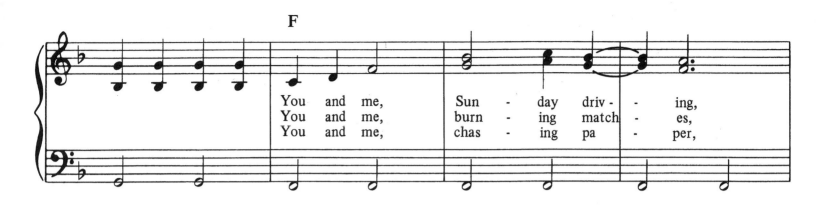

You and me,   Sun - day driv - - ing,
You and me,   burn - ing match - - es,
You and me,   chas - ing pa - - per,

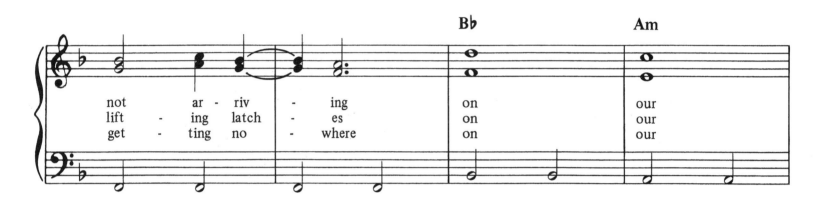

not   ar - riv - - ing   on   our
lift - ing latch - es   on   our
get - ting no - where   on   our

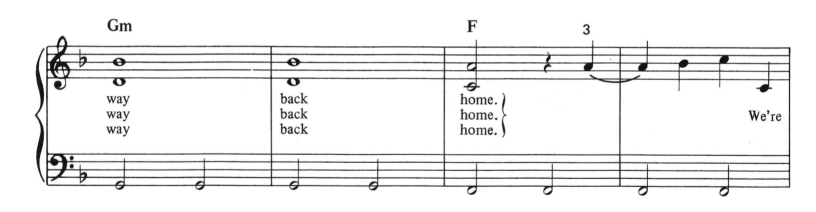

way   back   home.   We're
way   back   home.
way   back   home.

on our way   home,   We're   on our way

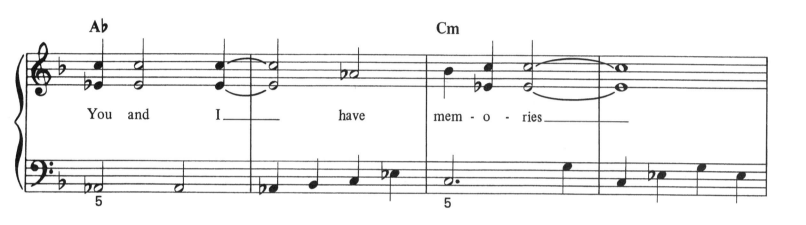

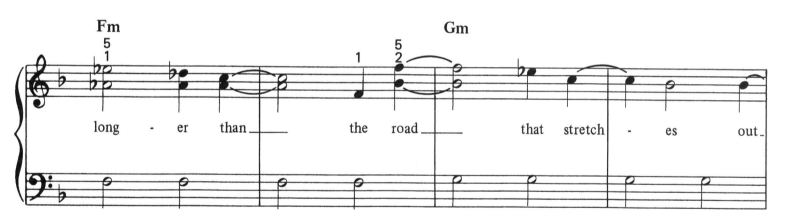

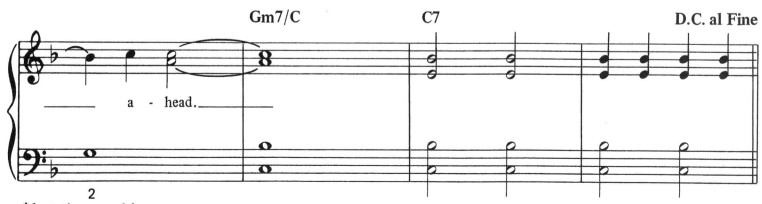

*last time, end here.

TWIST AND SHOUT

Words and Music by BERT RUSSELL
and PHIL MEDLEY

Moderate Rock and Roll beat

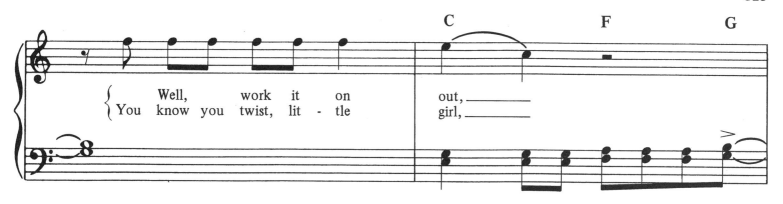

Well, work it on out, _____
You know you twist, lit - tle girl, _____

You know you look so good; ___
You know you twist so fine ___

You know you got ___ me ___
Come on and twist a lit - tle

go - in' now,
clos - er now,

Just like I knew you would.
And let me know that you're mine.

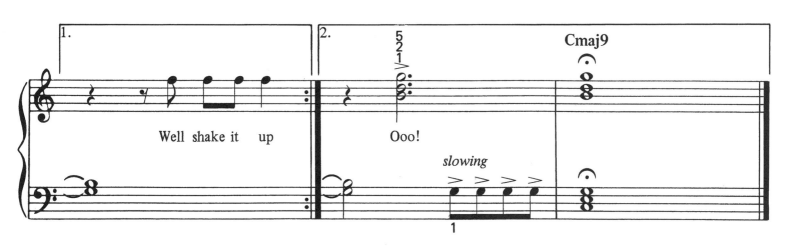

1.
Well shake it up

2.
Ooo!

slowing

Cmaj9

WE CAN WORK IT OUT

Words and Music by JOHN LENNON
and PAUL McCARTNEY

Slow and Steady

Life is ver-y short and there's no time_____ for

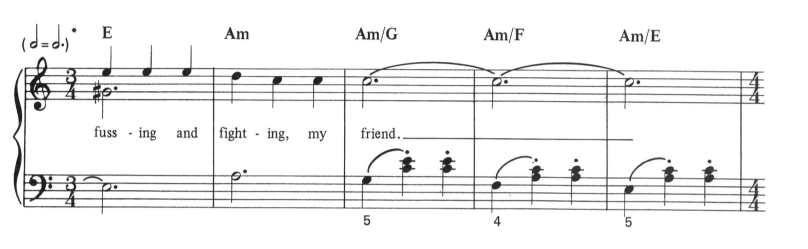

fuss - ing and fight-ing, my friend._____

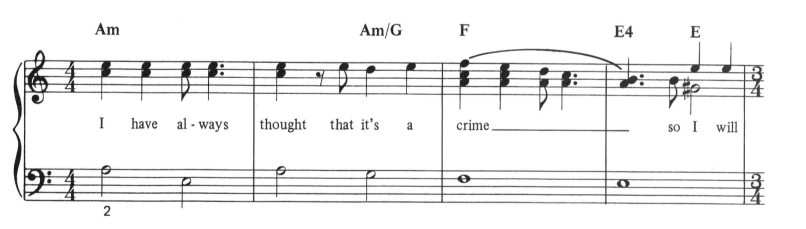

I have al-ways thought that it's a crime_____ so I will

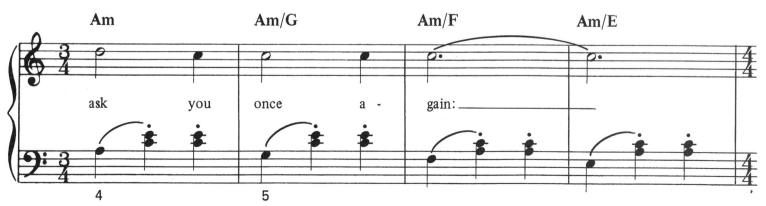

ask you once a - gain:_____

*Each 3/4 measure played in the same amount of time as the previous 2/4 measure.

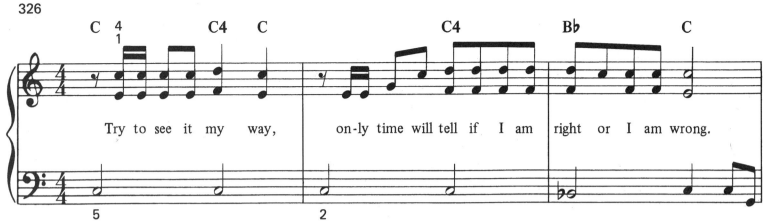

Try to see it my way, on-ly time will tell if I am right or I am wrong.

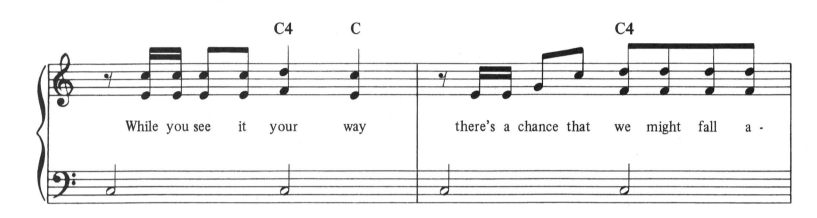

While you see it your way there's a chance that we might fall a -

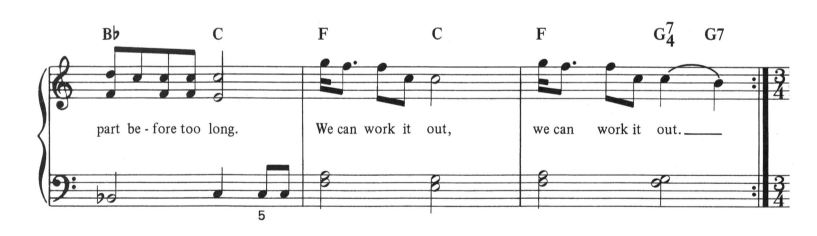

part be - fore too long. We can work it out, we can work it out._____

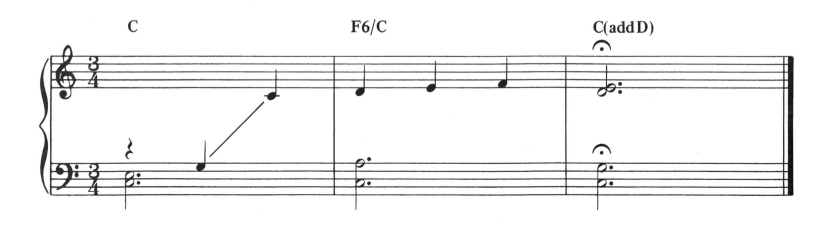

WHILE MY GUITAR GENTLY WEEPS

Words and Music by
GEORGE HARRISON

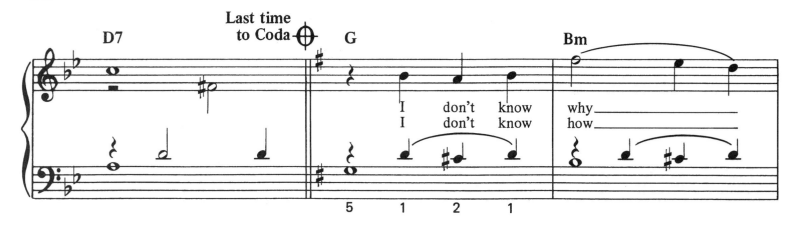

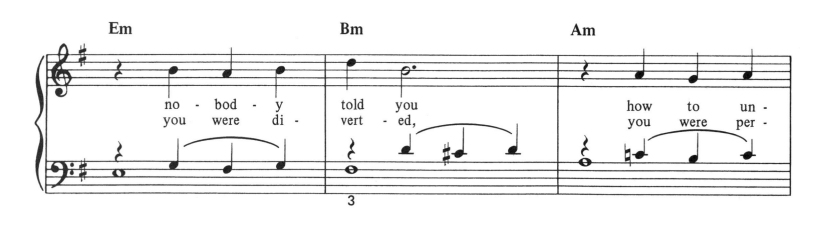

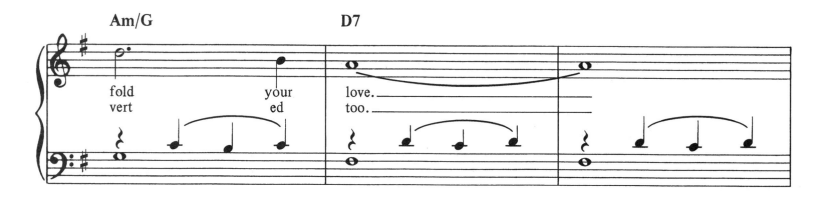

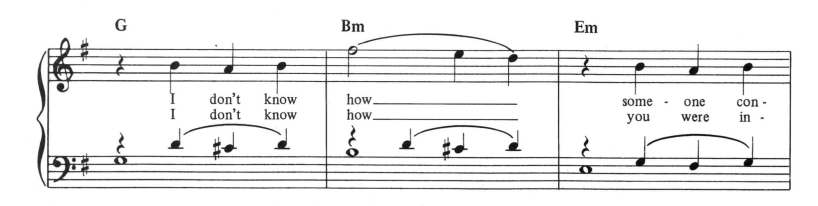

329

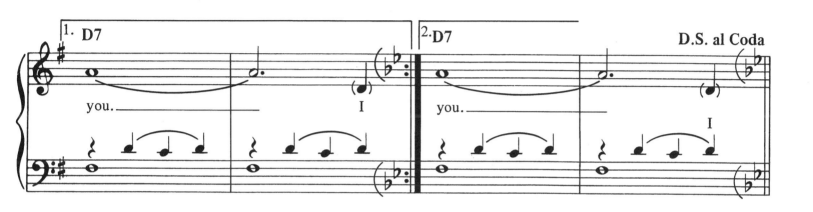

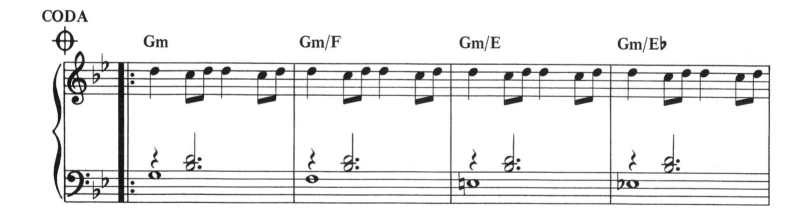

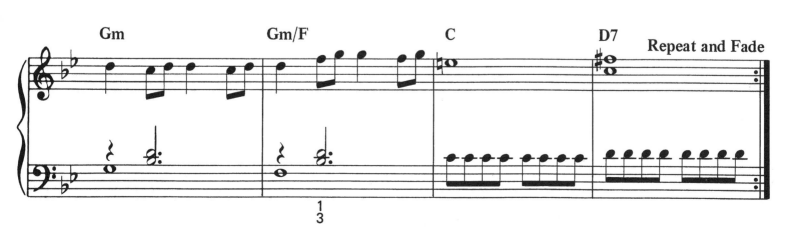

WHEN I'M SIXTY FOUR

Words and Music by JOHN LENNON
and PAUL McCARTNEY

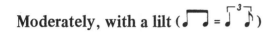

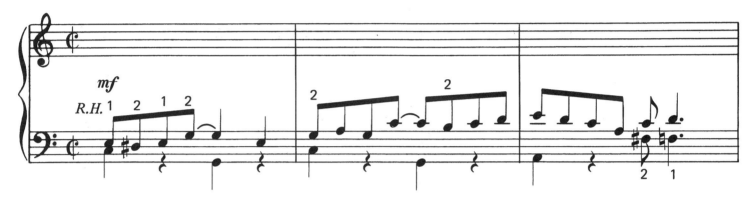

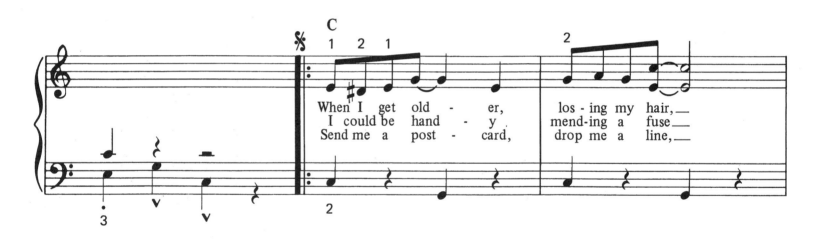

When I get old - er, losing my hair, ___
I could be hand - y, mend-ing a fuse ___
Send me a post - card, drop me a line, ___

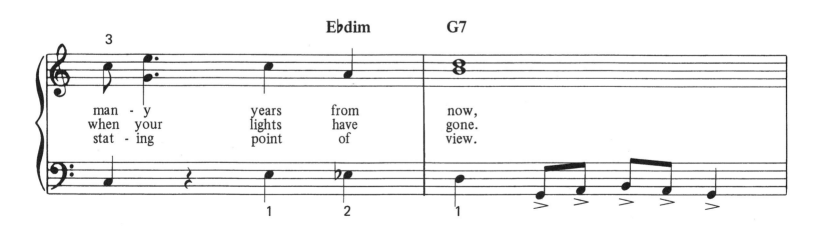

man - y years from now,
when your lights have gone.
stat - ing point of view.

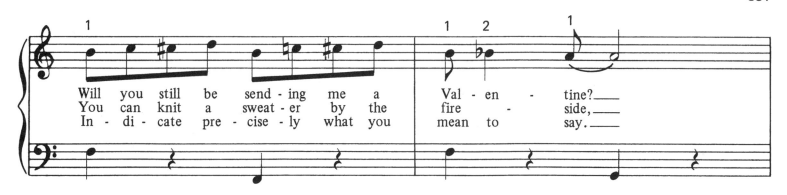

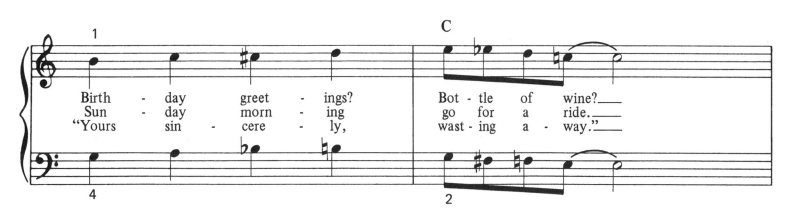

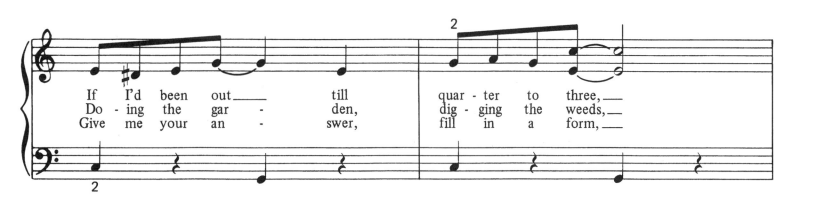

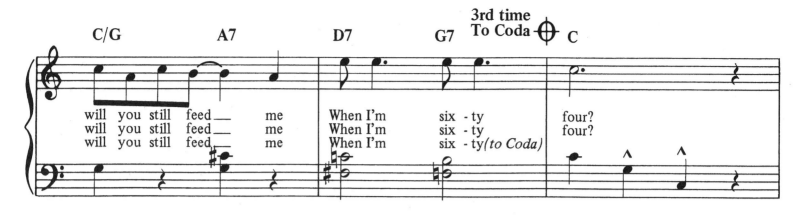

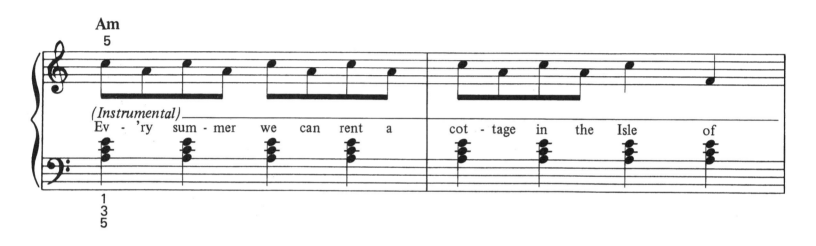

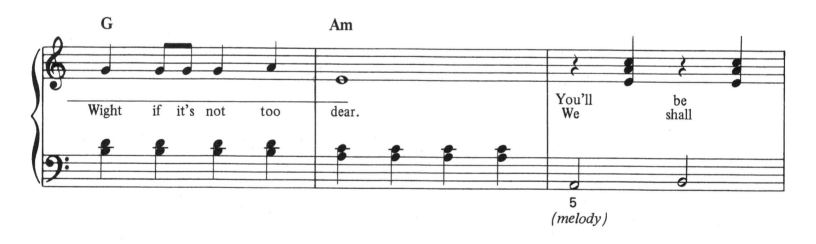

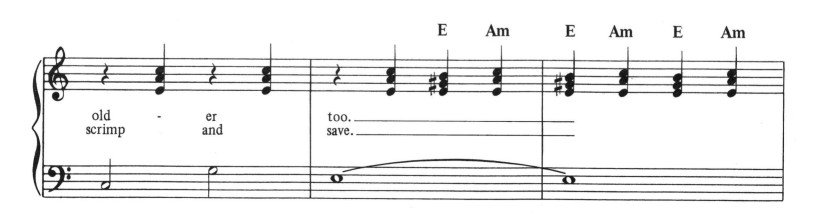

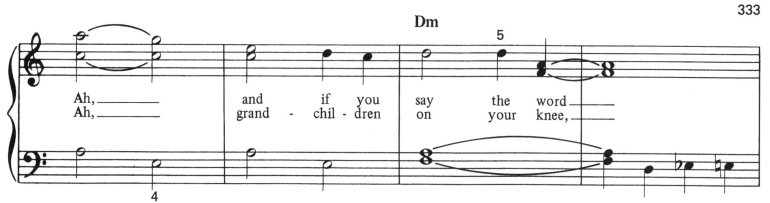

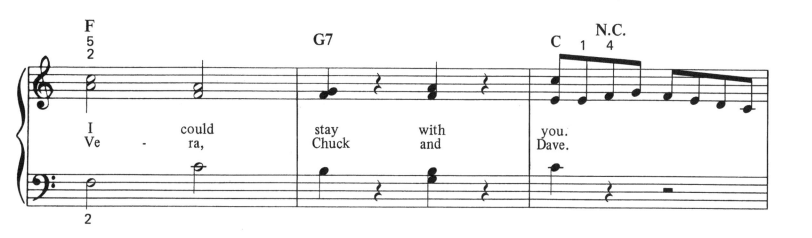

WITH A LITTLE HELP
FROM MY FRIENDS

Words and Music by JOHN LENNON
and PAUL McCARTNEY

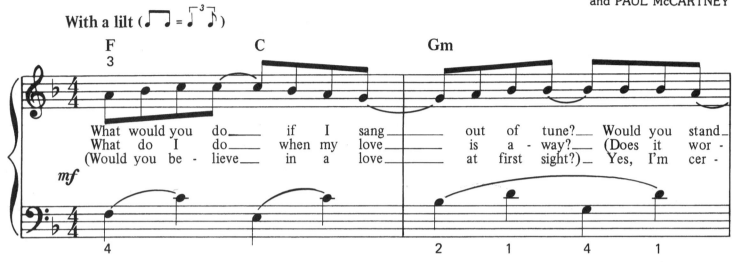

What would you do___ if I sang___ out of tune?___ Would you stand___
What do I do___ when my love___ is a-way?___ (Does it wor-
(Would you be-lieve___ in a love___ at first sight?)___ Yes, I'm cer-

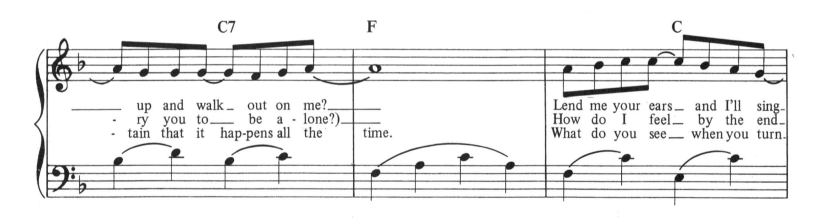

___ up and walk___ out on me?___ ___
-ry you to___ be a-lone?)___ time.
-tain that it hap-pens all the time.
Lend me your ears___ and I'll sing___
How do I feel___ by the end___
What do you see___ when you turn___

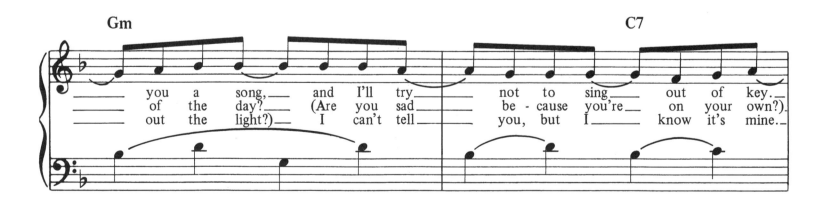

___ you a song,___ and I'll try___ not to sing___ out of key.___
___ of the day?___ (Are you sad___ be-cause you're___ on your own?)___
___ out the light?)___ I can't tell___ you, but I___ know it's mine.___

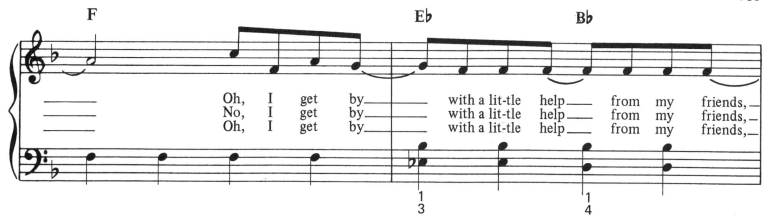

Oh, I get by___ with a lit-tle help___ from my friends,___
No, I I get by___ with a lit-tle help___ from my friends,___
Oh, I get by___ with a lit-tle help___ from my friends,___

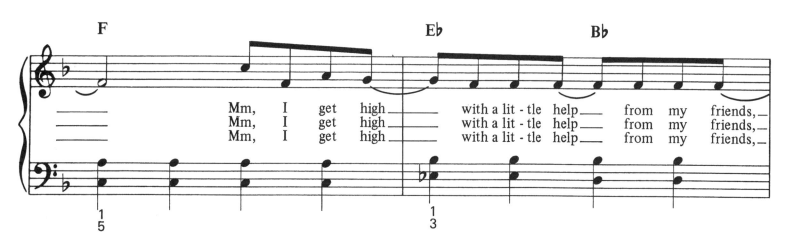

Mm, I get high___ with a lit-tle help___ from my friends,___
Mm, I get high___ with a lit-tle help___ from my friends,___
Mm, I get high___ with a lit-tle help___ from my friends,___

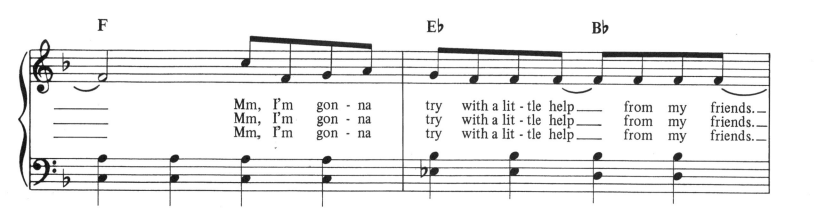

Mm, I'm gon - na try with a lit-tle help___ from my friends.___
Mm, I'm gon - na try with a lit-tle help___ from my friends.___
Mm, I'm gon - na try with a lit-tle help___ from my friends.___

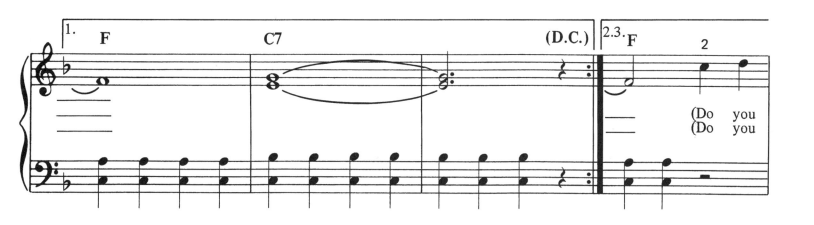

(Do you
(Do you

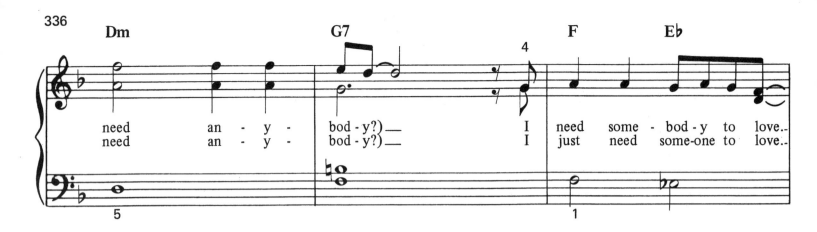

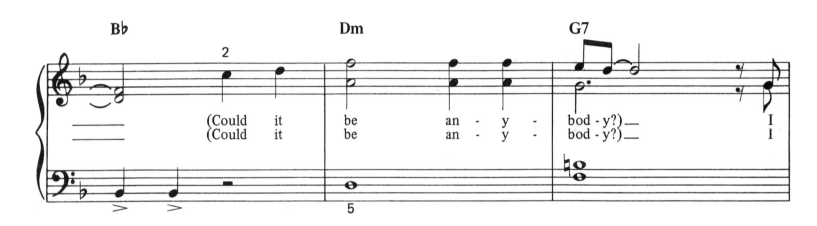

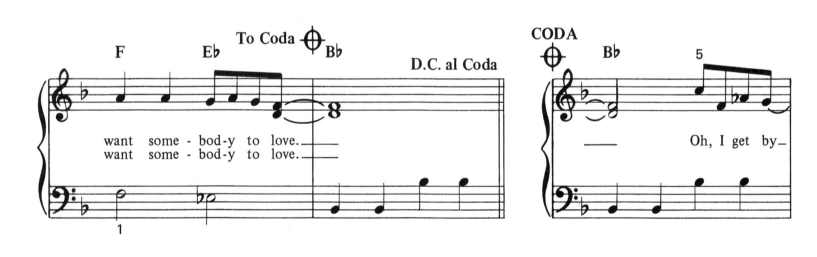

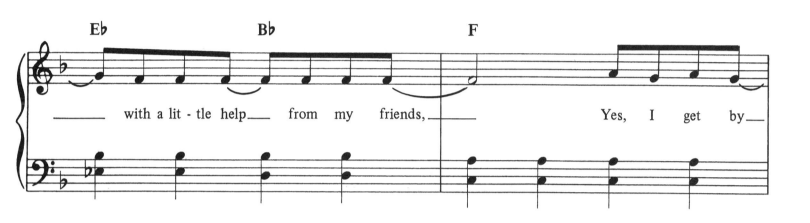

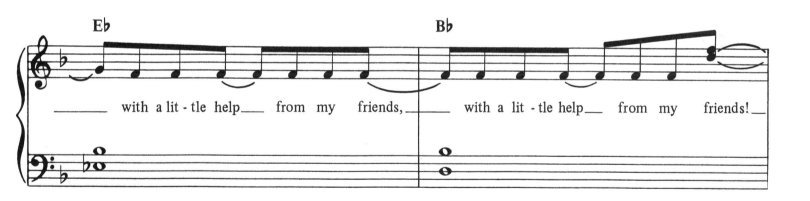

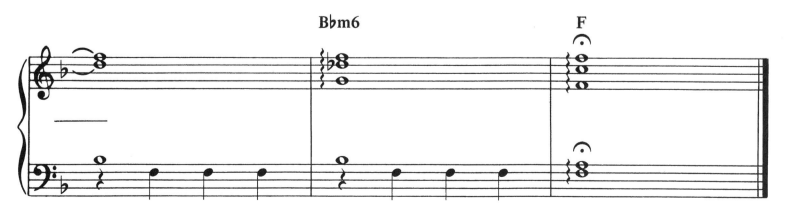

THE WORD

Moderate Rock

Words and Music by JOHN LENNON
and PAUL McCARTNEY

*The continual clash between the F♮ and F♯ in this song is part of its unique sound.

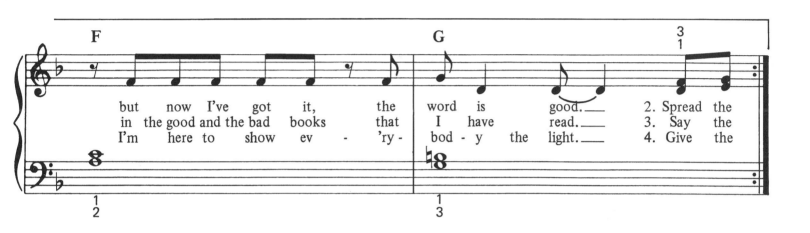

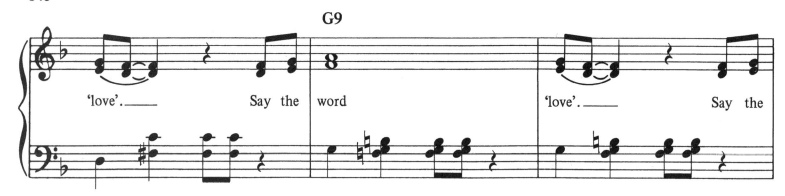

YELLOW SUBMARINE

Words and Music by JOHN LENNON
and PAUL McCARTNEY
Arranged by DAN FOX

March tempo

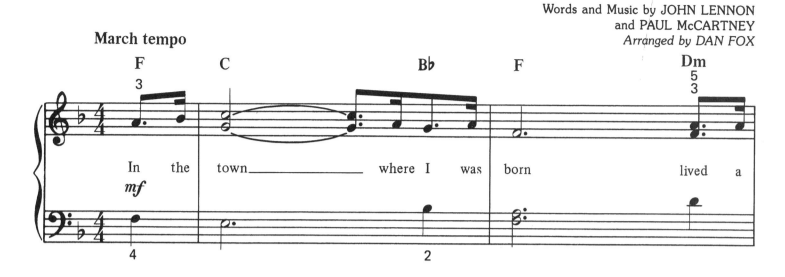

In the town_____ where I was born lived a

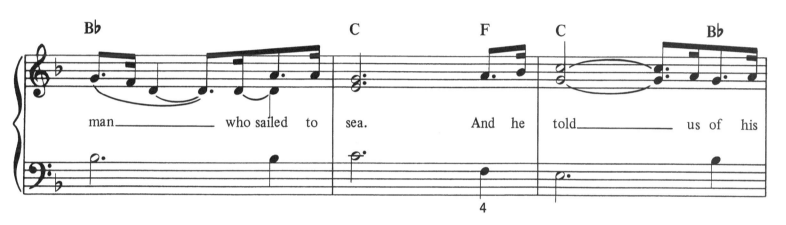

man_____ who sailed to sea. And he told_____ us of his

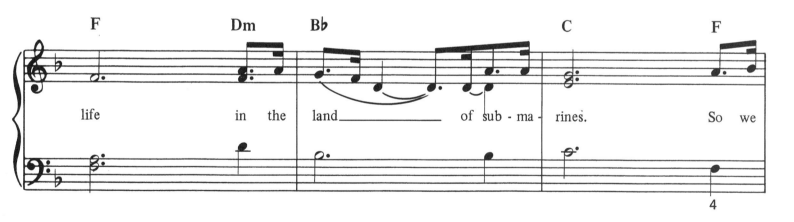

life in the land_____ of sub-ma-rines. So we

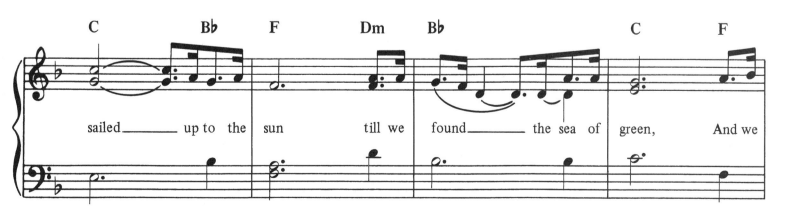

sailed_____ up to the sun till we found_____ the sea of green, And we

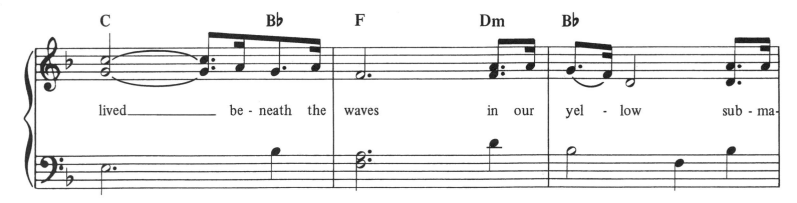

lived _____ be - neath the waves in our yel - low sub - ma-

rine. We all live in a yel - low sub - ma - rine,

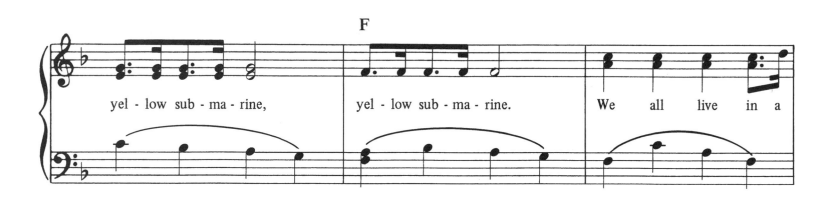

yel - low sub - ma - rine, yel - low sub - ma - rine. We all live in a

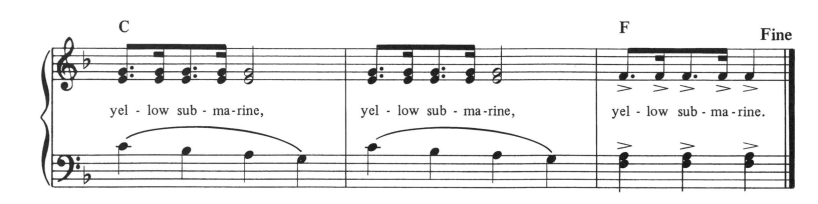

yel - low sub - ma - rine, yel - low sub - ma - rine, yel - low sub - ma - rine.

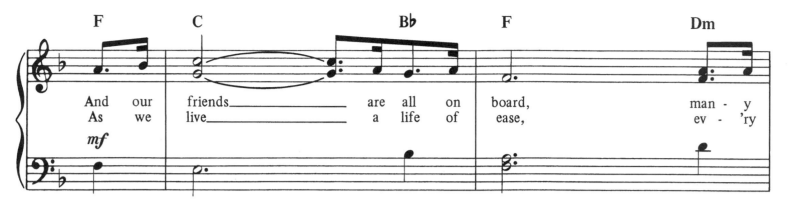

And our friends_____ are all on board, man - y
As we live_____ a life of ease, ev - 'ry

mf

more of them_____ live next door. And the band_____ be - gins to
one of us_____ has all we need. Sky of blue_____ and sea of

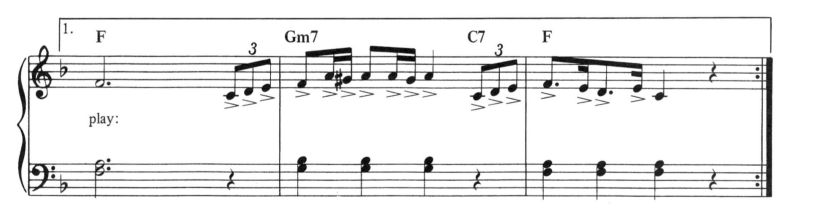

1.

play:

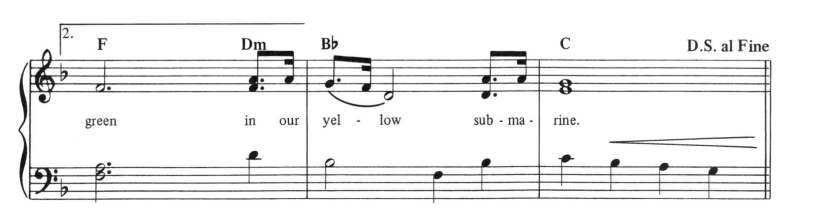

2.

green   in our yel - low sub - ma - rine.

D.S. al Fine

YES IT IS

Words and Music by JOHN LENNON
and PAUL McCARTNEY

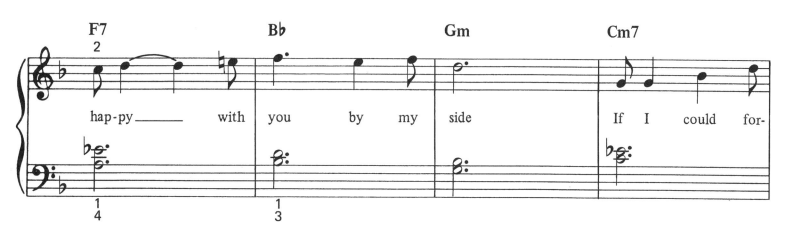

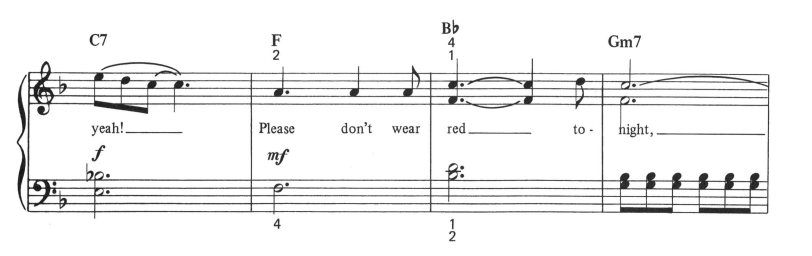

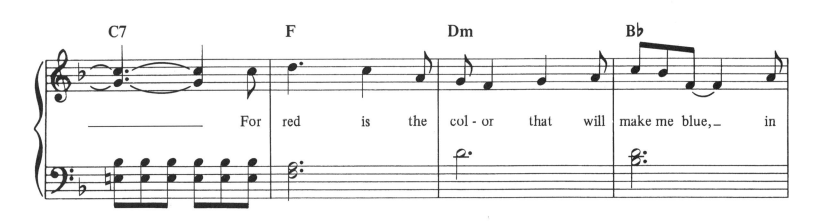

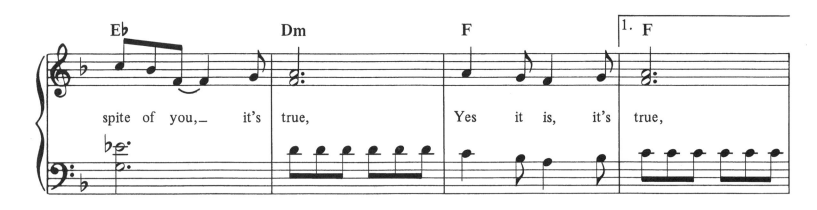

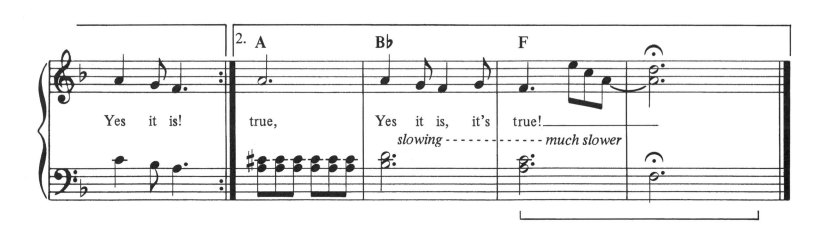

YOU CAN'T DO THAT

Words and Music by JOHN LENNON
and PAUL McCARTNEY

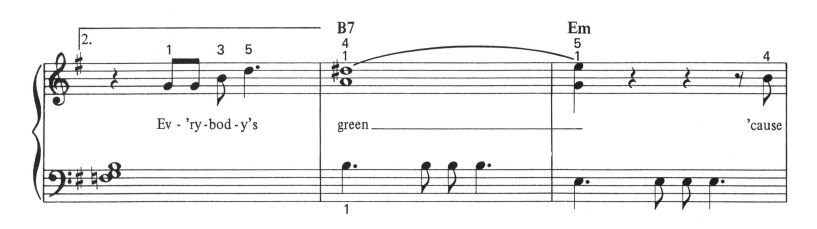

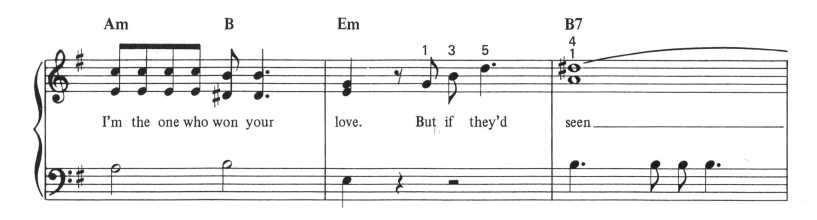

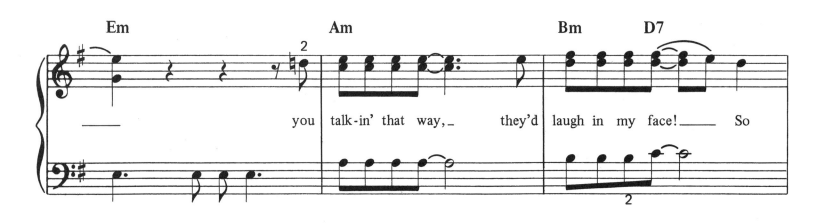

please lis-ten to me if you wan-na stay mine,_ I can't help my feel-ings I'll go

out of my mind,_ I'm gon-na let you down_____ and leave you

flat,___ Be-cause I've told you be-fore,

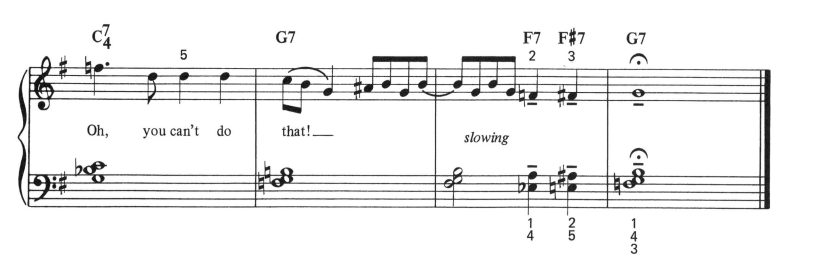

Oh, you can't do that!___ slowing

YESTERDAY

Words and Music by JOHN LENNON
and PAUL McCARTNEY

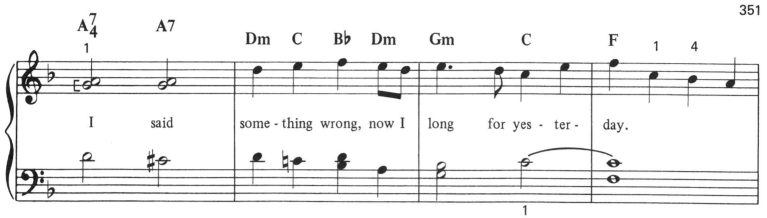

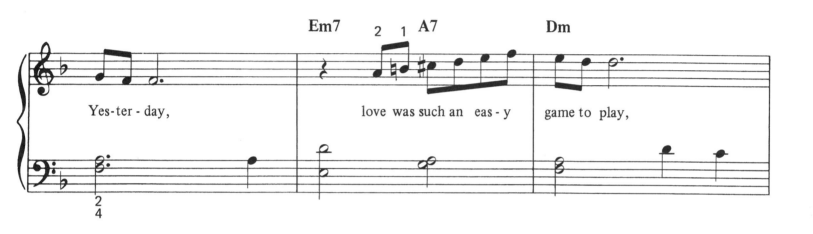

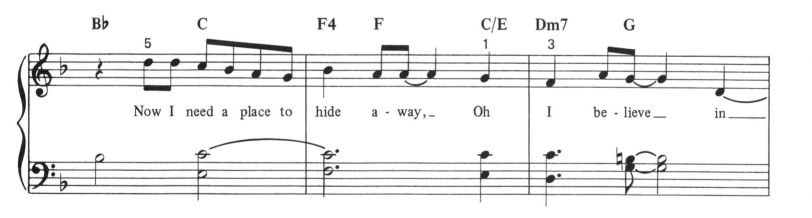

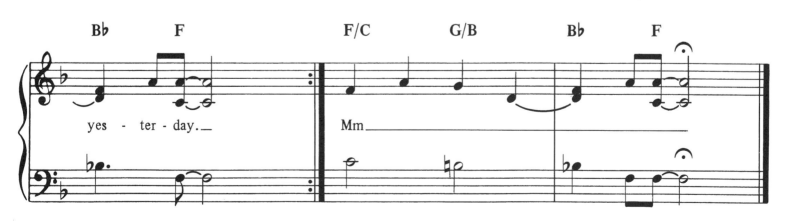

YOU NEVER GIVE ME YOUR MONEY

Words and Music by JOHN LENNON
and PAUL McCARTNEY

353

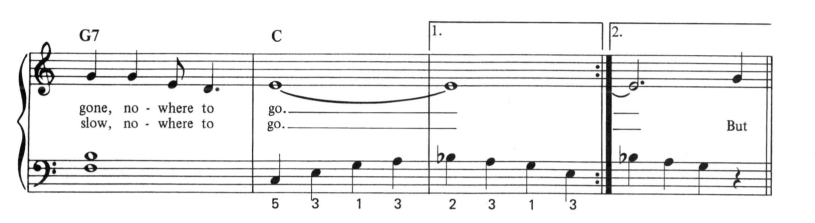

Original tempo and feel (♩♪ = ♩♪)

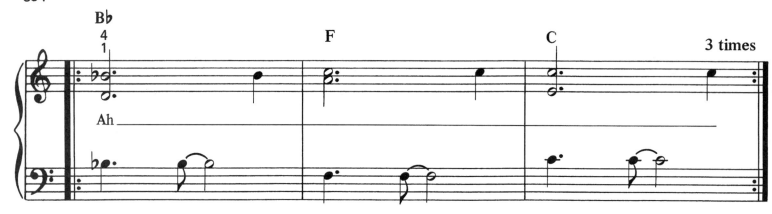

Bb   F   C   3 times

Ah _____

A   B

One sweet dream....

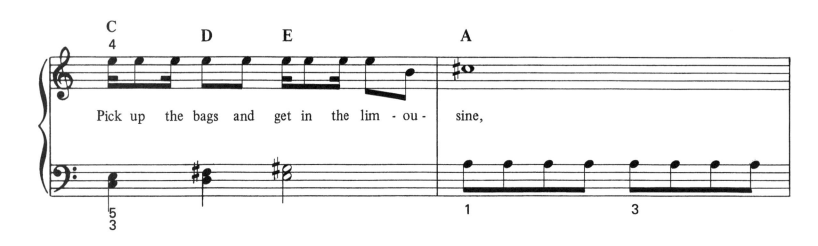

C   D   E   A

Pick up the bags and get in the lim-ou- sine,

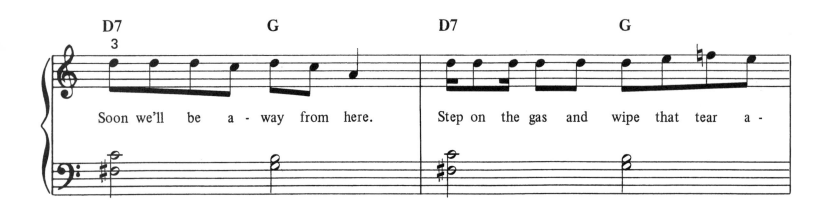

D7   G   D7   G

Soon we'll be a-way from here.   Step on the gas and wipe that tear a-

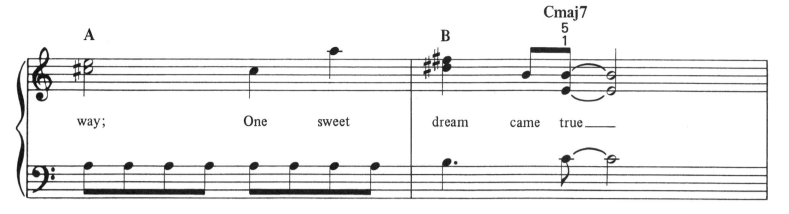

way; One sweet dream came true

to - day, came true to - day,

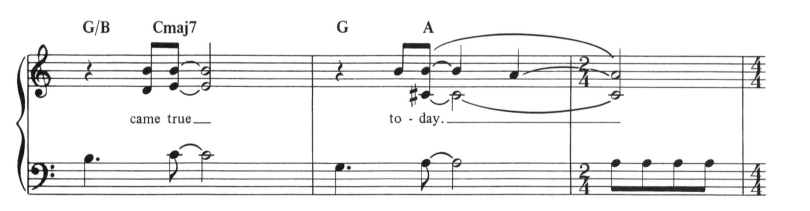

came true to - day.

One, two, three, four, five, six, sev-en, All good chil-dren go to heav-en.

YOU WON'T SEE ME

Words and Music by JOHN LENNON
and PAUL McCARTNEY

Moderate Rock

Last time to Coda

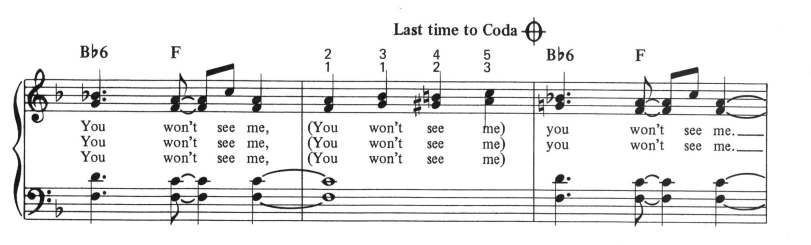

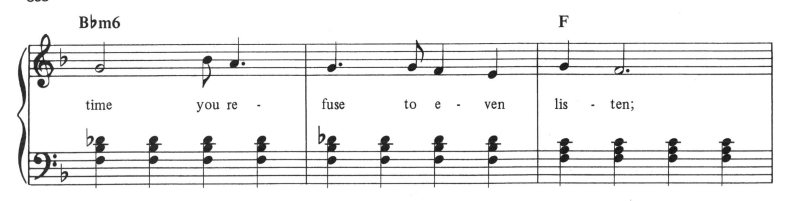

time you re- fuse to e- ven lis - ten;

I would-n't mind if I knew what I was

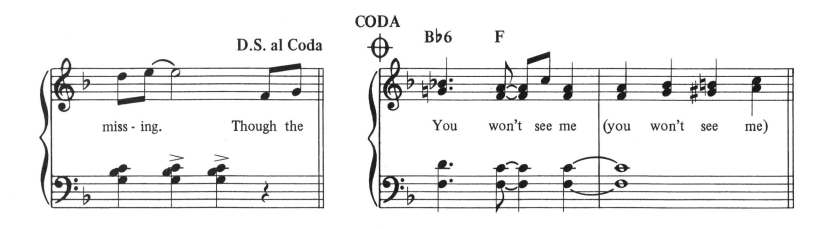

miss - ing. Though the

You won't see me (you won't see me)

La la la, la la la, la la la, la la la,

YOU'RE GOING TO LOSE THAT GIRL

Words and Music by JOHN LENNON
and PAUL McCARTNEY

You're gon-na lose that girl,__ you're gon-na lose that girl.___

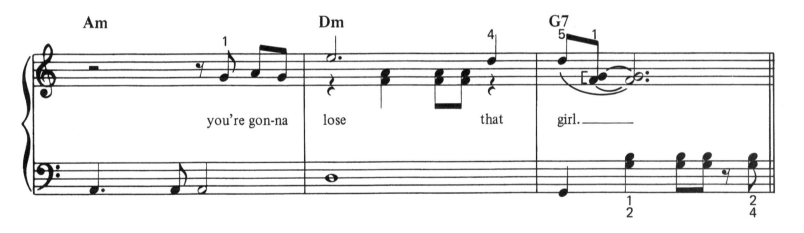

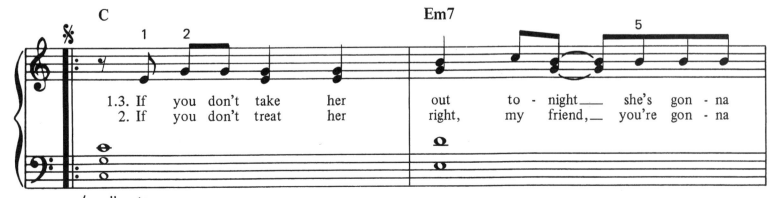

1.3. If you don't take her out to-night___ she's gon - na
2. If you don't treat her right, my friend,__ you're gon - na

(small notes
on D.S. only)

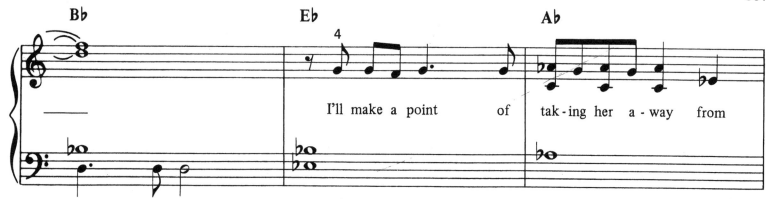

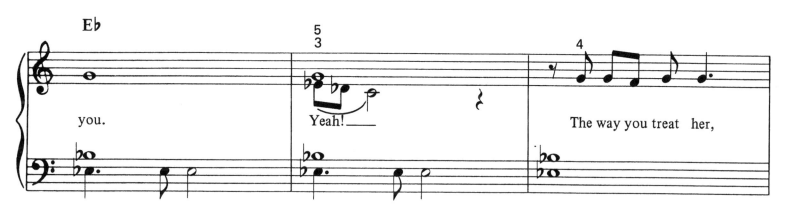

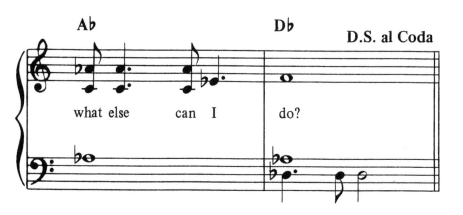

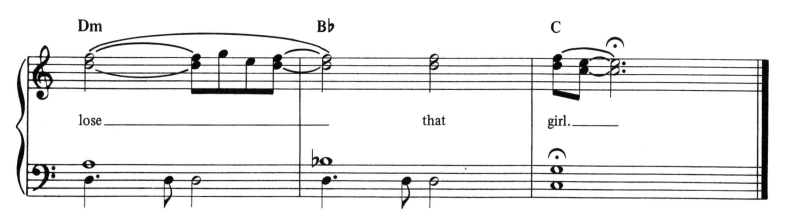

YOUR MOTHER SHOULD KNOW

Words and Music by JOHN LENNON
and PAUL McCARTNEY

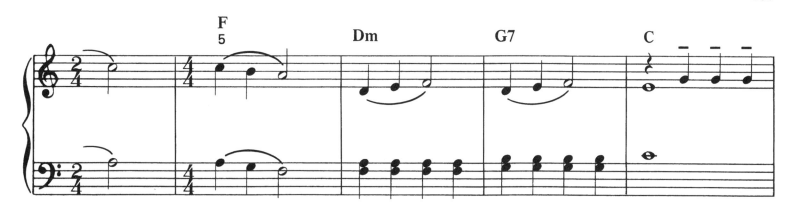

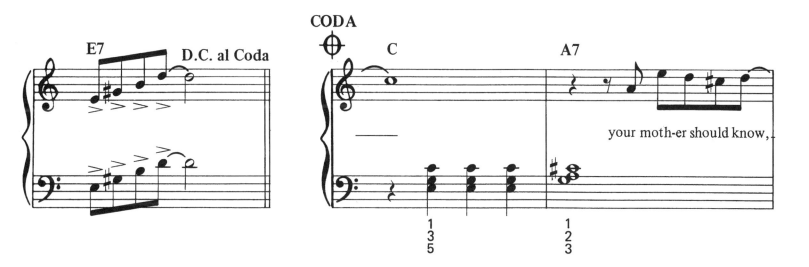

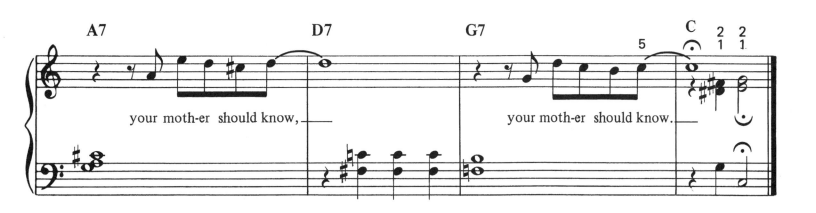

YOU'VE GOT TO HIDE YOUR LOVE AWAY

Words and Music by JOHN LENNON
and PAUL McCARTNEY

In one (each measure = 1 slow beat)

365

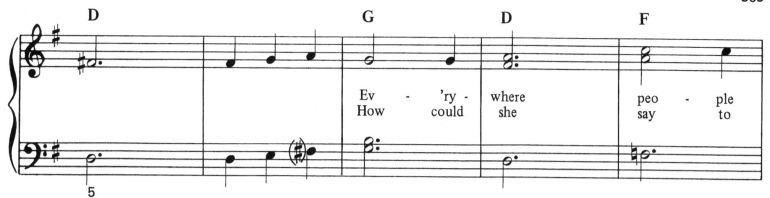

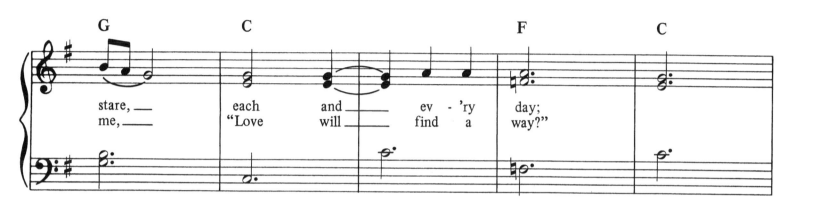

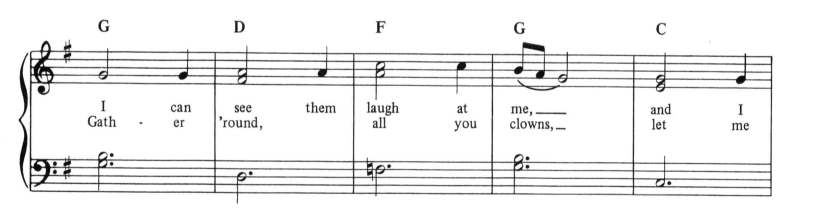

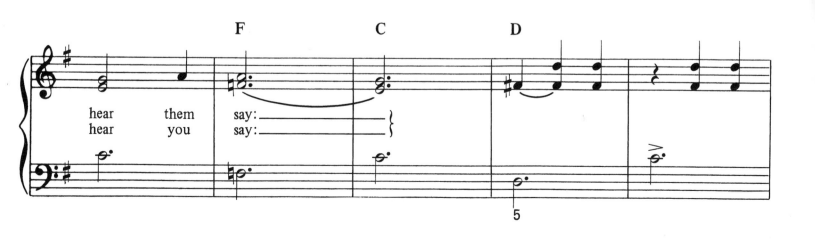

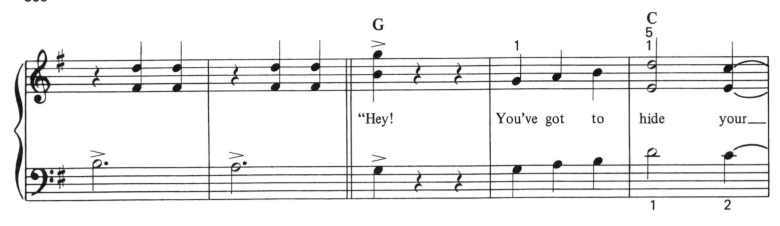

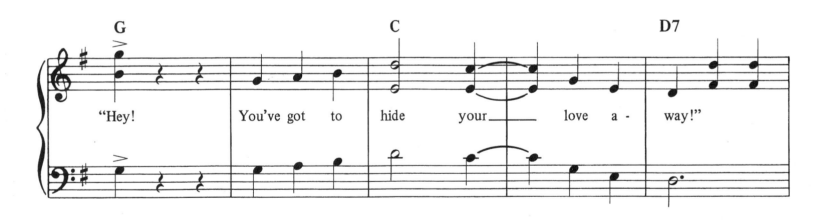